An Introduction
to the Pronunciation
of North American English

An Introduction
to the Pronunciation
of North American English

Jørgen Staun

UNIVERSITY PRESS OF SOUTHERN DENMARK 2010

University of Southern Denmark Studies in Linguistics vol. 19

© The author and University Press of Southern Denmark 2010
Printed by Special-Trykkeriet Viborg a-s
Cover by Donald Jensen, Unisats ApS
ISBN 978-87-7674-476-2

University Press of Southern Denmark
Campusvej 55
DK-5230 Odense M
Phone: +45 6615 7999
Fax: +45 6615 8126
Press@forlag.sdu.dk
www.universitypress.dk

Distribution in the United States and Canada:
International Specialized Book Services
5804 NE Hassalo Street
Portland, OR 97213-3644 USA
www.isbs.com

Distribution in the United Kingdom:
Gazelle
White Cross Mills
Hightown
Lancaster
LA1 4 XS
U.K.
www.gazellebooks.co.uk

Contents

Preface

This book is aimed at the undergraduate university student who has decided to learn about English pronunciation and the system this pronunciation is founded on when it is of the kind spoken in North America. The book assumes no prior knowledge of how language sounds are described, but all concepts used to explain both sound system (phonology) and pronunciation (phonetics) are defined as they are introduced.

As there is not just one North American English pronunciation, it has been necessary to choose one variety of North American English as the pronunciation which will be described and referred to throughout this book. This reference dialect, as such a variety is usually called, has been chosen so that it is both representative of North American speakers and simultaneously covers as much of the continent as possible. In the past, a variety known as General American has been used as a representative reference dialect in numerous not least European textbooks on North American English pronunciation. In such textbooks, General American is a contended representative pronunciation with neither southern nor eastern characteristics. However, General American has been criticised strongly by specifically American specialists, who have pointed out that it is a gross simplification to promote a northern variety of American English to a proto-type of North American English in general. The recent publication in 2006 of *The Atlas of North American English*, compiled by William Labov, Sharon Ash and Charles Boberg, has confirmed that a non-southern and non-eastern variety is not a homogeneous variety, but consists of a variety of dialects with no obvious over-arching common denominator.

In order to avoid the problems that surround General American, this book posits a reference dialect which allows for the findings of the Phonological Atlas of North American English, at the same time as this reference dialect is representative of as large a part of North America as possible. It has not proven easy to reconcile these two views. The difficulty is that the variation in dialect geography presented by the Atlas is extensive, so no dialect identified by the Atlas is the obvious representative choice. But the variation outlined by the findings of the Atlas is based almost exclusively on the pronunciation of vowels. Therefore, the reference dialect chosen here is somewhat restricted when it comes to the pronunciation of vowels, but includes more North American speakers when the pronunciation of consonants is incorporated, and even more inclusive when stress accent, intonation and rhythm are taken into account.

In particular, with regard to the pronunciation of vowels the reference dialect will exclude speakers in North America in whose speech sometimes quite radical shifts in the pronunciation of these sounds are currently taking place. In this way, varieties of not only New England and the Mid-Atlantic East, but also areas in the North, specifically those around the great lakes, as well as large parts of the South, are not included in the reference dialect. Instead the vowel pronunciations of the reference dialect are similar to those described by Peter Ladefoged in his influential *A Course in Phonetics* (2001), a type of pronunciation which he describes as typical of many North American newscasters and which also reflects the pronunciations used by John Wells in his authoritative *Longman Pronunciation Dictionary* (2000). This means that in the reference dialect the vowels of *bath, staff* and *dance* are assumed to be pronounced with the vowel of *trap* rather than the vowel of *palm*, and the vowel of *steady* does not sound like the vowel of *study*, and the vowel of *hide* does not sound like the vowel of *had*. With respect to other features of pronunciation, however, such as consonants and elements of the pronunciation larger than vowels and consonants like intonation, stress accent and rhythm, the reference dialect covers a considerably wider geographical area, so it excludes only relatively small regions, but sometimes containing many speakers, such as New York City or New England. Thus in words spelled with an *r*, as in *park the car in the yard*, all *r*'s are always heard in the reference dialect, which is not always the case in New York City or New England. Likewise *cube* and *bugle* – but not *tune* and *duke* – have *j*'s in their pronunciations, the *t*'s of *latter* and *party* are heard as *d*'s rather than as *t*'s in the reference dialect (known as taps or flaps), both of which pronunciations are heard almost everywhere in North America. The same goes for the pronunciation of *l* in *least, list* and *less* which is always said with a dark quality in the reference dialect, a pronunciation which is heard almost everywhere and probably only restricted by ethnic class. In sum, the reference dialect used in this book is then progressively more inclusive as the view of North American English changes from the pronunciation of vowels to the pronunciation of *r* and further on to the pronunciation of other consonants than *r* like certain *t*'s and *j*'s and all *l*'s. In fact, a yet wider view incorporating intonation, stress accent and rhythm makes the reference dialect fairly general covering most of North America.

One reason for taking this gradually more inclusive view on the reference dialect is that it does not conflict with the findings of the Atlas of North American English. But this choice of reference dialect also fulfils the second objective that the reference dialect should be typical and representative of English in North America. In fact, most native speakers of English outside North America not only regard it as typical of American speakers always to pronounce *r* after vowels and pronounce *t*'s in words like *party* and *letter* as *d*'s, or drop the *j*'s in *tune* and *duke*, but also not to pronounce *steady* as *study, hide* as *had* or *bath* with the vowel of *palm*. With the exception of such typical features, and few more not listed here, the reference dialect is not widely different from many other English varieties spoken across the world. For this reason, a popular and non-technical definition of the reference dialect is that it is the mainstream, neutral variety of North American English which mostly resembles English English without being non-American. Throughout this book the reference dialect will be referred to as the North American English Reference Dialect, abbreviated NAERD, thus avoiding a name involving the words 'general' and 'American', which when used to characterise a typical English pronunciation in North America tend provoke considerable resistance.

Since NAERD, with respect to the pronunciation vowels, is somewhat restrictive, readers who are familiar with northern, specifically inland northern, and southern and eastern varieties of North American English, will not always agree that the used pronunciation is as representative as its choice as reference pronunciation suggests. But in an introductory book to phonetics and phonology of North American English, it is necessary to simplify and restrict the description when the reader is assumed to be one who has no or very little prior knowledge of phonetics and phonology. The contention is that understanding and appreciating the subtle and extensive variation in North American English pronunciation, specifically among its vowels, requires a basic knowledge, and the reference dialect with a pronunciation which is fairly typical of North America, but lacking specifically the vowel pronunciations of, for example, the North and the South, constitutes a pedagogically functional and convenient variety from which this basic knowledge can be acquired. But sometimes considerable variation in North American English is ignored; yet all of this is in the interest of learning about North American English pronunciation and the system it builds on, and from this knowledge the more subtle details can be acquired and appreciated.

The book has been divided into three parts. Part I deals with the individual consonants and vowels of the reference dialect of North American English. One chapter has been devoted to obstruent consonants, one to sonorant consonants and one to vowels. Two chapters have a more general aim. The first of these, Ch. 1, outlines the main characteristics of North American English and defines in technical phonological terms the reference dialect which is the object of description of the following chapters. The aim of Ch. 2 is also general, positing the consonants and vowels that can contrast meaning in NAERD and describes the position of these sounds in the linguistic hierarchy. Throughout part I, the approach to sound description will not only consider how sounds are produced with the organs of speech, but it will also take into account how speech sounds are heard or interpreted by the human ear and what the physical sound wave properties of speech sounds are, the first type known as articulatory, the second one as auditory and the third type as acoustic. The description of consonants will be predominantly articulatory. Emphasising how this class of speech sounds is produced with the articulatory organs entails that some space is devoted to a more detailed explanation of the speech organs, whose three main systems, the articulatory, the phonatory and respiratory components, are outlined as part of Ch. 3, which is the first chapter dealing with the individual sounds.

Part II deals with what technically is known as supra-segmental entities. Supra-segmental entities are entities whose domain is larger than one consonant or one vowel (vowels and consonants are known technically as segments). Stress and tone are the most familiar supra-segmental entities. Ch. 7 and 8 outline the word stress and tone systems of American English. Word stress rules are described in Ch. 7 and will appear non-exhaustive but cover the main patterns, just like the outline of intonation in Ch. 8 far from covers all material and in its coverage employs British-oriented tone group units like nucleus, head and tail to express the information structure and more specific intonation-carried meanings of utterances. The syllable is also a supra-segmental entity. Ch. 6 of part II therefore outlines the basics of syllable structure, as well as giving the main rules for syllable boundary placement. Part II like part I is a description of NEARD, but since there exists no dialect geography which is based on supra-segmental variation, what is said in part II applies much more to North America English in general than the descriptions in part I, in which the focus specifically with regard to vowels has been narrowed somewhat and covers fewer speakers.

The last and third part of this book has variation and change as keywords. Ch. 9 covers both variation and change. The variation described in this chapter is such as occurs in present-day speech which is triggered by contiguous sounds. Pronouncing *happen* with a final *m*-sound or saying *good-bye* as if *good* had a final *b*-sound illustrates this kind of context conditioned but optional variation, and the chapter describes in a systematic way the targets and sources of such alternative pronunciations. Change in Ch. 9 stands for such transformations which have become permanent and which may originally have been the result of optional influence exerted by contiguous sounds. Input and output are then temporally separated in the latter case, often by several centuries. Variation in Ch. 10 refers to regional variation within North America. Elaborating on the brief introduction of Ch. 1, which delimits the reference dialect, this chapter outlines the main dialects of North America and lays out the defining sound system features of the five main North American dialects: the North, the South, the East, the West and Midland and Canada. The simplified view of the pronunciation of vowels which the choice of reference dialect entails is then compensated for in this last chapter.

It is a recurrent pattern that each chapter of each part concludes not only with a brief summary of the topic dealt with in the chapter in question but also with a list of suggested further reading. The summary allows the reader to reconstruct the main information of the chapter, whereas the provision of a list of suggested further reading gives the reader an opportunity to explore in more detail one or more of the topics discussed in the chapter in question. The list of further reading means that there is no or only very little reference to other books or articles in the actual running text. Experienced readers will probably find this annoying and miss such information in the text as they read along, whilst less experienced readers may be pleased not to get disturbed by references to other works before at the end of the chapter. Since it is an introductory textbook, the latter approach has been adopted here.

Needless to say, it is impossible to write a book of this kind without the help of other people. Numerous students and colleagues, sometimes without knowing, have made me get on with the work, helped with questions or commented (usually consciously) on draft versions. I would like to take this opportunity and thank these people. In particular I would like to mention: Penny Eckert, Heinz Giegerich, Christian Jensen, Cathrine Meinertz-Nielsen, William Labov, Peter Ladefoged, Hanne Lauridsen, Rikke Kvisgaard Laursen, Karsten Schou, Christian Brammer Prip, Robert Lee Revier. My absolutions on them all.

Jørgen Staun

Part 1

CHAPTER 1

Introduction to American English

1.1 American English Dialects

The history of English in North America begins in the early 17th century when English settlers within a time span of approximately 15 years found two successful settlements in Jamestown, Virginia, and Plymouth, Massachusetts. These settlements mark the beginning of a large-scale immigration of predominantly British settlers who in four great waves spread English to North America, so that at the declaration of independence some 150 years later English is the language of the new nation of united states. The English of the immigrants is generally known as **Early Modern English**., the English of the Elizabethan and Jacobean eras, differing from both **Present-day English**, which is assumed to have been used since approximately 1800, and from **Middle English**, the predecessor of Early Modern English, which spans the period from the time of the arrival of William The Conqueror in England in 1066 until 1500. The Early Modern English origin of American English explains some of the characteristic pronunciations, word meanings and grammatical features in present day North American English which many native speakers of English outside North America recognise as distinctly American. The characteristic American pronunciation of words like e.g. *staff*, *bath*, *dance*, with the vowel of the word *trap*, a vowel sometimes referred to as the flat 'a', dates back to the early modern English period, a pronunciation which standard present-day English English has lost and replaced by the vowel pronunciation found in *palm*. Word meanings like those associated with *mad* and *fall*, which in American English can mean 'angry' and 'the season following summer', also date back to this period, but these meanings are no longer current in English English. Grammatical traces left by Early Modern English are e.g. the past participle *gotten* of the verb *get* which was used in England until the mid 18th century but then supplanted by *got*, or the wider application of the present subjunctive form, as in a formal use of e.g. *We insist that John leave at once* where English English would express the deontic modal meaning of the sub-clause verb in terms of a modal verb (*should leave*) rather than by using the subjunctive form *leave*.

The development of a new variety of English in North America with for example such pronunciation, lexical and grammatical peculiarities is the result of what may be summed up with the two words: continuation and separation. By continuation is meant that English in order to start a life of its own which could lead to the development of a new variety had to be brought to North America and continued to be used as a common language in the new colonies. Separation, on the other hand, refers to the fact that the development of a new variety was optimised by, if not dependent on, the colonists being cut off physically, mentally and politically from the old English-speaking world of the mother countries. Both continuation and separation have not only helped preserve in present-day North American English such Early Modern English examples as those just listed in the previous paragraph. For example, the pronunciation of *bath, staff, dance* with a 'flat *a*' as in *trap* is a continuation of English English 18th century usage which separation aided to preserve and shielded against the influence of English English, which developed a pronunciation with the vowel of *palm* in these words. But the creation of new North American English forms and meanings, for which this variety is also famous, (*apartment, truck, gas, color, center* to mention a few classic examples not typical of English English) have also been facilitated by if not resting on separation and continuation. The numerous new forms, not least lexical ones, which are absent in English English but prominent in and characteristic of American English, result largely from settlers' contact with speakers of other languages and their response to a new environment in the new world, but because of separation the speakers of the mother countries did not adopt such new forms. Yet such new forms could not have arisen in North America if English had not continued to be the mutual language among the colonists.

However, although they spoke early Modern English, the immigrants arriving within the first 150 years far from spoke a homogenous type of Early Modern English. England at the time of the departure of the settlers hosted numerous regional dialects and had not yet developed a non-regional standard pronunciation, or English speaking settlers came from Scotland and Ireland with a very different linguistic background. This lack of homogeneity inevitably left linguistic marks on the North American Continent. As pointed out earlier, English speaking settlers arrived in four great waves. Of these the first wave, constituted mainly by the Puritans, came mostly from East Anglia and the East Midlands and thus spoke a south-eastern variety of English English. Consequently, New England and the north, where they established themselves, came to be influenced by this kind of south-eastern speech. The second great wave of immigrants, the Cavaliers and their followers, who settled mainly in Virginia, had their origin mostly in the west and south of England or to a lesser degree in the London area. For this reason, American English in the South is often said to be influenced by the speech of the south and west of England. Unlike the first two waves, who came from relatively confined areas, the settlers of the third wave, the Quakers and their sympathisers, were much more mixed, but their main source of origin was the North Midlands. This third wave settled areas in between the North and the South. Pennsylvania and nearby West Jersey and northern Delaware and Maryland, that is, areas in between the northern and the southern settlements, therefore came to be influenced by a north Midland variety of English English. The fourth and last wave is the group of settlers who are traditionally referred to as the Scotch-Irish, although they also contained people from the north of England. These immigrants were predominantly frontiersmen settling inland in between the North and the South, specifically in western Pennsylvania and the mountains of Maryland, Virginia and Carolina, just as they became the inhabitants of the Appalachian mountains. The speech of these inland areas can thus be said to be a continuation of or influenced by the English used by the people of this last predominantly Scotch-Irish wave.

Since the foundation for the introduction of English to North America was laid by the settlement of English speakers from Britain and Ireland, settlement history is said to have shaped the main dialect areas of present-day North American English. From New England where the first wave of immigrants settled, colonists migrated eastward to Maine, northward to Canada, southward to New Jersey and westward to upper New York and further beyond. The English of the first wave then formed the basis of a northern and north-eastern dialect of North American English. The second major wave, settling mainly in Virginia, spread gradually southward into South Carolina and Georgia, excluding Florida, which was only ceded by Spain in the 19th century, and from there westwards. The English spoken by these Virginia colonists therefore became the basis of a second main North American English dialect, viz. that of the South. The third and fourth waves colonised areas in between the north and the south. The quakers and their followers (the third wave) settled chiefly in Pennsylvania, and areas closest to the east coast, whilst the Scotch-Irish (the fourth wave) settled further inland from where they moved southward and westward. The English of these two quite mixed groups formed the basis of a third main dialect of North American English (usually regarded as two separate dialects), the dialect of the Midland and the West. The four main settlement waves, their origins (indicated in brackets inside text boxes) and their target areas in North America are summarised in the map in (1.1) with arrows indicating the direction of further movements of these settlement groups. The lines on this map separating the three main dialect areas are rough guidelines but not real boundaries between dialects. Such dialect boundaries will be taken up shortly.

The establishment of actual dialect boundaries, the so-called **isoglosses**, which indicate the borders between competing linguistic forms, began with the formation of the American Dialect Society in 1889. The work undertaken after its establishment laid the foundation of several important dialect projects outlining North American English dialects in the following decades. At least four of these projects are particularly relevant in the present context, as they serve to refine the broad outline shown in (1.1). The first project is the Linguistic Atlas of New England (abbreviated LANE), which was compiled by Hans Kurath and others and pub-

(1.1)

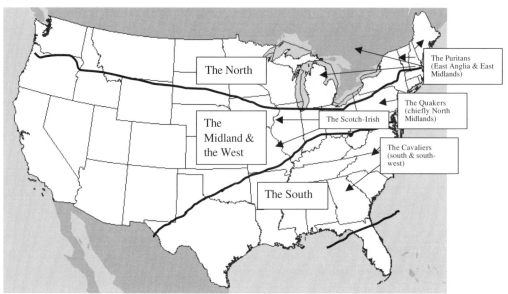

lished in 1943. LANE reported both lexical differences and variation in pronunciation, and showed these differences on maps. But LANE covered only New England. Therefore, the Linguistic Atlas of the Middle and South Atlantic States (abbreviated LAMSAS) and the Pronunciation of English in the Atlantic States (abbreviated PEAS) were important supplements. LAMSAS and PEAS, which were directed by Hans Kurath too and appeared in 1949 and 1961 respectively, the former dealing with lexical differences, the latter with pronunciation differences, provided maps of these differences and were the first to divide North American English dialects into northern, midland and southern types, thus confirming the linguistic impact of the different settlement waves. This appears from the reproduction of a LAMSAS map in figure (1.2), showing the dialect divisions of the eastern United States.

Although they confirmed the division into at least three main dialect areas which settlement history has shown to be relevant, LAMSAS and PEAS, like LANE, also covered a geographically restricted area. Subsequent dialect projects helped refine and extend the boundaries between these three dialects, specifically in the westward direction. In particular, Craig Carver's American English Regional Dialects, published in 1987, contributed to completing the picture, redrawing isoglosses established by LANCS, the Linguistic Atlas of North Central States, which extended the evidence provided by LAMSAS. But both Carver's results and the evidence made available by earlier projects, with the exception of PEAS, were based upon lexical data. Pronunciation and sound system were not investigated, so from the point of view of the present book the last and most recent dialect pro-

(1.2)

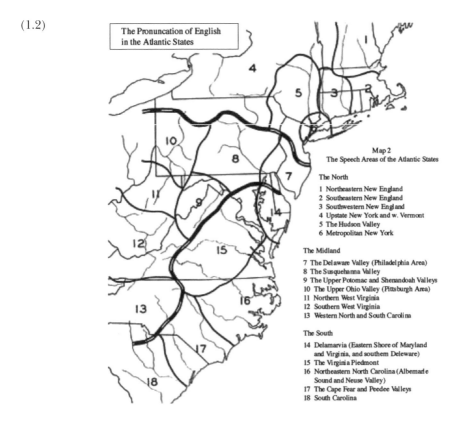

The Pronunciation of English
in the Atlantic States

Map 2
The Speech Areas of the Atlantic States

The North

1 Northeastern New England
2 Southeastern New England
3 Southwestern New England
4 Upstate New York and w. Vermont
5 The Hudson Valley
6 Metropolitan New York

The Midland

7 The Delaware Valley (Philadelphia Area)
8 The Susquehanna Valley
9 The Upper Potomac and Shenandoah Valleys
10 The Upper Ohio Valley (Pittsburgh Area)
11 Northern West Virginia
12 Southern West Virginia
13 Western North and South Carolina

The South

14 Delamarvia (Eastern Shore of Maryland
   and Virginia, and southern Deleware)
15 The Virginia Piedmont
16 Northeastern North Carolina (Albemarle
   Sound and Neuse Valley)
17 The Cape Fear and Peedee Valleys
18 South Carolina

ject, the Atlas of North American English, compiled by William Labov, Sharon Ash and Charles Boberg and published in 2006, which deals with pronunciation and sound system only, is the most relevant of all the projects which followed the establishment of the Dialect Society more than a century ago.

Basing itself on previous work, most notably LAMSAS and PEAS, The Atlas of North American English (abbreviated ANAE), is not only relevant in this context because it deals with pronunciation only, but also, and more importantly, because it attempts to include all North American speakers of English (with the exception of Alaska) and records an up-to-date pronunciation of these speakers within a time span of approximately 7 years (from 1992 to 1999). The detailed maps, which loom large in ANAE, reflect urban speech, in particular describe the pronunciation of 762 English-speaking North Americans in cities of 50,000 or more citizens. The present book will draw widely on ANAE data, since they cover all of English-speaking North America. Evidently, a sample based on only 762 subjects whose pronunciation was obtained through telephone interviews (ANAE builds on the TELSUR project which sampled data through telephone interviews) and who do not represent rural speech or the speech of cities of less than 50,000 citizens leaves out considerable detail. Sampling urban speech is also in contrast to earlier projects such as, for example, LANE which investigated rural speech. But concentrating on urban speech is motivated by sociolinguistic research such as William Labov's investigation of New York speech which has shown that linguistic changes in progress are most advanced in urban areas. Urban speech is then probably the most up-to-date and the kind of North American English which best illustrates its most recent state of development.

The division into the North, the West and Midland and the South, supported by settlement history and confirmed by dialect projects such as LANE and PEAS, also appears clear and distinct according to ANAE. But the maps in ANAE add considerable more detail. Inner areas in the North and the South are added and in the east the Mid-atlantic states constitute a separate area. The dialect divisions according to ANAE appear as shown in (1.3), with inner areas inside both the North and the South and other small dialect regions, as will be discussed in more detail in specifically Ch.10 below.

(1.3)

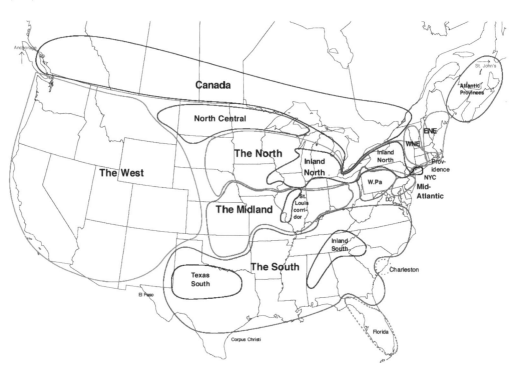

The boundaries drawn on this map reflect competing pronunciation features among specifically vowels. ANAE is unique in that it shows boundaries between different English sound systems, and sound systems only, for all of North America. Earlier projects, as pointed out above, were as much concerned with lexical as pronunciation differences. However, by and large boundaries drawn on the basis of pronunciation and underlying sound systems such as those presented by

ANAE coincide with boundaries based on lexical differences. The frequent concurrence of lexical and pronunciation boundaries explains in part why there is
no single non-regional standard American English pronunciation in North
America comparable with Received Pronunciation (RP) in English English,
which is the standard non-regional pronunciation in England. The existence of
a non-regional standard pronunciation like RP in England has lead to the notion of **accent**, which refers to a typical and specifiable pronunciation of a language which is characteristic of a geographical region or a social group. Such a
standard non-regional pronunciation is justifiable in England because – so sup-
porters of this concept argue – RP is characteristic of a social group and because
other accents than RP can be used with the standard grammar and lexicon. The
absence of such a variety in North America explains why the term **dialect**, rather
than accent, is used to describe linguistic varieties in North America, as has been
the case so far in this chapter, because dialect refers to a typical variety of a language which is characterised not only by a particular pronunciation but also by
a specific lexicon and grammatical system. But although the term dialect thus
encompasses other components of language than pronunciation, the present
book will deal with the pronunciation of dialects only. In fact, the focus will be
more specific than on just the pronunciation of North American English dialects. This book will focus on the pronunciation of a restricted form of North
American English, a form which is representative and regarded as typical of
North America. The following section will look further into the delimitation of
this reference dialect, as such a chosen representative dialect is traditionally
called.

1.2 The delimitation of a reference dialect

A textbook like the present one, whose aim is to introduce students to North
American English pronunciation and the sound system that this variety of Eng-
lish is founded on, must necessarily restrict its description to a kind of American
English which is fairly general and typical of English in North America. However, to choose one pronunciation that is general and typical of North American
English is not easy and likely to involve a good deal of subjectivity and prejudice.
For example, is it typical of American English to pronounce *steady* so it is heard
as *study* or to pronounce *hide* so it is heard as *had*? Or is it typical to pronounce
to park the car in the yard so *park*, *car*, and *yard* are said without an *r*, or to pronounce *ask* and *dance* so their vowels sound like the vowels of *ma* and *pa*? One
could also ask whether it is typical of American English to stress and pronounce
distinctly the penultimate syllables (last but one) and their vowels in *cemetery* and
obligatory, or whether a speaker from North America would typically utter *to park
the car in the yard* with a speech melody (pitch or intonation contour) which
starts at a relatively high pitch level and falls towards the end with some kind of

pitch variation associated with *yard*. Some will answer yes to these questions, but probably a majority will not be sure that such pronunciations are common or simply answer no. The assumption of this section and of the book in general is that it is not so typical of North American speakers to use any of the pronunciations mentioned above. This does not mean that such pronunciations are non-existent and are never encountered. Instead it means that they are not taken as representative of English in North America. But if they are not typical what kind of pronunciations is then representative in this continent?

Answering this question is to identify the **reference dialect,** which is the selected representative type of pronunciation that will be dealt with in the following chapters. Choosing a North American English reference dialect is controversial and likely to create considerable disagreement between linguists. The reason for this is that such a choice inevitably involves omission and simplification. In general, European textbooks describing North American English pronunciation such as Bauer et al., *American English Pronunciation* (1980), and Giegerich, *English Phonology* (1992), employ a reference dialect which is simply called **General American**. General American is also the point of reference in Wells' comprehensive three volume study, *Accents of English* from 1982, describing English pronunciations across the world. Geographically, General American in such descriptions refers to a variety which is spoken in the most of North America except for eastern New England, New York city and an area encompassing all of the states of Virginia, Kentucky, Tennessee, the Carolinas, Georgia, Alabama, Mississippi, Arkansas, Louisiana, some of Florida and the most of the state of Texas, i.e. the area which in a dialect context usually is referred to as the South. Thus General American refers to the variety spoken in the area not marked by a shaded colour on the map in (1.4).

The notion of General American dates back to George Krapp's study, *The English Language in America*, published in 1925, in which he identified three main dialects in North America: a New England dialect, a southern dialect and a general mid-western and western dialect covering the rest of the country. This third dialect Krapp called General American. As is apparent from the previous discussion, this division has been refuted and cannot be said to reflect the factual dialect geography in North America today. But Krapp's identification of General American reappeared in Kenyon and Knott's influential *A Pronouncing Dictionary of American English* from 1953 which, they say, represents 'standard speech'. Although firmly rooted in Kenyon's native Ohio speech, this standard is neither eastern nor southern, but what they refer to as northern, which in fact comes close to what Krapp called General American. Outside North America, specifically in Europe, Kenyon and Knott's dictionary earned considerable prestige as an accurate source of information about North American English pronunciation, so much that it is one important reason why John Wells in 1982 in his *Accents of English* calls his North American reference accent General American.

(1.4)

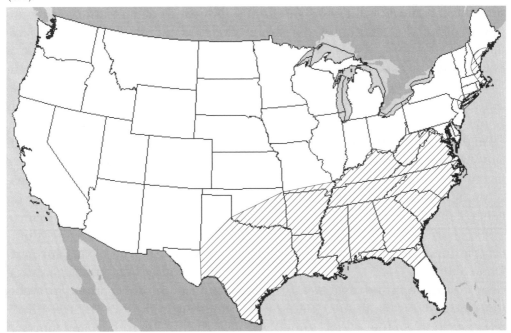

Other textbooks have followed this practice, and all assume it to have the geographical extension as shown in (1.4). Among North American linguists General American has long been considered a doubtful simplification or plainly a fiction which cannot be related to real data. The previous brief account of North American English dialect projects and their results establishing four main dialect areas seem to confirm the view that General American is an invention with little or no foundation in present-day North America.

No matter how useful, General American must then be rejected as an actually existing reference dialect, because it ignores such regional distinctions as those established most recently by ANAE and shown in (1.3). But ANAE boundaries are drawn on the basis of the pronunciation of vowels. This reflects a general approach in English dialectology, highlighted by John Wells' *Accents of English*, that the pronunciation of vowels is the key to the identification of different English regional pronunciations in both North America and elsewhere. As will become clear in specifically chapter 5, vowels are the sound types which allow most variation in pronunciation and which shifts and changes mostly and much more than other sound types. Dialect boundaries drawn on the basis of the pronunciation of vowels are then likely to be fine-grained and show much more regional variation than those drawn by investigating consonant pronunciation, and quite possibly those drawn by investigating variation in word stress and intonational patterns. Therefore, the above questions which were meant to expose what is characteristic and typical of North American English pronunciation such as whether it is typical of American English to pronounce *steady* so it is heard as *study* or pronounce *park the car in the* yard without an *r* will concern the pronunciation of vowels much more than other aspects of speech, even if these questions are meant to exhaust all the characteristic features of a North American English pronunciation.

ANAE is then an obvious source of information to use when a reference dialect of North American English pronunciation should be established with its primary focus on vowels. From the ANAE data, based on urban speech, it is clear that four main dialect areas are relevant: the North, the East, the South and the Midland and the West. The pronunciation of *steady* as *study* and also the pronunciation of *block* as *black* plus in fact a host of other somewhat unusual pronunciations are typical of the North. These pronunciations follow from a general shift of vowel pronunciations which affects short stable vowels (the so-called short monophthongs, see Ch. 5 below) in specifically many Northern cities around the great lakes, a shift which is known technically as **the Northern Cities Shift** (see Ch 5. below for discussion). On the other hand, the pronunciation of *hide* as *had* and also *slade* as *slide* plus in fact a series of other somewhat unusual pronunciations are typical of the South. As in the North, these follow from a general shift of vowel pronunciations, affecting both short and long stable vowels (short and long monophthongs, see Ch. 5 below), as well as unstable vowels consisting of two vowels with the first gliding towards the second (the so-called diphthongs, see again Ch. 5 below). This southern shift is known technically as **the Southern Vowel Shift**. Vowel pronunciations following from both the Northern Cities Shift and the southern Vowel Shift are not so characteristic of North American English that they will be regarded as unmarked and typical in this context. Many native speakers of English outside North America will also consider them uncharacteristic or local and for non-native speakers of English, to whom this text is also addressed, pronouncing *steady* as *study* or *hide* as *had* is certainly not typical of North American English.

The first delimitation of a reference dialect using vowel pronunciation points then to a non-northern and non-southern variety. But vowel pronunciations call for more subdivisions, as is obvious from the ANAE map. Above one question was whether it is typical to pronounce words like *staff*, *ask* and *dance* so they are heard with the vowel of *ma* or *pa*. Probably, most Americans as well as many non-American native speakers, let alone non-native speakers of English, will reject this pronunciation as characteristic of North America. Instead, probably, the vowel heard in the word *trap* will be suggested as an appropriate and typical North American pronunciation heard in these words. Geographically, a pronunciation of *staff*, *ask* and *dance* with the vowels of *ma* and *pa* is characteristic of the Northeast, an area which historically has maintained close contact with England where the *ma* and *pa* pronunciations developed in post-settlement eras and became typical of the standard English English pronunciation.

Further eastern peculiarities suggest that it is not in the East a reference dialect is to be found. In the East, the vowel found in *trap* has quite regularly two pronunciations. Either the *trap*-vowel sounds like the pure stable vowel of *lack* and *mat* or it is heard as the second vowel of *idea*, that is, it has the quality of an unstable bi-componential vowel sound also heard in the r-less, non-rhotic English English pronunciation of *fear* and *hear* (this pattern is also heard in the North). Again such a pronunciation of *trap*, although on the increase in North America, will at least by most native speakers of English outside North America be judged as untypical or local rather than as one which is typical of the continent. Another bi-componential pronunciation which is also characteristic of eastern speech further rules out eastern speech as reference pronunciation. The pronunciation in question is the one found in, for example, New York speech where the vowels of *York* (in exactly *New York*) or *talk* are heard as if they are pronounced with the vowel of *duel* or *cruel*. Although well-known to some American speakers, testified by the popular spelling of *New York talk* as *Noo Yawk tawk*, this pronunciation with two vowel elements will usually be considered local rather than general and typical of North America. For non-American native speakers of English it is likely to be considered unusual and non-representative, as will most certainly the majority of non-native speakers of English.

With respect to the pronunciation of vowels, the delimitation of a reference dialect narrows down to an area not mentioned so far, the Midland and the West. Florida, Canada and the north-eastern Atlantic provinces where English is also spoken can be disregarded. Since they fall outside the original English-speaking settlement areas, or are populated by a substantial number of speakers who do not speak English, these areas will be considered subsidiary. But although they appear as good candidates, the vowel pronunciations of the Midland and the West are not homogenous, but vary considerably as is expected of such a large geographical area. However, no extensive shift like the Northern Cities Shift or the Southern Vowel Shift applies in the Midland and the West. Nor can these areas be aligned with distinct splits such as the two alternative realisations of the trap-vowel in the East or the typically English English pronunciations found in New England. On the other hand, no vowel pronunciation unites them completely. One vowel pronunciation is fairly widespread in the Midland and the West and expanding. For many speakers of English word pairs like *dawn* versus *don*, *hawk* versus *hock* are distinct. The former member of the pair has a long stable vowel, the latter member a short stable vowel. In the Midland and the West this distinction is receding, so such word pairs are increasingly homophonous and often pronounced with the vowel of *pa* or *ma*. This merging of two distinct vowel pronunciations affects vowels which are articulated with the back of the tongue in a fairly low position (see Ch. 5 below for discussion). This loss of distinction is therefore referred to as **the low back merger.** The low back merger is neither typical of the North nor of the South, but it is found in Eastern New England and also characteristic of Canadian English. Wolfram and Estes report in their book, *American English*, from 1998 that they have encountered North American speakers who do not know that *don* and *dawn* can be distinct in the speech of some North Americans. Outside North America, the low back merger is also judged typical of North America, even sometimes used to describe a North American stereotype. With the low back merger, the characteristic pronunciations of the East and the quite radical shifts in the North and the South, a reference dialect based on the pronunciation of vowels begins to take shape.

Rather than saying that the vowel pronunciations of the Midland and the West should serve as a model for the reference dialect, the vowels of this very large region will be taken as a representative starting point. The contention is that the reference dialect with respect to vowels involves a vowel system which excludes speakers whose vowel pronunciation demonstrates evidence of the Northern Cities Shift, the Southern Vowel Shift and the characteristic diphthongs of the East as well as the English English influenced vowels in New England. The exclusion of such vowel pronunciations means that the reference dialect largely becomes negatively defined, described by what vowel pronunciations it does not include. Positively defined, the reference dialect has predominantly merged the distinction between the vowels of *dawn* and *don* so they sound as if they are more and more said with the vowel of *ma*. Its vowel system is also close to the system used and described by Peter Ladefoged in his authoritative *A course in Phonetics* (2001), a North American English variety which he terms **Standard American Newscaster English**. The same pronunciation underlies the American English renderings in John Wells' *Longman Pronunciation Dictionary* from 2000, which gives both English English RP and North American pronunciations of more than 75,000 words. Interestingly, in ANAE Labov et al. state that if any dialects were to be recognised as constituting a general American variety, then it should be the speech of the Midland and the West along with the pronunciation used in Canada. When all these observations are added up, it makes reasonable sense to say that a reference dialect must be associated with at least the vowel system found mainly in these areas. It is probably best to exclude Canadian speech, which has two vowel shifts (see Ch. 10 below) not found in the US. Such a vowel system is very close to what Ladefoged has used and called Standard American Newcaster English. The vowel pronunciations of the reference dialect are thus the mainstream characteristic standard without the obvious systematic shifts and splits of the North, the South and the East. In very general terms, it is the North American pronunciation which probably mostly resembles English English without being non-American, and it can be heard in the speech of at least some North American television presenters.

Some vowel pronunciations which are typical of the reference dialect can also be said to be standard in the areas excluded from the reference dialect by way of vowel shifts and splits. One such is the use of the *trap* vowel in words like *bath*, *staff*, *dance* which is typical of most parts of North America (except eastern New England). Another very widespread feature in North America is the nasalisation of vowels when these stand next to the nasal consonants as in, for example, *lamb*, *fan*, *sang*. In this position the vowels assume some of the nose quality (the nose acts as a resonator along with the mouth, see Ch. 4 below) of the contiguous nasal consonant. This nasalisation of vowels again is not restricted to a particular area but widely distributed in North America, yet not heard so often and to the same degree outside North America.

The tendency that the reference dialect area widens with certain vowel pronunciations as with the two above-mentioned cases characterises even more the pronunciation of consonants. A classic example of this is the pronunciation of *r* after a vowel as in *car* and *yard*. Above this pronunciation of *r* was used as one way to elicit what is typical of North American speech. A variety of English which has *r* in both these words is called **rhotic** and its users **rhotic speakers**. Most forms of North American English are rhotic. By contrast, most forms of English English are **non-rhotic** because in these varieties *r* is never pronounced in *yard* and only sometimes pronounced in *car* if the following sound is a vowel. Probably most settlers were rhotic, but under English English influence specifically areas along mainly the east coast developed non-rhotic pronunciations. According to ANAE, present-day non-rhotic speakers are centred around eastern New England and New York City and in the South around Charleston, Savannah, Atlanta and on the Gulf coast New Orleans. It is most stable in eastern New England and among black Americans in the South, but variable in other areas and on the whole receding on the model of the rest of rhotic North Americans. The assumption is here that the reference dialect is rhotic and given the limited geographical extension of non-rhotic pronunciation this widens the reference dialect area to cover most of North America.

The same geographical width seems to apply to three further consonant pronunciations typically associated with North American English. The first is the pronunciation without a *j*-sound in words like *tune*, *duke*, *new*. In such words, English English, and in fact most types of English pronunciations, pronounce a *j* after the first consonant. Technically *j* is known as **jod** and because it has lost jod in such words, North American English is described as **jod-dropping**. Jod-dropping is found throughout North America and thus not just characteristic of the reference dialect. The second pronunciation which will be considered standard and part of the reference dialect, thus extending it, is the common pronunciation of *t* and *d* as a quickly articulated *d*-like sound, known as the **flap** (also referred to as *t*-voicing, see Ch. 3 below for discussion). This pronunciation is found when unstressed *t* and *d* occur between vowels or between an *r* and a vowel, as in *matter*, *ladder*, *fourty*, *party*. Again, flapping is found throughout North America and only restricted by various speech situations (known as registers) where lan-

guage serves different social roles, but not by geography. The third and last pronunciation which is assumed to be characteristic of the reference dialect and not
restricted by geography is the pronunciation of *l*. In most English varieties outside North America (except Ireland), this consonant can be pronounced as a
clear or a **dark** *l* (see Ch. 4 below for discussion). As the name suggests, the dark
l has a dark resonant sound and outside North America it is found before consonants and in word-final position as in *film, tall, cattle,* whereas clear *l*, whose resonance is light, is found before vowels as in *let, last, lost, loom.* In North America the
pronunciation is typically dark in all these words but to a varying degree. It is
most dark in *film, tall, cattle* and less dark in *lost* and *loom* but least dark in *last* and
let. If it is restricted in North America, dark *l* is chiefly less frequent among specific ethnic groups. Among Black Americans, for example, there is a tendency to
replace the dark *l* with a vowel or drop it all together. It is also reported among
white speakers in the Midland but receding, but the overall general picture is that
dark *l*, varying as described above, is found throughout North America.

The picture of the reference dialect which arises on the basis of the pronunciation of individual consonants and vowels is then that whereas it is somewhat
geographically restricted when defined by major vowel shifts and splits, it widens
after the inclusion of consonant pronunciations and other vowel pronunciations than the major shifts and splits. This picture is not disturbed when phenomena like word stress and intonational patterns are considered. There exist
no examinations which document clear regional differences in intonation contours. Instead factors like ethnicity and gender have been shown to create variation in theses areas of speech. Thus the pronunciation of black Americans supposedly involves a wider pitch range than that of other speakers in North
America, and women employ a very high pitch level (also claimed to be characteristic of British women) absent in the speech of male speakers. Variation in
stress and rhythm has also been shown to be ethnic. Spanish influenced varieties of North American English can show features of the rhythm associated with
this language, which is governed by syllable structure rather than by stress accent as in English (see Ch. 6 below). The absence of clear indications of region-
ally based variation in stress and intonation leaves us with a reference dialect
predominantly determined by variation in the pronunciation of vowels and to a
lesser degree by variation in the pronunciation of consonants. The features restricting the reference dialect mostly are then:

The Northern Cities Shift
The Southern Vowel Shift
The split of the *trap* vowel in the East
The Low Back Merger

with the last feature restricting it positively as the merger is characteristic of the reference dialect, and the first three features restricting it negatively by occurring outside the reference dialect. The features that expand the area of the reference dialect so it includes the North, the South and the East partly or fully are these:

Trap vowel in *bath, staff* etc.
Rhoticity, pronunciation of *r* in e.g. *yard, car*
Dark *l*, dark resonant quality especially in e.g. *tall, cattle, film, lose, lust*
Flapping of *t* and *d* in words like *better, ladder, party, porter*
Jod-deletion, no *j* in such words as *duke, tune, new, sue*
Nasalisation of vowels, nasal quality of vowels in such words as *nun, ram, ring*
Stress and intonation patterns

A choice of reference dialect, as has been done here, on the basis of primarily regional variation inevitably involves omission of detail, simplification of variation and not least a considerable amount of subjective selection. It is very difficult to avoid subjective judgement in selecting a reference dialect. The tradition of textbooks whose main aim is to provide students with the basic tools of sound description based on North American English is bound to influence the biased chooser in a way which reflects his own non-native preferences. But caution has been exercised so that the above mentioned authoritative accounts of Peter Ladefoged or John Wells, combined with the recent findings of ANAE all have been considered and applied in identifying a representative dialect of English in North America. Attempts will be made to make up for the omission and generalisation following from choosing a particular variety as reference dialect. The first compensation is a brief mention of an ethnic rather than regional dialect which from time to time will be mentioned in the following account of the reference dialect's sound system. The ethnic dialect in question is known under the name of **African American Vernacular English**, abbreviated **AAVE**, which is the dialect spoken by some, but by no means all, African Americans. AAVE, according to one view, although this is debated, is originally a **pidgin** which grew out of contact between the African slaves who did not speak the same language and the English-speaking people they worked under in the early days of slave-hood. Gradually, this reduced pidgin language, which was a mixture of several African languages and English, acquired native speakers and became a **creole** with a fully fledged non-reduced sound system, grammar and lexicon. As it was originally based on English, and therefore had many English features in it, this creole became **decreolised** under the influence of the **Anglo American English** which surrounded the AAVE speakers. As a result of this decreolisation, AAVE changed into something very similar to Anglo American English, preserving, however, some features of the original creole which today serve to identify this variety as different. Some of these features are listed below:

- Absence of third person present tense -*s*
  he drink for *he drinks*
- Use of stressed *been* to indicate a remote action or a state
  I been known him a long time for *I got to know him a long time ago and I still know him*
- Reduction of a consonant cluster before a following vowel
  lif up for *lift up*
  bussing for *busting*
- Devoicing of voiced consonants in stressed syllables
  [bit] for *bid*, [bæk] for *bag*
- Absence of post-vocalic *r*
- Use of vowel instead of dark *l*

AAVE will be referred to from time to time whenever relevant in connection with the discussion of individual sounds. Another compensation for what is excluded and generalised as a result of choosing a particular variety of North American English as reference dialect will be a more extensive treatment of the sound systems of the major North American dialects. Chapter 10 will be devoted to a description of such regional variation by using the data provided by ANAE, and the chapter will identify the characteristic and diagnostic sound system features of the main regional dialects in North America. First, however, the sound system of the reference dialect will be described in greater detail. In the past, the reference dialect of North American English has been called General American which is basically a non-eastern and non-southern variety of North American English, as pointed out earlier. Since the reference dialect proposed here is much more than just non-eastern and non-southern, the term General American will be abandoned. Instead the reference dialect referred to throughout this book will simply be called North American English Reference Dialect and abbreviated NAERD. Before the individual sounds, first consonants and later vowels, of NAERD can be described, it is necessary that we know how many vowels and consonants there are and what is criterial for their being members of the sound system of NAERD. These issues will be the topics of the immediately following chapter, which then is an introduction to some important theoretical concepts in the description of linguistic sounds.

1.3 Summary of the main points

As pointed out in the preface, each chapter will be concluded with a brief summary of the main points of the chapter in question. The main points of this chapter can be summarised as follows:

- English was brought to North America in the 17th and 18th centuries in four great waves which largely shaped the present-day dialect geography
- A detailed description of North American English dialects started in the 20th century culminating in 2006 with the Atlas of North American English (ANAE) which identifies five main areas in the US, the North, the South, the West, the Midland and the East and one in Canada
- ANAE provides detailed maps of borders between dialects on the basis of pronunciation only and identifies several sub-dialects within the main areas
- A pronunciation is chosen as reference dialect which is taken to be representative of North America. This dialect is abbreviated NAERD (North American English Reference Dialect). With respect to the pronunciation of vowels this reference dialect is non-northern, non-eastern and non-southern. With respect to consonants (and certain vowels) as well as stress and speech melody, the reference dialect covers also northern, eastern and southern areas either partly or fully. The main characteristics of the reference dialect are:
- Exclusion from the Northern Cities Shift and the Southern Vowel Shift as well as vowel splits in the East
- Rhoticity, that is *r* is pronounced in postvocalic position as in *yard, car,* *l* is pronounced as the so-called dark *l* in all positions, unstressed *t* and *d* are pronounced as flaps between vowels or an *r* and a vowel and, finally, *j* is dropped after certain consonants as *in new, tune, duke, sue*
- The *trap*-vowel, sometimes referred to as the 'flat *a*', is pronounced in about 150 native words such as *bath, staff, mass.* Nasalised vowels next to nasal consonants as in *men, lamb, sang.*

Further reading
Comprehensive accounts of most aspects of American English are Algeo 2001, Wolfram and Estes 1998, Tottie 2002. The best detailed account of settlement history and its effect on English in North America is Fischer 1996. An early very comprehensive description of English in North America is Krapp 1925. The first detailed descriptions of English dialects in North America are those of Kurath 1939-1943, 1949, 1965 and Kurath and McDavid 1961. A more recent description in particular extending the dialects in a westward direction is Carver 1987. For a recent and very comprehensive description of American English dialects see Labov et al. 2006 dealing with sound system only but covering all of North America. A now somewhat dated but nonetheless very detailed account of American English sound systems is found in Wells 1982. The best dictionaries on American English pronunciation are Kenyon and Knott 1944 and Wells 2000. On African American English see, among others, Green 2002 and Wolfram and

Thomas 2002. Comprehensive introductory textbooks to English pronunciation dealing partially or fully with American English are Giegerich 1992, Bauer et al 1980 and Ladefoged 2001.

CHAPTER 2

The phoneme and the phoneme inventory of North American English

2.1 Introduction

Having established that the reference dialect, NAERD, is predominantly non-northern, non-southern and non-eastern when it comes to the pronunciation of vowels but much more inclusive comprising also the North, the South and the East partly or fully when other aspects of pronunciation are considered, it is now time that the sound system of this reference dialect is examined more closely. By sound system is meant at this stage the individual consonants and vowels of the reference dialect and not properties such as stress, intonation or rhythm. Although equally important, the latter properties of the reference dialect will only be dealt with once the individual consonants and vowels have been described in detail and therefore not considered until part II.

This chapter will examine the sound system in two ways. Firstly, it will establish what makes a consonant or a vowel a member of the sound system, in particular how the ability to contrast meaning is essential for membership, and outline how each consonant or vowel constitutes a building block in a larger hierarchical system in which they interact with other entities of linguistic structure such as word, phrase and sentence. Secondly, the chapter will establish exactly how many consonants and vowels the reference dialect NAERD has, what its contrasting vowels and consonants are and show how a limited set of words can elicit the contrasting sound inventory. The chapter begins with the more general issue of identifying the contrastive sounds and how they fit into the hierarchical system of language.

2.2 The phoneme and the linguistic hierarchy

The linguistic tradition on which the present description is built views language as an entity which consists of building blocks of variable size that make up a **structural linguistic hierarchy**. According to this tradition, the largest structural building block of language is the **clause** and the smallest structural building block of language is the individual **consonant** or **vowel**. The clause belongs to grammatical structure and the individual consonant or vowel belongs to sound structure. The best way to illustrate how the clause and the individual consonant or vowel are building blocks at opposite ends of the structural hierarchy of language is to show how a string like the following can be analysed (divided) into successively smaller structural units:

(2.1)

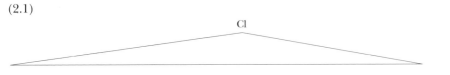

the faithful painters located in the open square gave the chairman a promising answer very quickly

First this string is analysed as one clause as shown in (2.1). The next step of the analysis divides the clause into its clausal functions. The clause in (2.1) has the **clausal functions** shown in the tree diagram in (2.2):

(2.2)

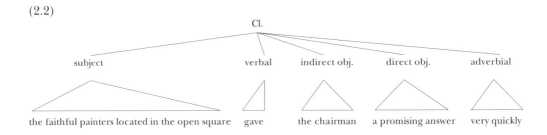

Each clausal function is then described in terms of a **phrasal category** (noun phrase (NP), verb phrase (VP) etc.), reflecting the head of the material which makes up each clausal function, so that a NP, for example, is used to describe a clausal function whose head is a noun:

(2.3)

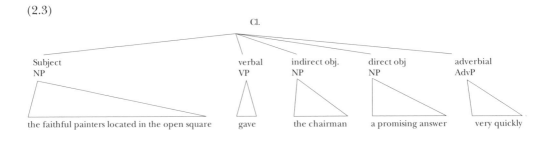

The subsequent step subdivides each phrase into its functional elements (prm (premodifier), head and pom (postmodifier)) whose material is specified in the following step. The result of these analyses is shown in (2.4):

(2.4)

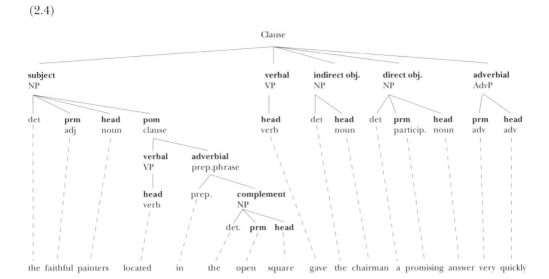

When each word has been described in detail by having been separated from any other word by being aligned with a single node in the tree (in the way e.g. 'faithful', and only this word, is aligned with the leftmost adj.-node), the analysis of the clause has been concluded.

Whilst the syntactic analysis of the clause terminates once the material and function of each word have been fully described, the linguistic analysis does not necessarily stop here. Individual words may be divided into smaller building blocks, as shown by the vertical lines in (2.5):

(2.5)

the faith|ful paint|er|s locat|ed in the open square gave the chair|man a promis|ing answer very quick|ly

Two types of building blocks arise as a result of this further division. The first type, exemplified by *faith, print, chair*, simply constitutes individual words. The second type is characterised by being smaller than individual words. *painters*, for example, consist of two such elements, namely *er* and *s*; other elements smaller than words are *ing* and *ly* which form part of *promising* and *quickly*. Although they differ from words by being unable to occur independently, these elements share with words the property that they have meaning. This meaning is not lexical, but typically more general and grammatical. For example, the meaning of *s* in *painters* is 'plural' and the meaning of *ly* in *quickly* is 'adverb'. Building blocks which cannot be divided further into meaningful elements are called morphemes, so *faith, paint, er, ly* are morphemes, allowing no further subdivision into meaningful blocks. A **morpheme** is then the smallest **meaningful** unit of language.

But as anticipated above, the morpheme is not the smallest structural building block of language. The individual morphemes may be further subdivided into building blocks, only these smaller blocks are not meaningful. Consider the one-morphemic word *might*. Evidently, *might* consists of several successive blocks as reflected by the use of different spelling symbols. More accurately, the spelling reflects that *might* consists of three successive sounds (written in right-angled brackets), namely [m] + [aɪ] + [t], i.e. two consonants [m] and [t] and one vowel [aɪ], which is in this case a diphthong. But unlike morphemes, these individual sounds – unless they also function as morphemes – are not meaningful. The sound reflected by the representation [t] and found as the last sound of *might* or the first sound of *two* (although the two *t*'s are not completely identical) does not in itself have meaning. Instead, such a sound is characterised by distinguishing meaning. This becomes evident when the *t*-sound is replaced with other sounds, as illustrated below in (2.6a), where the vertically arranged sound symbols in angled brackets indicate sound substitutions and the word arranged to the right of each arrow the result of such substitutions:

(2.6)

a. [maɪ t] → *might*   b. [maɪt]   → *might*
   [s] → *mice*   [æ] → *mat*
   [n] → *mine*   [e] → *met*
   [m] → *mime*   [i] → *meet*
   [l] → *mile*   [oʊ] → *moat*

When each of the sounds in the vertical row in (2.6a) is inserted into the position after [maɪ-], this insertion results in a change of meaning. For example, the insertion of the sound [t] results in the word *might*, the replacement of [t] by the sound [s] results in the word *mice*, the replacement of [s] by the sound [n] results in the word *mine* and so on. A sound which is able to change meaning in this way is called a **phoneme**. A phoneme does not have meaning then, only morphemes and larger building blocks have meaning. Instead phonemes distinguish meaning. So in North American English the consonant sounds [t, s, n, m, l] are all phonemes when they occur finally in a word, because they can all change meaning in this position. Similarly, the insertion of the vowel sounds [aɪ, æ, e, i, oʊ] (see Ch. 5 for an explanation of these symbols) one after the other into the context of a preceding [m] and a following [t], shown in (2.6b), shows that these vowel sounds should be regarded as phonemes in medial position, since the insertion of each vowel sound results in a change of meaning. A sound which functions as a phoneme is written between '//', so the representation /t/ refers to one among several of the smallest building blocks of language which is able to distinguish meaning. This building block combines with other phonemes to form meaningful blocks, for example morphemes and words. The representation between angled brackets refers to the actual pronunciation of the phonemes, whereas the representation between slashes ('//') refers to the sound which can distinguish meaning in the language in question. This difference in representation will be taken up again shortly.

The test for phonemehood by inserting sounds into the same context is called the **commutation test**, and the word pairs which arise as a result of this test such as, for example, *might – mice* are termed **minimal pairs** because they differ in the smallest possible way, the former having final /t/ and the latter final /s/. However, it is in fact possible to be more specific than describing the difference between *might* and *mice* as one where the former has the phoneme /t/ and the latter the phoneme /s/, and show that it is not quite accurate to define the phoneme as the smallest building block of the linguistic hierarchy. But to show that the phoneme is not the smallest building block requires that we anticipate some of the slightly more technical descriptions of how speech sounds are produced, which will be found in Ch. 3 below.

Both /t/ and /s/ are consonants, that is, such sound types which, unlike vowels, cannot typically form syllables alone (also described as non-syllabic). At the same time, they are both what is referred to as voiceless because the vocal folds (also known as the vocal cords), which are located in the Adams apple, do not vibrate during their articulation. /t/ and /s/ also involve a major obstruction in the mouth because the tongue tip or tongue blade or both are raised against the gum ridge behind the upper teeth (what is known as the alveolar ridge, see Ch. 3 below) when they are articulated. But they differ from one another in one respect: the tongue is not raised equally much when the two consonants are pronounced. When /t/ is pronounced, the tongue forms a complete closure at the alveolar ridge followed by a release of the outgoing air, whereas during the pronunciation of /s/ the outgoing air escapes through a narrow passage at the alveolar ridge, causing a frictional, hissing noise as the air flows out continuously. The closure characteristic of /t/ is what makes this consonant a stop and the narrow passage of /s/ is what makes this consonant a fricative (both articulations are described in more detail in Ch. 3). So to return to the minimal pair *might – mice*, the difference between these two words is, strictly speaking, not one of /t/ versus /s/, but one that boils down to closed stricture (/t/) versus narrow stricture (/s/). In other words, it is just one articulatory property (closure of air stream versus narrow passage of air stream) which serves to distinguish /t/ and /s/ and hence *might* and *mice*. In all other respects, /t/ and /s/ are identical as they are both voiceless, articulated at the alveolar ridge and consonants. Such properties as closure, stricture, alveolar, voiceless are called **distinctive features**, because they serve to distinguish phonemes uniquely. In fact, any phoneme is made up of several distinctive features. This is illustrated in the following diagram in which the distinctive features of /t/ and /s/ are listed vertically below /t/ and /s/ in large angled brackets:

(2.7)
might / m aɪ t /   *mice* / m aɪ s /

The distinctive features are then the ultimate and smallest contrastive units in the linguistic hierarchy and smaller than the phoneme. The distinctive features 'closure' versus 'stricture' keep the two phonemes /t/ and /s/ distinct, as is apparent from (2.7). The status of the phoneme does not change as a result of recognising distinctive features. The distinctive features of e.g. /t/ are characterised by being simultaneous, all occurring at the same time when this phoneme is pronounced, which explains why the distinctive features are arranged vertically in (2.7) rather than one after the other, i.e. consecutively. By contrast, phonemes are characterised by occurring one after the other, i.e. they are consecutive. For this reason the phoneme is still the smallest contrastive unit among the **consecutive** units of language. But among all linguistic units, consecutive and non-consecutive, the distinctive feature is the smallest contrastive unit of language.

   Let us sum up the main points about sound structure and the linguistic hierarchy. The distinctive feature is the smallest structural unit in the linguistic hierarchy. Distinctive features make up phonemes. Distinctive features and phonemes distinguish meaning but do not have meaning. Phonemes combine and form the smallest meaningful strings, the morphemes. Morphemes combine and form words and words in turn enter into combinations which constitute phrases. Lastly concatenations of phrases make up clauses. The clause is the largest structural block. Above clause level relations are semantic and pragmatic rather than structural. Therefore the clause is considered the largest structural entity. At the bottom of the hierarchy no further decomposition of the distinctive feature is possible. However, it is common to operate with different kinds of distinctive features, depending on the tradition followed in a given context. What is not questioned is that the distinctive features constitute a finite set which is very often assumed to be applicable to all languages.

2.3 Phonemes and allophones

Establishing the consonants [t, s, n, m, l] and the vowels [aɪ, æ, e, i, oʊ] as phonemes in North American English by substitution in the way illustrated in (2.6),
requires that the sounds tested for phonemehood can occur in the same context, in (2.6a) in the context of preceding [maɪ] and in (2.6b) in the context of
a preceding [m] and a following [t]. But there also exist sounds which can occur in the same context where the substitution of one for the other does not
lead to a change in meaning. For example, the final *t*-sound of *might* can be pronounced in at least two different ways. Recall that this consonant is a stop and
produced by raising the tongue tip against the alveolar ridge whereby the outgoing air is blocked. Often the blocked-off air is released very quickly after the
closure. This results in what could be called a *t*-sound with a release, written [tʰ].
But it is also common that the *t*-sound is articulated without an audible release.
This pronunciation is written [t˺]. Both these *t*-pronunciations can occur in the
same context. For example, they are both possible as the last sound of *might*. But
substituting [tʰ] for [t˺] (released [t] as opposed to unreleased [t]) does not
lead to a change of meaning. *might* does not have one meaning when pronounced with a final [tʰ] and another meaning when pronounced with a final
[t˺]. In other words, it is not possible to say that [tʰ] and [t˺] are different phonemes. When substitution of one for the other fails to change meaning, the two
t's are instead variant pronunciations of one phoneme, in this particular case
the phoneme /t/, and because a speaker can choose freely between these two
pronunciations, [tʰ] and [t˺] are **free variants** or **free allophones** of the phoneme /t/.

Let us briefly consider two other examples of free variants. The final sound of
might may serve as illustration again. In the string *might agree* a third pronunciation of the final *t* of *might* is frequent in American English. In the string *might
agree*, where the *t* occurs before an unstressed vowel, it is likely to be pronounced
as what in Ch. 1 was called a flap, viz. a quick flick of the tongue tip against the
alveolar ridge, like the *t* in *letter* and *party* (the flap is transcribed [D], see Ch.3
for further discussion). Although it is frequent in most speech styles, this pronunciation is not obligatory but an option available to the American speaker.
Because the use of this pronunciation does not change the meaning of *might*,
the flap is a free variant of the phoneme /t/ (and in fact /d/) alongside with
other possible pronunciations like [tʰ] and [t˺]. The other example of a free
variant involves also partly a flap-like pronunciation. The example comes from
English English and may be illustrated with the word *very*. The *r* of this word
may be pronounced in up to three different ways in an English English pronunciation: firstly as an approximant [ɹ], an articulation which involves open approximation, secondly as a flap [D], similar to the flapped pronunciation of /t/
or /d/ in American English, and thirdly (but rarely) as a trill [r] which involves

several successive flaps. Again these three pronunciations all occur in the same context, viz. between vowels (what is known as intervocalicly). Moreover, the speaker may choose freely between the three possibilities (this is probably not quite accurate for trilled [r] which is strongly dependent on speech style), and since, as with the different *t*-pronunciations, the substitution of one for the others does not lead to a change of meaning, [ɹ], [D] and [r] are not phonemes but free allophones or variants of the phoneme /r/ in English English.

The free allophones or free variants are thus non-contrastive or non-phonemic sounds which occur in the same context. But there also exist sounds which never occur in the same context, and therefore cannot contrast meaning, but which are still variants of the same phoneme. As illustration of this possibility, consider the pronunciation of the phoneme /l/. Above in Ch. 1 it was said that this consonant usually has a dark quality in North American English in words like *film, tall, law, lust*. This quality is called dark *l*, and it is a feature which is characteristic of North American English, as it is found in more contexts in this variety than in other non-American kinds of English (English English RP, for example, would not have it in *law* and *lust*). However, some North American English speakers fail to use dark *l* in words like *least, list, less, last*. Before certain vowels, specifically what is called front vowels as in these words (see Ch. 5 below), /l/ instead has a lighter quality resulting in what is called clear *l*. This pattern of pronunciation is always found in English English, but such that clear *l* has a wider distribution than in North American English, occurring before all vowels and /j/ and not just before front vowels as in *least, list, less, last* and dark *l* elsewhere. The situation in North American English is then the following for those speakers who use clear *l*:

(2.8)

clear *l* [lʲ]	dark *l* [ɫ]
before: front vowels	before: all other vowels
/j/	consonants (except /j/)
	in word-final position

What (2.8) summarises is that clear and dark *l*'s are mutually exclusive: clear *l* occurs in exactly those positions where dark *l* does not occur and vice versa. The technical term for this kind of occurrence or distribution of sounds is **complementary distribution**. This was what was meant when it was said above that two sounds may belong to the same phoneme, although they never occur in the same context. Because they do not occur in the same context but are bound to particular positions or environments, such sounds are called **bound variants** or **bound allophones**. Unlike free allophones, bound allophones then cannot occur in the same context and will therefore never be potential contrasts. But the two *l*-sounds will still be interpreted as belonging to the same phoneme, the phoneme /l/, because they are very similar as far as pronunciation is concerned. '

Let us consider another example of bound variants or bound allophones. Consider the pronunciation of the two words *keep* and *cool*. In a broad transcription *keep* and *cool* will be represented as [kip] and [kul]. But a closer examination of the initial stop consonants of these two words reveals that, although they are transcribed with identical symbols (the symbol [k] denoting a voiceless stop articulated by raising the back of the tongue against the soft back part of the mouth, see Ch. 3 for discussion) the two stops are not completely identical. [k] of *keep* is distinctly marked or 'coloured' by the following front vowel ([i]), so the place where it is articulated has been pushed forward and the tongue is raised where the roof of the mouth is hard rather than soft. The [k] of *cool*, on the other hand, remains retracted and is articulated by raising the tongue against the soft back part of the mouth, because it is followed and influenced by the following back vowel [u]. In other words, the [k]'s of *keep* and *cool* vary according to context. The fronted articulation in *keep* is bound to a following front vowel and the more retracted articulation in *cool* is bound to a following back vowel, and the fronted variant does not occur where the retracted variant occurs, and the retracted variant does not occur where the fronted variant occurs. As such, they stand in complementary distribution, excluding one another mutually, and the two [k]'s are therefore examples of bound allophones or variants of the phoneme /k/, because they are also very similar in pronunciation.

However, two sounds which stand in complementary distribution are not always allophones of the same phoneme such as the two pronunciations of the first consonants in *keep* and *cool*. In NAERD, and in most varieties of English, the first and last sounds of the word *hang*, i.e. what is transcribed as [h] and [ŋ] (the latter is a nasal like /n/ articulated by the air escaping out through the nose, see Ch. 4 below), stand in complementary distribution too. In words of one syllable, the sound [h] occurs only in initial position and [ŋ] occurs only in final or near final position, but [ŋ] is not found initially and [h] never occurs finally. Nevertheless, [h] and [ŋ] are not assigned to the same phoneme. Unlike clear *l* and dark *l* and unlike fronted [k] and retracted [k], which also excluded each other mutually, [h] and [ŋ] do not share any distinctive features apart from both being consonants. That is, they are not pronounced alike to the same extent as clear *l* and dark *l* and fronted [k] and retracted [k] are pronounced alike. For this reason, it does not make sense to consider them to be bound variants of one phoneme. The fact that they are not pronounced in a similar way instead opts for a solution where they are assigned to two different phonemes: the pronunciation [h] is assigned to the phoneme /h/ and the pronunciation [ŋ] to the phoneme /ŋ/. Each of these phonemes then has a limited or **defective distribution**, /h/ never occurring finally and /ŋ/ never occurring initially.

2.4 The phoneme as an organising unit of sound structure

It was pointed out in the discussion of free variants that the phoneme /t/ has at least three different variant pronunciations: [t⁺], released /t/, [t], unreleased /t/ and [D], the flap. But a closer inspection reveals that in words like *two, cattle, button* and *stake* another four different pronunciations of the sound spelled *t* occur. In *two* /t/ is pronounced with a following short period of voiceless breathing adding a *h*-quality to the stop. This feature is called **aspiration** and indicated in the transcription of the sound which has this feature with a raised *h*, so the /t/ in *two* is transcribed [tʰ]. In *cattle*, on the other hand, the *t*-sound is influenced by the following lateral *l*, so that when the stop is released the release occurs with a tongue position identical to that found with the *l*. This is notated with a raised *l*, i.e. [tˡ]. In *button* the stop is also influenced by the following sound, resulting in a release through the nose like that found and characteristic of a nasal sound like *n*. The notation for this pronunciation is a raised *n*, i.e. [tⁿ]. Finally in *stake* the stop written *t* lacks aspiration, the *h*-like quality found in *two*, as a result of its position after the initial sound [s]. This will be written with a plain *t*, i.e. simply [t]. More pronunciations of the stop written *t* can be shown to exist. For example, pronunciations with variable degrees of aspiration occur, but it is not important to list all possible variants. What is important to observe is that the concept of phoneme enables us to organise and draw together this multitude of pronunciations. By operating with the phoneme /t/ it is possible to show that although they differ from each other, the different *t*-pronunciations are systematically the same and that there exists an underlying system behind the wealth of speech variation. Viewed from this angle, the phoneme becomes a unit which is a head of a family where the members of the family are the individual and sometimes quite excessive number of pronunciations. This organising property of the phoneme is illustrated in the following simple diagram (which does not include all variants of /t/):

(2.8)

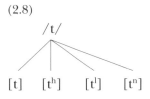

Any phoneme in NAERD can be shown to be the head of a family of sounds, a family of variant pronunciations. Sound structure is then viewed as consisting of two levels. First a level which organises sound structure into a manageable entity with a limited number of elements. These elements or **segments**, as they are very often referred to, are the phonemes, and the level they form or belong to is called the **phonological** level and the discipline which describes them is termed **segmental phonology**. The phoneme is then an abstract entity which is a kind of common denominator for the speech sounds which are similar in pronunciation. These actual pronunciations make up the other level of sound structure. This level is called the **phonetic** level and the elements of this level are called **allophones**. The phonetic level, whose indvidual vowels and consonants appear in square brackets, is then the concrete level of pronunciation from which phonemes are set up. The phonemes, by contrast, are represented in slashes (//) which then signal underlying contrasting sound element.

Although it is an abstract entity, the phoneme has a very concrete use. As will become clear below, the existence of phonemes enables us to posit a limited number of consonants and a limited number of vowels for any language or language variety, including NAERD, namely only those consonants and vowels which can contrast meaning. This is an advantage when we want to describe a variety of English like NAERD and compare it with other varieties of English. The phoneme also facilitates the historical description of how pronunciation has changed. As a manageable entity, it optimises the systematisation of how, for example, the pronunciation of Middle English has changed to that found in Early Modern English and subsequently to that of present-day English. The phoneme is also a natural entity given a structuralist view on language, as illustrated in § 2.1 above, by being the smallest successive structural unit. Lastly, the phoneme can be put to a very concrete use in foreign language learning. As an entity which restricts the number of sounds that a foreign language contains, the phoneme not only helps the learner to get an overview of the sound system of the foreign language to be learned, but the existence of the phoneme also makes it easier to identify the difficult areas of pronunciation, as these often coincide with areas where the learner language and the foreign language differ in phoneme inventory. As a final point it should be stressed that the phoneme has a long history in the consciousness of speakers. To be true, most speakers are not aware of the existence of phonemes, but the finite number of letters in written alphabets is proof that phonemes, and a finite number of phonemes, have been tacit knowledge for many centuries. The letters of written language were exactly devised to represent the contrasting sounds of language.

2.5 Establishing the phoneme inventory of NAERD

Given the necessary background knowledge of phonemes as outlined in the preceding, it is now time that the commutation test is put to concrete use in order to establish how many phonemes NAERD has, that is, how many sounds can contrast meaning in this variety of English. By inserting consonant sounds into the environment of a following [aɪ] and [u], it is possible to show that 22 consonant sounds can change meaning in initial position in NAERD and hence are phonemes, as shown in (2.10a):

(2.10)

	a. **initial position**			b. **final position**		
a.	[-aɪ]	[-u]	phoneme	[li-]	[ru-]	[ræ-]
	pie	*pooh*	/p/	*leap*		*rap*
	buy	*boo*	/b/		*Rube*	
	tie	*two*	/t/	*leet*	*root*	*rat*
	die	*do*	/d/	*lead*	*rude*	*rad*
	kye	*coo*	/k/	*leak*		*rack*
	guy	*goo*	/g/	*league*		*rag*
		chew	/tʃ/	*leech*		*ratch*
		Jew	/dʒ/	*liege*		
	fie	*Fu*	/f/	*leaf*	*roof*	*raff*
	vie		/v/	*leave*	*roove*	
	thigh		/θ/	*wreath*	*Ruth*	*wrath*
	thy		/ð/	*wreathe*		
	sigh	*Sue*	/s/	*lease*		
		zoo	/z/	*lees*	*ruse*	*razz*
	shy	*shoe*	/ʃ/	*leash*	*ruche*	*rash*
			/ʒ/	*liege*	*rouge*	
	high	*who*	/h/			
	my	*moo*	/m/	*leam*	*room*	*ram*
	nigh	*new*	/n/	*lean*	*rune*	*ran*
			/ŋ/			*rang*
	lie	*Lou*	/l/		*rule*	
	rye	*rue*	/r/	*leer*	*Ruhr*	
		you	/j/			
	why	*woo*	/w/			

But consonants occur not only initially but also finally. An examination of final position by substituting consonant sounds in the environments of preceding [li-], [ru-] and [ræ-] results in two more than the 22 contrasting sounds found in initial position. At the same time, three consonant sounds found in initial position turn out not to contrast in final position. (2.10b) illustrates the finally contrastive consonant sounds found in NAERD.

A further search for contrastive consonants will be futile. The total number of consonant phonemes in NAERD (and most varieties of American English), counting both (syllable) initial and final positions, is then 24. Of these /j/, /w/ and /h/ occur only initially, whereas /ŋ/ and /ʒ/ are found only finally, not counting foreign loan words. The remaining 18 phonemes occur both finally and initially.

Turning to vowel sounds, the contrastive vowel sounds of NAERD can be established by the following lists of words:

(2.11)

beat	*feel*	/i/
bit	*fill*	/ɪ/
bet	*fell*	/e/
bat		/æ/
but (unstressed)		/ə/
Burt		/ɜ/
butt		/ʌ/
boot	*fool*	/u/
	full	/ʊ/
bought	*fall*	/ɔ/
Bart		/ɑ/
bait	*fail*	/eɪ/
bite	*file*	/aɪ/
	foil	/ɔɪ/
bout	*foul*	/aʊ/
	foal	/oʊ/

According to this chart, 16 vowels are then contrastive in NAERD. Of these one, viz. /ə/, never occurs in stressed syllables. Arguably, /ə/ thus fails to comply fully with the criterion that phonemes should occur in identical environments. The same applies to /ɜ/ which is followed not only by a *t*, as required, but also by an *r* in the chart in (2.11) (the same applies in fact to /ɑ/). Indeed, /ɜ/ always occurs before an *r* and as such fuses with the *r* and becomes an *r*-coloured vowel, something which explains why the vowel of *Burt* in a phonetic transcription is represented as [ɜ] (a similar fusion/colouring characterises /ə/ when followed by *r*, giving the phonetic representation [ə] for the last syllable of, for example, *finer* ([ˈfaɪnə], see Ch. 5 below for discussion). But whilst /ə/ occurs both with and without a following *r*, /ɜ/ is only found before *r*. It is then defensible to analyse the vowel of *but* as /ə/, provided its occurrence in unstressed syllables is ignored. The vowel in *Burt* is more of a problem, as, unlike /ə/, it always is bound to a following *r*. One analysis often adopted for the vowel of *Burt* is therefore to consider this vowel a bound allophone/variant of another vowel phoneme, either /ə/ or /ʌ/, both of which are phonetically quite similar to the vowel of *Burt*, and thus not posit an independent /ɜ/ phoneme. However, since it makes for ease of comparison between other varieties of English, many of which have /ɜ/, /ɜ/ will here be recognised as an independent phoneme alongside with other vowel phonemes which occur both with and without a following *r* in NAERD. But it is important to emphasise that this solution is not quite accurate, as it disregards for this vowel the fundamental principle that phonemes should contrast in identical environments.

As with consonants, a further search for contrastive vowels will be futile. The total number of contrasting vowels in NAERD is then 16. Before *r*, however, there is not only the special case of /ɜ/, as just pointed out. The environment of a following *r* also restricts the number of contrasting vowels. Much fewer vowels contrast in NAERD before *r* than before other consonants. This lack of contrast will be dealt with in connection with the discussion of the individual vowels. The total number and types of vowel phonemes which occur in the words lists of minimal pairs in (2.10) and (2.11) are the results of choosing a variety of American English as reference dialect which neither shows obvious effects of the Northern Cities Shift nor of the Southern Vowel Shift. Likewise the vowel system set up here does not show signs of specifically eastern vowel changes. Readers who are familiar with American English pronunciation as it is found in these areas will therefore not always agree with the set of contrasting vowels posited here, nor the words associated with these vowels. Choosing a reference dialect is always controversial and bound to lead to accusations of generalisation and inaccuracy. However, the aim of actually introducing students to how American English speech sounds can be described outweighs, in the view of the present author, the simplification that the choice of NAERD as reference dialect results in. And, as pointed out above, attempts will be made to compensate for the generalisation following from the position of a reference dialect like NAERD, so the following descriptions of individual vowels and consonants will incorporate variation in the pronunciation of these sounds in the North, the South and the East, as well as describe the dialects of these areas in more detail in Ch. 10.

2.6 Summary

The main points of this chapter may be summarised as follows:

- The phoneme is the smallest consecutive building block in the linguistic hierarchy which can contrast meaning
- Phonemes consist of non-consecutive distinctive features which are the smallest building blocks in the linguistic hierarchy
- Phonemes and distinctive features distinguish meaning, but are not in themselves meaningful
- Above the level of phonemes, the linguistic building blocks are meaningful
- Phonemehood is established by means of the commutation test and minimal pairs

- Phonetically similar sounds which may occur in the same environment, but cannot contrast meaning, are free allophones of one phoneme
- Phonetically similar sounds which cannot occur in the same environment stand in complementary distribution and are bound allophones of one phoneme
- Phonemes belong to the phonological level of language. The actual pronunciation of the phonemes constitutes the phonetic level of language
- There are 22 consonant phonemes and 16 vowel phonemes in NAERD.

Further reading
One of the best introductions to phonemes and phonological analysis is Lass 1984. See also Sommerstein 1977 and Laver 1994. As for the phoneme inventory of American English, Wells 1982 should also be consulted. See also Bauer et al. 1980. The idea behind the linguistic hierarchy and its manifestation is discussed in, among others, Lyons 1968.

CHAPTER 3

Obstruent consonants in American English

3.1 Articulatory, acoustic and auditory descriptions

As anticipated earlier, this chapter and chapters 4 and 5 are devoted to the description of the individual consonant and vowel phonemes of the reference dialect NAERD. The consonant and vowel phonemes, as established in Ch. 2, are the smallest consecutive speech sounds which can contrast meaning. But consonants and vowel phonemes only exist as phonemes because they are pronounced in the actual world. A description of the consonant and vowel phonemes therefore must start with their actual pronunciation. Phonetics is the scientific study of the actual pronunciation of speech sounds. Conventionally, a phonetic description can be articulatory, acoustic or auditory. The description below of the NAERD phonemes will therefore take into account, but to a varying degree, these three phonetic aspects of speech sounds.

More specifically, by an **articulatory** description is meant that the consonants and vowels will be described according to how they are produced with the articulatory organs. For example, according to an articulatory description the first sound of the word *zoo*, what is transcribed [z], is produced by placing the tip or the front of the tongue close to the alveolar ridge (the gum ridge behind the upper teeth), at the same time as the sides of the tongue are raised, and with this tongue configuration air escapes out through the mouth along the middle of the tongue while the vocal cords vibrate partly or fully. Although it may appear complex and technical, such a description has proven useful because it can be understood by all students after a few hours of teaching. It has the advantage that the student can quickly check such a description of [z] against the way he uses his own articulatory organs, which creates an awareness of how his articulatory organs work. Also with this knowledge it is easier to learn how other sounds are articulated and teach new students how to pronounce a consonant like [z]. Articulatory knowledge also provides valuable help in a foreign language learning context.

An **acoustic** description, by contrast, investigates the physical characteristics of the sound waves which make up speech sounds rather than the movement and position of the articulatory organs. An acoustic description makes heavy use of a variety of electronic instruments such as the sound spectrograph, with which it is possible to measure frequency and intensity of speech sounds as a function of time. Much of what will be said about intonation below in Ch. 8 will be based on the acoustic analysis of the pitch frequency produced by the vibrating vocal cords. Similarly, vowels are often distinguished on the basis of concentration of energy within specific frequency bands, known as formants, which result from the vocal tract (the entire length of the speech apparatus from lungs to lips) forming a series of varying resonators whose modulation of the speech sound aligns each vowel with a unique acoustic sound picture. ANAE, referred to in Ch.1, uses acoustic data extensively to determine the vowel differences of North American English dialects. Since data of ANAE play a significant part in the present book, much of what will be said about vowels is founded on acoustic analyses. Acoustic properties can also support the general division into speech sound types like vowel and consonant, and the division of consonant types into obstruent and sonorant and sub-categories of these, although such classifications are as much defined by articulatory as by acoustic properties. As a rule, the technical reference to the acoustic properties of speech will be limited, as this requires a comprehensive introduction to acoustic analysis, which has been judged too ambitious in an intoductory textbook like the present one, but acoustics underly much of what is said below about both vowels and intonation.

Lastly, whilst an acoustic approach bases itself on physical facts like frequency and intensity, the **auditory** approach to sound description is impressionistic and investgates how the human ear perceives, interprets and processes speech sounds. Some use will be made of this method too. When consonants like /s, z, ʃ/ (the first sounds of the words *sip, zip, ship*) are described as sibilants, then this characterisation is auditory, reflecting the relatively high degree of hissing noise associated with these consonants. Descriptions of intonation and rhythm also rely on the auditory properties when we compare the acoustic interpretations of these phenomena with our own production or with what we hear others say. In controlling and amending own speech, speakers also rely on auditory feedback from what they hear in the air or through the bones of their heads, feedback which is essential when first learning a language and in second language learning. But as far as the description of individual consonants is concerned, the approach of this book is predominantly articulatory, concentrating on how the organs of speech are used in producing the NAERD consonants. Consequently, this chapter begins with an outline of the organs of speech and how they function in speech production.

3.2 The organs of speech and their three systems: articulatory, phonatory and respiratory

The present-day shape and position of the human organs of speech are usually assumed to be essential for the production of speech. Thus humankind has neither produced speech nor probably possessed language for very long, comparatively, in its 3 million years old history, as the present-day position of the organs of speech supposedly dates back only some 175,000 years. Athough it will never be known exactly how language developed as a result of evolution, it is very likely that the development of a large brain and an anatomical reconfiguration of the mouth and throat in our ancestors have played major parts in the process of language development. The reconfiguration involved, as can be seen when the mouth and throat of apes are compared with those of humans, that the larynx, or Adam's apple, descended to occupy the position it has today between the mouth and lungs, a position it does not have in apes. In this way the mouth became a resonator, or, as mentioned above, a series of resonators, and the vocal cords, located in the larynx, and which for very long served the function of preventing food (or water when our ancestors were still aquatic) from entering the wind-pipe, became positioned such that they could modulate the outgoing air coming from the lungs in a variety of ways which are relevant for the production of individual speech sounds as well as pitch and prominence. In the course of evolution the individuals with a lowered Adam's apple adapted most successfully to the surrounding environment and survived as the fittest. If this had not happened and another species had prevailed with a different anatomical development, the following outline of the organs of speech, let alone other details in this book, would not be relevant nor probably ever written. But we know now that these humans who developed, among other capacities, the abilty to produce speech because of this reconfigurating descend and other factors fared well and passed on their genes and came to dominate the human race.

The organs of speech are divided into three main categorial systems whose existence depends on the above-mentioned descend: **the articulatory system**, **the phonatory system** and the **respiratory system**. Figure (3.1) illustrates this common subdivision:

Beginning from the bottom, the respiratory system consists of the lungs, the muscles which control the inhalation and exhalation of air and the bronchi and the wind-pipe. In English, only the flow of air out of the lungs is relevant. This **egressive** air stream is the source of energy on which English speech is based. The ingressive airstream is not utilised systematically in English, but can be heard if a speaker is out of breath or excited. Many African languages make systematic use of an **ingressive** airstream. The sound used in English to signal horses to move forward or go faster is a consonant, known as a click, in several African languages. In a click air is sucked into the mouth by an inward movement of the front part of the tongue. Clicks are then formed on an ingressive airstream.

As the outgoing air leaves the lungs and the wind-pipe, it enters the phonatory system. The phonatory system comprises the **larynx**, also known as the Adam's apple. The larynx, whose forward part is prominent in men, is a chamber of cartilage which contains two muscles termed the **vocal cords**. The space between the vocal cords is called the **glottis**. (3.2) illustrates the larynx seen from above:

(3.1)

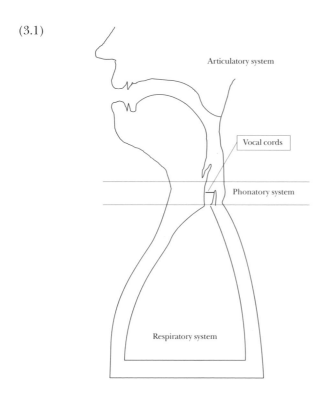

(3.2)

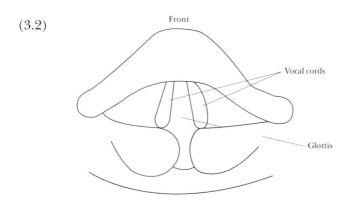

The glottis can assume a number of shapes of which three are relevant in the present American English context:

1. The glottis can be closed, a state which occurs when the vocal cords form a closure so no air can escape; this state is found as a reinforcement of word-final English /p, t, k/ or, in some varieties, as a replacement of /t/. This is referred to as the **glottal stop** and written [ʔ].

2. The glottis can be open because the vocal cords are pulled apart. This state results in a completely **voiceless sound**. /p, t, f, s/ in NAERD, for example are always pronounced voiceless. In some stop consonants, the glottis is open for a period of time after the release of the closure creating an *h*-like sound after the stop referred to earlier in Ch. 2. This period of voiceless breathing is known as **aspiration** and notated with a raised *h* after the stop so that aspirated /p/ as in *pull* is transcribed [pʰ].

3. The glottis can be a narrow passage as a result of the vocal cords being pulled closely together. When the air escapes out through this narrow passage, the vocal cords vibrate. This state results in a **voiced sound**; English vowels and some English consonants are normally voiced. Voicing is also essential for the creation of pitch and different rates of vibration create a variation of pitch which contributes to intonational contours (see Ch. 8 below).

As it leaves the larynx, the egressive air enters the **articulatory system**. The articulatory system consists of three cavities or resonators and the articulatory organs in them. These cavities are the pharynx, the nasal cavity and the oral cavity. (3.3) shows this subdivision of the articulatory system:

(3.3)

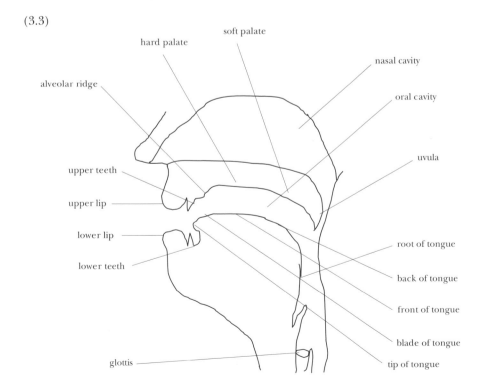

Of these only the oral cavity requires further subdivision. First the articulators in the oral cavity are divided into **active articulators** and **passive articulators**. The passive articulators are those articulators which are attached to the upper jaw and which cannot in principle move. The active articulators, on the other hand, are those articulators which can move and which are attached to the lower jaw.

Beginning with passive articulators, these may be divided first up into **upper lip** and **upper teeth**. Behind the upper teeth there is a bony gum ridge. This ridge is called the **alveolar ridge**. After the alveolar ridge, the roof of the mouth domes. The first part of this dome is also hard and bony and is termed the **hard palate**. Moving backwards, the texture of the roof changes and becomes soft. The soft part of the roof is called the **soft palate** or **velum**. Finally, the roof ends in the **uvula** which may be raised and close off the nasal cavity or lowered so air can escape out through the **nasal cavity**.

Turning to the active articulators, which are attached to the lower jaw, these are first divided up into **lower lip** and **lower teeth**. The tongue constitutes the remaining active articulator. The tongue is divided into a number of areas which are not physiologically but phonetically motivated. The point of the tongue is referred to as the **tip**; then comes the **blade** and the area following the blade is called the **front** of the tongue which in resting position lies immediately under the hard palate. Finally, the **back** of the tongue is the area which in resting position lies under the velum, whilst the **root** refers to the tongue part which is opposite the **pharynx** wall.

The reader is asked to identify the various active and passive articulators in the diagram in (3.3). It should also be noted that an active articulator typically interacts with the passive articulator immediately opposite. If they occur, displaced articulations usually involve the front part of the active and passive parameters with several closely successive articulators and usually a displaced articulation does not involve a deviation of more than one degree. Thus the labio-lingual consonant found in some Oceanic languages which is produced by the tongue tip making contact with the upper lip is a highly marked and very unusual type of articulation, whereas the displaced articulation found in /f, v/ is very common.

3.3 The classification of the consonant system

The class of NAERD consonants is the topic of the present chapter and chapter 4. More specifically, this chapter deals with the class of so-called obstruent consonants, while the class of consonants known as sonorants is the topic of chapter 4. But before we describe the individual members of these consonant classes, it is necessary to define what kind of sound a consonant is and how these two main classes of consonants, obstruents and sonorants, differ from one another.

A first attempt at a definition of a consonant would be to say that it is a sound type which, articulatorily, is produced with either a complete closure or a narrow constriction in the oral cavity. Although it defines sounds like, for example, /p, dʒ/ as in *pie* and *Jew* and sounds like /f, ð/ as in *fine* and *they* as well as the nasals /m, n, ŋ/ as consonants, (the latter are included by this definition as they involve an open nasal passage but a closed mouth), this description fails to cover all sounds generally considered to be consonants. The definition does not include /r, l, j, w/, but these sounds are nevertheless held to be consonants, even though they lack oral closure/constriction. Therefore closure/constriction is not enough, but other properties must be invoked to delimit consonants uniquely from other sound types. Acoustic properties do not help much either. On the one hand, consonants like /p, dʒ/ and /f, ð/ show either no acoustic or irregular and non-periodic output, whereas all of /m, n, ŋ/ and /r, l, j, w/ like vowels possess a regular periodic wave structure. Instead the property that unites all consonants, not only those like, for example, /p, dʒ, f, ð/ and those that differ both articulatorily and acoustically like /r, l, j, w/, is the inability of all these sounds to constitute the peak or centre of a stressed or prominent syllable. Vowels, on the other hand, can be the central element around which other sounds cluster in stressed syllables, indeed always are with the exception of the vowel /ə/ (see Ch. 5 for further discussion). A unique definition of consonants must therefore invoke not only phonetic properties, such as eg. closure/constriction, but also phonological (functional) properties such as ability to serve as the central element of syllables. So, to return to the question of what kind of sound a consonant is, the answer is that a consonant is a sound which articulatorily involves either closure/constriction or a stricture of open approximation in the mouth and acoustically anything from zero to clearly periodic output, at the same time as this sound cannot act as the peak or central element of a stressed syllable.

Given this definition of consonants, the next step is to consider how this large group of sounds can be sub-classified. The difference, mentioned above, between, on the one hand, /r, l, j, w/ and, on the other, consonants produced with oral closure/constriction corresponds approximately to a division into two main classes of consonants, viz. the division into **sonorants** and **obstruents**. Obstruents are those voiced or voiceless consonants which are produced with either a narrow constriction or a complete closure in the vocal tract and acoustically with no or irregularly organised output, at the same time as there is no nasal air passage. Sonorants are those voiced consonants which are produced in such a way that there is a free air passage either through the nose or through the mouth, at the same time as they are aligned with an acoustically periodic and regular output. Auditorily, sonorants never involve audible friction, whereas the constriction in obstruents always aligns them with fricative or plosive noise. Also obstruents are usually never syllabic (but see Ch. 5), whilst sonorants may constitute the syllabic peaks of unstressed but not of stressed syllables, as pointed out earlier.

Both sonorants and obstruents can be divided into further sub-classes. Obstruents consist of two main classes, **stops** and **fricatives**. Stops are those consonants which involve a complete but brief closure of the articulators and acoustically brief zero output. There are two types of stops: affricates which are stops whose blocked air is released gradually, thus creating clearly auditory frictional noise, and **plosives** whose blocked air is released abruptly (see § 3.4.1 below). /tʃ/ and /dʒ/, as in *chew* and *Jew*, are **affricates** and /p/ and /b/, for example, as in *pace* and *base*, are plosives. Unlike stops, fricatives are not produced with a complete closure but involve only a narrow constriction and not a complete closure of the articulators. Fricatives, which thus involve frictional noise caused by the narrow constriction as well as continuous acoustic output, also fall in two types: those that as a result of concentration of energy are produced with a characteristically hissing noise and those which due to less energy concentration are less noisy. The first class is termed **sibilants** and the second class **non-sibilants**. The obstruent types mentioned so far are summarised below:

(3.4)

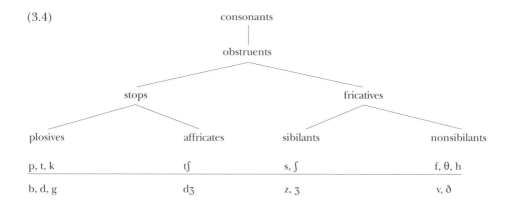

Sonorants, the other main class of always voiced and acoustically periodic consonants, may also be divided into subclasses. One class of sonorants is articulated with a lowered velum and a closed mouth so the air only escapes out through the nose. These sonorants are termed **nasals**. A second class contains those consonants in whose articulation there is no contact between active and passive articulators. As they lack frictional noise and are articulated with open approximation, these consonants are termed **semivowels** or **approximants**. Finally, there is one sonorant consonant, viz. /l/, which is articulated with constriction centrally at the alveolar ridge and with open approximation along one or both sides of the tongue. As another term for open approximation along the sides of the tongue is lateral, this sonorant consonant is called a **lateral**. The sonorant classes are shown in (3.5):

(3.5)

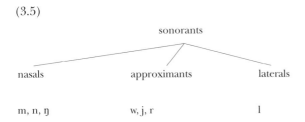

A classification of consonants as summarised in (3.4) and (3.5) is a classification specifying the generally phonetic (predominantly articulatory) properties of the consonants. The nodes in the tree diagrams specify whether the outgoing air is impeded completely, whether the air has to pass through a narrow constriction, whether there is an open oral passage, whether the nasal cavity is invoked and so on. Since terms like blockage, constriction, approximation, voicing describe the general way or manner in which consonants, in particular classes of consonants, are produced, this classification is termed **manner of articulation**.

Describing manner of articulation, i.e. the general articulation of consonants, is in contrast to two other ways of describing consonants. The first is a description of the point or place where a particular sound is articulated. Describing the place where there is closest contact between active and passive articulator is a description of **place of articulation**. Place of articulation can be specified for any consonant type and although it refers to the point in the vocal tract where there is closest contact between active and passive articulator, a place description typically mentions the passive rather than the active articulator, because it is assumed that the active articulator is the one immediately opposite the passive articulator, except in the case of consonants produced with the lips (bilabial) or lips and teeth (labiodental) which refer to active articulators too. Thus when the plosive /t/ is described as alveolar, it means that the alveolar ridge is the passive articulator and the immediately opposite tongue tip is the active articulator, just like it means when /g/ is described as velar that the velum is the passive articulator and the immediately opposite tongue back is the active articulator. How many places of articulation are relevant for the description of the NAERD consonants appears from the following diagram, which specifies the places of articulation of the obstruents and sonorants shown in (3.4) and (3.5):

(3.6)

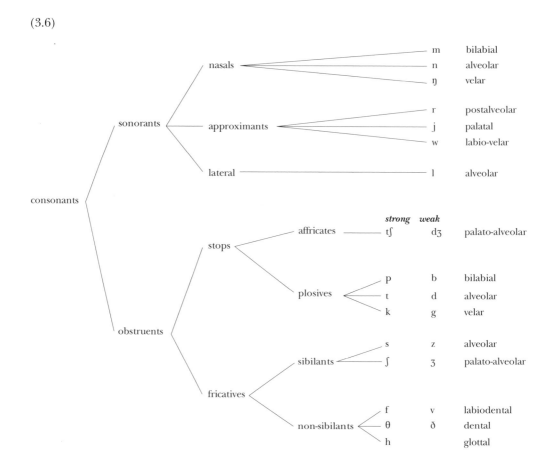

The other way to describe consonants applies to obstruents only and involves what is referred to as **strength**. Those obstruents placed above the horizontal line in (3.4) involve more muscular energy and greater acoustic intensity, are relatively more noisy, lack vocal cord vibration, and shorten the preceding sound. These obstruents are termed **strong** and differ from those placed below the horizontal line which instead are **weak**, as they involve less muscular energy, are comparatively less noisy, frequently involve vocal cord vibration and do not shorten the preceding sound. The energy of obstruents serves an important function in the classification of both stops and fricatives, cutting across the classes of obstruents established on the basis of manner of articulation. A comprehensive description of a consonant should then establish the manner of articulation, the place of articulation and, in the case of obstruents, the energy of articulation of the consonant in question.

3.4 Classes of obstruents in NAERD – stops

As is apparent from (3.6), stops are a major class of obstruents in NAERD. This class of consonants is produced with an oral closure at the same time as the velum is raised so no air escapes out through the nasal cavity. According to the way the blocked air is released, stops can be divided into two classes: plosives and affricates. It is equally apparent from (3.6) that stops may also be divided into a strong and a weak class cutting across the division into plosive and affricate. This section looks in more detail at these manner-and energy-based classes, including properties specifically related to the release of the stop closure. The third classification of stops (and fricatives) according to place of articulation, also apparent from (3.6), will only be taken up in § 3.5 where each individual stop is dealt with in detail.

3.4.1 Plosive versus affricate

As a consonant type which is articulated by closing off the egressive airstream orally at the same time as the velum is raised, a stop typically consists of three distinguishable phases. These phases are:

- the **closing phase** is the phase in which the articulators approach each other and form a closure
- the **closure** is the phase during which the air is compressed behind the closure
- the **release** is the phase in which the articulators diverge and the compressed air is exploded

In a diagram, the three phases of stops are commonly illustrated as follows:

(3.7)

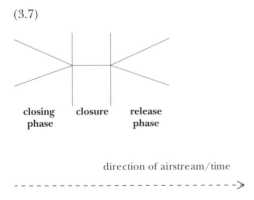

closing   closure   release
phase   phase

direction of airstream/time

in which the non-vertical lines represent the active and passive articulators and the vertical lines the borders between the three phases.

The distinction between plosives and affricates pertains to the third phase, the release phase. The abrupt release, illustrated in (3.7), is characteristic of /p, t, k/ and /b, d, g/. In these stops, articulators diverge from one another quickly, as is apparent from the release phase in (3.7). The hissing noise characteristic of the affricates /tʃ/ and /dʒ/, on the other hand, is a result of a gradual release of the compressed air; in particular, the articulators first form a narrow stricture before they diverge and the air is allowed to flow out unhindered. In a diagram this looks as follows:

(3.8)

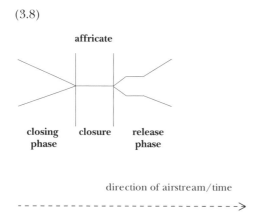

affricate

closing   closure   release
phase   phase

direction of airstream/time
- ->

The second symbol of the affricates (/ʃ/ in /tʃ/ and /ʒ/ in /dʒ/) then corresponds to the first part of the release phase when the articulators have not yet diverged completely but still form the stricture of close approximation. This stricture is identical to the stricture of the individual fricatives /ʃ/ and /ʒ/ (see § 3.6.1 below). For this reason the second symbols of the affricates (/ʃ/,/ʒ/) are also reused for these fricatives which are articulated with an identical stricture. Despite the use of two symbols for these stop types, affricates are interpreted as single consonants because they behave like other single consonant stop phonemes such as /p/ and /b/.

3.4.2 Strong versus weak

Whereas the distinction plosive versus affricate divides stops exhaustively into two neat release-defined categories, the division according to energy into strong and weak plosives cuts across these categories. But given that it results in two equally exhaustive classes, the distinction between strong and weak is just as neat and uniform as the release-based division. But unlike the release-defined division, the strong-weak division is more general and also applies to the class of fricatives, if not exhaustively then almost exhaustively. This will be discussed in more detail in § 3.6.2 below.

Although somewhat controversial, the strong-weak distinction will be used here to cover a number of more or less constant properties:

- **force of articulation** referring to muscular energy, air-pressure, duration of closure and noise. Stops in which these properties are prominent are **fortis**; stops in which these properties are less prominent are **lenis**
- **voicing** (see § 3.2 above) referring to whether the vocal cords vibrate or fail to vibrate. Stops which in some positions exhibit full or partial vocal vibration are **voiced**, and consonants which never involve vocal cord vibration are **voiceless**
- **aspiration** (see § 3.2 above) referring to whether the glottis is open and the out-going air produces a period of voiceless breathing, an *h*-like sound, after a consonant. Stops which are followed by this voiceless breathing are **aspirated**, stops which are not followed by this breathing are **unaspirated**
- **length of the preceding sound** referring to whether the length of the preceding sound, specifically a vowel, is or is not affected by a following consonant

Given these properties, /p, t, k, tʃ/ are strong stops as they are fortis, voiceless, aspirated (except /tʃ/) and shorten the preceding sound, whereas /b, d, g, dʒ/ are weak stops as they are lenis, partially or fully voiced, unaspirated and do not shorten the preceding sound. Thus the horizontal line in (3.9) divides the class of obstruents into strong and weak with the former listed above the line and the latter listed below the line. The horizontal line shows how the distinction strong-weak cuts across other categories:

(3.9)

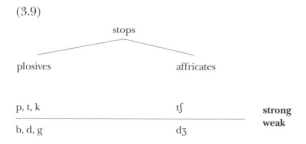

The degree to which these properties contribute to the distinction between strong and weak depends on the position that the sounds occupy within the syllable. Three positions are relevant in this connection, viz. initial, medial between voiced sounds and final positions. The three positions may be illustrated by the following word pairs:

(3.10)

	[p/b]	[t/d]	[k/g]	[tʃ/dʒ]
initial	pill bill	till dill	kill gill	chill Jill
medial	caper caber	latter ladder	vicar vigour	riches ridges
final	cap cab	hat had	lack lag	rich ridge

More specifically, the four properties contribute as follows:

- **Force of articulation**. In all positions, strong /p, t, k, tʃ/ are fortis whereas weak /b, d, g, dʒ/ are lenis
- **Voicing.** In initial, medial and final position, strong /p, t, k, tʃ/ are always voiceless. In initial and final position weak /b, d, g dʒ/ are either completely voiceless or partially voiced, so that when it occurs voicing is found in those parts of the weak stops which adjoin the contiguous voiced sounds, i.e. in the last part of the stop when this is followed by a voiced sound and in the first part of the stop when this is preceded by a voiced sound. In medial position between voiced sounds, weak /b, d, g dʒ/ are fully voiced
- **Aspiration**. Strong /p, t, k/ (note that /tʃ/ is never aspirated) are aspirated, most especially in initial position, in particular if the syllable is also stressed, less aspirated in other positions. Weak /b, d, g, dʒ/ are unaspirated in all positions
- **Length of the preceding sound**. Strong /p, t, k, tʃ/ shorten the length of the preceding sound, weak /b, d, g, dʒ/ do not shorten the preceding sound. This characteristic and for non-native speakers often difficult feature of English plays an important part in differentiating word pairs like *cup – cub, felt – felled, dock – dog, rich – ridge* in which the first member of these pairs has a distinctly shorter [ʌ], [l], [ɔ] or [ɪ] which are followed by strong /p, t, k, tʃ/ than in the second members of these pairs which contain weak /b, d, g, dʒ/

No single property then serves to distinguish strong from weak stops. Instead an interplay of properties preserves the distinction, and their relative contribution depends on where the stops occur in the syllable. The following diagram summarises the main points:

(3.11)

p t k tʃ b d g dʒ	initial	medial	final
force	fortis / lenis	fortis / lenis	fortis / lenis
voicing	voiceles / voiced/voiceless	voiceles / voiced	voiceles / voiced
aspiration	strongly aspirated / unaspirated	aspirated / unaspirated	aspirated / unaspirated
length		shorten preceding sound / no shortening of preceding sound	shorten preceding sound / no shortening of preceding sound

where in each box the terms listed above the diagonal line describe the properties of the strong stops, and the terms listed below the diagonal line describe the properties of the weak stops in the three positions, initial, medial and final.

3.4.3 Different kinds of release

In Ch. 2 above it was described how the phoneme from one point of view can be seen as an organising unit of sound structure, unifying different but related pronunciations of, say, one stop consonant. For example, it was pointed out that /t/ may be pronounced unreleased or released, as a flap or *l*-released or *n*-released. This sections looks in more detail at such variant pronunciations which concern the release phase of stops.

The first release-based variant to be discussed is the stop pronunciation without an audible release. Inaudible release is not found with the affricates /tʃ/ and /dʒ/ but is only a possibility with the plosives /p, t, k, b, d, g/. **Inaudible release** is found in the following cases:

- finally before a pause; thus in *give up!*, *it's good!*, *at stake!* one option for the final stops is to be realised as a free allophone without audible escape of compressed air
- when two stops with the same place of articulation (**homorganic** stops) occur next to each other. Thus in *bad tape* or *can't take*, the /d/ of *bad* and the /t/ of *can't* are unreleased. Instead the two alveolar stops merge as one long plosive. Note that the second stop in these pairs of stops also lacks the closing phase. Unlike the inaudible releases before a pause, these inaudibly released pronunciations are bound vari-

ants as they occur in the context of another contiguous stop consonant.

- When two non-homorganic plosives occur next to each other; thus in
  captain, in which /p/ and /t/ are contiguous, the release of /p/ is
  normally inaudible because the closure of the following stop means
  that only a very small volume of air is released. Similarly, in *bad boy* the
  release of /d/ is not heard because a following labial closure prevents
  the air from being released. Again these inaudibly released pronunciations are bound variants as they occur in the context of another contiguous stop consonant.

The second type of release to be mentioned is when the release of a plosive is
determined by the following consonant. There are two such bound variant pronunciations, viz. nasal and lateral releases:

- **Nasal release** occurs when a plosive is followed by a homorganic nasal
  as for example in *sudden, rip them, bacon* which are typically pronounced
  ['sʌdn̩], ['rɪpm̩], ['beɪkŋ̩]. In such pronunciations the compressed air
  of [d], [p] and [k] is not let out through the mouth but out through
  the nose. Because they are all followed by a nasal articulated in the
  same place, the closure of these three plosives is maintained, and the
  air is released through the nose which is open for the following nasal.
  In each of these words, the nasal moreover becomes syllabic, constituting the single sound of the second syllable of these words (see Ch. 4
  below).
- **Lateral release** occurs when the lateral /l/ (see Ch. 4 below) follows
  homorganic /t/ and /d/ as in, for example, *cattle* and *middle*. Just like
  in nasal release, the closure of the plosives is maintained and the air
  escapes along a route determined by the following nasal; in lateral release the closure of the stops /t/ and /d/ is maintained and the compressed air escapes in a way determined by the following /l/. This way
  is along one or both sides of the tongue, but not centrally, since /l/ is
  articulated by letting the tongue tip closing off the airstream at the alveolar ridge, at the same time as air can escape out through the mouth
  on one or both sides of this closure. Just like the nasals become syllabic in connection with nasally released plosives, /l/ becomes syllabic
  in laterally released words like *cattle, middle*, constituting the single
  sound of the second syllable (see Ch. 4 below).

Nasal and lateral releases are shown in the following diagrams:

(3.12)

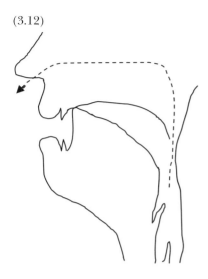

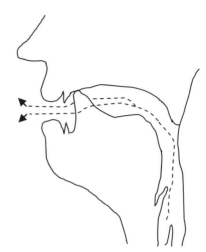

nasal release   lateral release

3.4.4 Summing up the manner and energy of stops

This concludes the description of manner-based classes of stops and important variation associated with manner of articulation. Before proceeding with a description of each individual NAERD stop, to which the rest of this chapter is devoted, a brief summary of the manner of articulation of stops is in order:

- stops belong to the class of obstruent consonants, which are consonants produced by complete closure or close approximation of the articulators
- stops are articulated with complete closure, fricatives with close approximation
- typically, a stop consists of three articulatory phases: the closing phase, the closure and the opening phase
- the stops are divided into plosives and affricates according to the opening phase; plosives have an abrupt opening, affricates a slow gradual opening resulting in frictional noise
- plosives may be exploded nasally or laterally when followed by a nasal or /l/ respectively
- stops, like other obstruents, are divided into strong and weak. /p, t, k, tʃ/ are classified as strong, /b, d, g, dʒ/ as weak
- strong stops are fortis, voiceless, aspirated (except /tʃ/) and shorten the length of the preceding sound; weak stops are lenis, fully or partially voiced, unaspirated and do not shorten the length of the preceding sound.

3.5 The individual stops

Following established practice, the description of each stop, indeed of each consonant below in this and chapter 4, will concentrate on the following points:

1. articulation of the consonant with special emphasis on place of articulation specified in a diagram showing the position of the articulatory organs
2. variation, i.e. important free and bound allophones of each consonant
3. spelling, i.e. the typical orthographic renderings of each consonant.

3.5.1 The affricates

On the basis of manner of articulation, as described in § 3.4, the affricates /tʃ/ and /dʒ/ can be described as stop consonants with a slow and gradual release which gives them their distinctive frictional noise. The position of the articulatory organs during the articulation of /tʃ/ and /dʒ/ is shown in the following diagram:

(3.13)

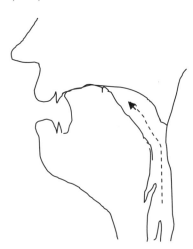

/tʃ/

Articulation: as is apparent from the diagram in (3.13), /tʃ/ is articulated by the tongue blade forming a closure against the hard palate just behind the alveolar ridge at the same time as a raised velum closes off the nasal cavity. The air compressed behind this closure is subsequently let out as the tongue is lowered gradually. The gradual release, accentuated by a groove-formed tongue shape, creates the distinctive friction of /tʃ/, so that when its energy of articulation is added,

/tʃ/ can be classified as a **strong, alveopalatal affricate** where alveopalatal describes the place of articulation of /tʃ/. As a strong obstruent consonant, /tʃ/ is not only fortis but also always voiceless, i.e. articulated with an open glottis, as well as it has a shortening effect on a preceding sound as described in § 3.4.2. The slow and gradual release generates a [ʃ]-like sound similar to the fricative /ʃ/. The second symbol of /tʃ/ refers to the opening phase, the first symbol to the closing phase and the closure, but the two symbols in /tʃ/ still represent one phoneme, as /tʃ/ phonologically behaves as one segment. Some speakers produce /tʃ/ with a raised tongue tip, some with a lowered tongue tip.

Variation: unlike plosives, /tʃ/ is never produced with the inaudibly released variant, but after /t/ and /d/ as in *just choose* and *had chosen*, /tʃ/ has no closing phase.

Spelling: /tʃ/ is regularly spelled *ch* or *tch* as in *church, such, catch, itch*. Less frequent spellings are *tu* as in *adventure, nature*, and *te* as in *righteous*.

/dʒ/

Articulation: /dʒ/ is articulated in the same way as /tʃ/ except that with respect to energy it is weak and not strong, so /dʒ/ may be classified as a **weak, alveopalatal affricate** where alveopalatal describes the place of articulation of /dʒ/. As a weak obstruent consonant, /dʒ/ is lenis and articulated with partially or fully vibrating vocal cords as described above in § 3.4.2. The slow and gradual release which involves a grooved tongue shape, as in /tʃ/, generates a [ʒ]-like sound similar to the fricative /ʒ/. Thus the second symbol of /dʒ/ refers to the opening phase, the first symbol to the closing and the closure, but the two symbols still represent one phoneme as /dʒ/ phonologically behaves as one segment. Some speakers produce /dʒ/ with a raised tongue tip, some with a lowered tongue tip.

Variation: unlike plosives, /dʒ/ is never produced with the inaudibly released variant, but after /t/ and /d/ as in *best judge* and *had judged* /dʒ/ has no closing phase. The voicing of /dʒ/ also varies so that it is fully voiced between voiced sounds as in *judging*, voiceless or partially voiced in initial and final positions as in *jet* and *edge* (see § 4.3.2 above)

Spelling: /dʒ/ is regularly spelled *j* or *g* before *a, e, i, y* (often in words of French or Latin origin) as in *jaw, Jew* and *general, ginger*. /dʒ/ is also frequently represented by *dg* as in *edge, judging*. *dg* always represents /dʒ/ before *e, i, y*. *gg* is also a possible rendering as in *suggest, exaggerate*, as are the *d*-spellings *dj, de* as in *adjective* and *grandeur*.

3.5.2 The plosives

The manner of articulation of the plosives /p, t, k/ and /b, d, g/ is such that these can be described as stops with a quick and abrupt release. Unlike affricates, plosives are then released without frictional noise. They also differ from affricates by often lacking the release phase and by potentially allowing nasal and lateral releases. Below the plosives will be described in pairs whose members have the same place of articulation.

/p/ and /b/

The position of the articulatory organs during the pronunciation of the plosives /p/ and /b/ is shown in the following diagram:

(3.14)

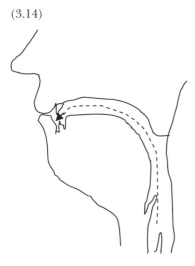

/p/

Articulation: From the diagram in (3.14), it is apparent that /p/ is articulated by the lower lip forming a closure with the upper lip at the same time as the velum is raised, so no air can escape out through the nose. The air compressed behind this bilabial closure is subsequently let out as the lower lip and jaw are lowered. This release is abrupt and quick as is distinctive of plosives. Given this articulatory description and its strong energy, /p/ can be described as a **strong, bilabial plosive** where bilabial describes the place of articulation of /p/. As a strong obstruent consonant, /p/ is not only fortis but also always voiceless, i.e. articulated with an open glottis, as well as it has a shortening effect on a preceding sound as described in § 3.4.2 above.

Variation: /p/ has the following variant pronunciations:

1. aspirated, specifically strongly aspirated in stressed initial position be-fore vowels as in e.g. *peace, pause, oppose*; less aspirated in other posi-tions
2. unaspirated after syllable-initial /s/ as in *speak, sport*
3. nasally released as in *rip them*, cf. § 3.4.3 above
4. inaudibly released when followed by another stop as in *stop Peter, apt, stop chewing, sip coffee* and in utterance final *stop!*, cf. § 3.4.3 above
5. without a closing phase when preceded by another bilabial stop as in *stop pulling*
6. reinforced or replaced by a glottal stop particularly wordfinally; the glottal stop, [ʔ] see § 3.2 above, may completely supplant /p/ in e.g. *rap* so it is pronounced [ræʔ], or reinforce it so the pronunciation is [ræʔp]; glottal replacement/reinforcement is not so common in American English as in English English, and as a variant pronuncia-tion in American English much more common of /t/ than of /p/

Spelling: /p/ is regularly spelled *p* or *pp* as in *put, flap, appear, happy*. Notice that /p/ is not pronounced in *receipt, pneumonia, psychology* and other foreign loan words; in *unkempt* and *empty* /p/ may or may not be pronounced.

/b/

Articulation: /b/ is articulated in the same way as /p/ except that with respect to energy it is weak and not strong, so /b/ may be classified as a **weak bilabial plosive** where bilabial describes the place of articulation of /b/. As a weak ob-struent consonant, /b/ is lenis and articulated with partially or fully vibrating vocal cords as described in § 3.4.2 above.

variation: /b/ has the following variant pronunciations:

1. voiced, partially voiced or voiceless depending on context so that it is fully voiced between voiced sounds as in *rubber*, partially voiced or voiceless in initial and final positions as *belt, curb* (see § 3.4.2 above)
2. inaudibly released when followed by another stop as in *rob banks, robbed, Bob chose, Bob called* and optionally in utterance final *follow Bob!* (see § 3.4.3 above)
3. without a closing phase when preceded by another bilabial stop as *rob banks*
4. nasally released as in *submarine* (see § 3.4.3 above)

spelling: /b/ is regularly spelled *b* or *bb* as in *bow, cab, sobbing, pebble*. Notice that /b/ is not pronounced after /m/, cf. *climb, tomb*, unless /b/ belongs to the following syllable as in *tumble, tombola*, nor before syllable final /t/, cf. *doubt, debt*.

/t/ and /d/

The position of the articulatory organs during the articulation of the plosives /t/ and /d/ is shown in the following diagram:

(3.15)

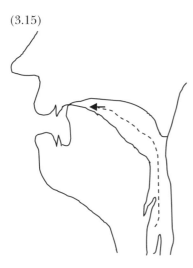

/t/

articulation: from the diagram it is apparent that /t/ is articulated by the tongue blade or tip forming a complete closure at the alveolar ridge at the same time as the velum is raised, so no air can escape out through the nose. The air compressed behind this closure is subsequently let out as the tongue is lowered, releasing the air in an abrupt and quick way as is distinctive of plosives. Given this articulatory description and its strong energy, /t/ can be defined as a **strong alveolar plosive**. As a strong obstruent consonant, /t/ is not only fortis but also always voiceless, i.e. articulated with an open glottis, as well as it has a shortening effect on a preceding sound, as described in § 3.4.2 above.

variation: /t/ has the following variant pronunciations

1. aspirated, specifically strongly aspirated in stressed initial position before vowels as in *tune, task, atomic*; less aspirated in other positions (see § 3.4.2 above)
2. unaspirated after syllable-initial /s/ as in *steal, stall*
3. inaudibly released when followed by another stop as in *right time, right choice, light blue, fast girl* and optionally in utterance final *get out*! (see § 3.4.3 above)

4. without a closing phase when preceded by another alveolar stop as in *night train, could try* (see §3.4.3 above)

5. nasally released as in *button, sweeten* (see §3.4.3 above)

6. laterally released as in *bottle, castle* (see §3.4.3 above)

7. reinforced or replaced by a glottal stop particularly wordfinally; the glottal stop may completely supplant /t/ in e.g. *what*, so it is pronounced [wɔʔ] or reinforce it so it is pronounced [wɔʔt]. Medially, /t/ may also be realised as [ʔ] in the nasally released environment (cf. *button, sweeten* under 5 above.). Pronouncing /t/ as a glottal stop is not as common in American English as it is in English English.

8. flapped, that is, realised as what is often referred to as the **flap** (or sometimes tap; also called *t*-voicing). Realising /t/ (or /d/) as a flap is a striking characteristic of American English pronunciation. Flapping involves two processes: i) changing the sound undergoing the process into a voiced sound if it voiceless, and ii) pronouncing the /t/ or /d/ not as a comparatively slow and distinct stop with a closure and a release, but by quickly flicking or tapping the tongue tip once against the alveolar ridge. The classical environment of flapping is when /t/ or /d/ occurs between vowels or between /r/ and a vowel, provided the second vowel is unstressed. Thus the words in (3.16a) are potentially pronounced with a flap, whereas the stress pattern of those in (3.16b) prevents a pronunciation with a flap. Following many American specialists, the flap is here written [D]. Other symbols used are [ɾ] or [ṭ] and [ḍ].

(3.16)

a.   b.

atom [ˈæDəm]	*atomic* [əˈtɑmɪk]
beauty [ˈbjuDi]	*beautician* [bjuˈtɪʃn]
party [ˈpɑrDi]	*partition* [pɑrˈtɪʃn]
ridicule [ˈrɪDɪkjul]	*ridiculous* [rɪˈdɪkjʊləs]
laudable [ˈlɔDəbl]	*laudation* [lɔˈdeɪʃn]

Flapping occurs not only word-internally, as in the examples in (3.16a), but also across word boundaries as illustrated in (3.17):

(3.17)

It is part of the city   [ɪD ɪz ˈpɑrD əv ðə ˈsiDi]
The word about the kid in the class [ðə ˈwɜrD əbaʊt ðə ˈkɪD ɪn ðə ˈklæs]

Flapping is also often assumed to apply when /t/ or /d/ occurs after /n/ or /l/ and before a vowel or after a vowel and before a syllabic /l/, provided the stress pattern is correct:

(3.18)

winter   ['wɪnDər]
builder   ['bɪlDər]
bottle   ['bɑDl]
middle   ['mɪDl]

Auditorily, these pronunciations of /t/ and /d/ are very similar to intervocalic flaps and hence transcribed as such, but strictly speaking they are not true flaps since the tongue tip cannot make one flick against the alveolar ridge, as it is either already in contact with the alveolar ridge (*winter, builder*) or remains in contact with the alveolar ridge (*bottle, middle*).

An important effect of flapping is that numerous word pairs are pronounced identically because flapping also involves the voicing of /t/. Thus the following word pairs are homophonous if pronounced with a flap:

(3.19)

atom   *Adam*   ['æDəm]
writer   *rider*   ['raɪDər]
putting   *pudding* ['pʊDɪŋ]

just like it is not possible to say whether [ðə 'læm ɪz 'bliDɪŋ] means 'the lamb is bleeding' or 'the lamb is bleating'. The loss of distinction between /t/ and /d/ as a result of flapping is a case of **neutralisation**.

It is important to stress that /t/ and /d/ are not always pronounced as flaps when occurring in the correct environment. The rule of flapping depends on the following: i) register, i.e. speech situation, so flaps are more likely to occur in conversational speech style than in more formal speech styles, ii) word frequency so the more frequent a potential flap word is the more likely it is that this word will be pronounced with a flap, iii) morphological complexity so morphologically more complex words like *beating, hater* are less likely to be pronounced with flaps than morphologically simple words like *city, duty*. Flapping is then an optional and not an obligatory rule in American English.

As mentioned above, the flap is a distinctive characteristic of American English. It is probably an American innovation and its appearance in Australian English and English English can be seen as an example of American English influence. In Cockney, the London working class accent, flapping represents a step on a scale of 'broadness' so that the pronunciation of the word *better* in this variety is posh when said with a [t], normal or standard when said with a [D] and broad when said with a [ʔ].

spelling: /t/ is regularly spelled *t* or *tt* as in *tap, fat, matter, shutter*. No /t/ is pronounced in *listen, christen, often*. In a few instances, mostly in proper nouns, /t/ is spelled *th* as in *Thomas, Thames, thyme*.

   /t/ is also spelled *-ed* when this is the inflectional suffix on verbs indicating past tense or past participle. More specifically, the verbal inflectional suffix *-ed* represents three different phonemes/phoneme combinations only one of which is /t/. For details see the comments below on /d/-spellings.

/d/

Articulation: /d/ is articulated in the same way as /t/ except that /d/ is weak and not strong, so /d/ is defined as a **weak, alveolar plosive** where alveolar describes the place of articulation of /d/. As a weak obstruent consonant, /d/ is lenis and partially or fully voiced depending on context as described in § 3.4.2 above.

variation: /d/ has the following variant pronunciations:

1. voiced, partially voiced or voiceless depending on context so that it is fully voiced between voiced sounds as in *ladder* partially voiced or voiceless in initial and final positions as in *dealt, told* (see § 3.4.2 above).

2. inaudibly released (see § 3.4.3 above) when followed by another stop as in *feed Bob, bad choice, could call* and, optionally, in utterance final *home made*!

3. without a closing phase when preceded by another alveolar stop as in *could do*

4. nasally released as in *sudden, couldn't* (see § 3.4.3 above)

5. laterally released as in *middle, fiddle* (see § 3.4.3 above)

6. flapped, that is, realised as what is often referred to as the flap (or sometimes tap); see the description of flapping under /t/

spelling: /d/ is regularly spelled *d* or *dd* as in *dull, mad, ladder*. In *handsome, handkerchief d* is always silent. Other words with *d* after *n* often drop *d*, as in for example *grandmother, landslide*.

   /d/ is also spelled *-ed* when this is the inflectional suffix on verbs indicating past tense or past participle. In fact, the verbal inflectional suffix *-ed* represents three different phonemes/phoneme combinations only one of which is /d/. What *-ed* should be identified with phonemically appears from the following rules describing the three possible pronunciations of the verb suffix *-ed*:

1. as [ɪd] or [əd] when *-ed* is added to a verb stem ending in /t/ or /d/. Thus the past tense and past participle forms of the verbs *fit* and *scold*, i.e. *fitted* and *scolded*, are pronounced (assuming a flapped pronunciation) ['fɪDɪd] or ['fɪDəd] and ['skoʊldɪd] or ['skoʊldəd]. Phonemically, these pronunciations of the suffix represent /ɪd/ or /əd/.

2. as [d] when *-ed* is added to a verb stem ending in a weak obstruent (except /d/), a sonorant or a vowel. Thus the past tense and past participle forms of the verbs *judge*, *kill* and *enjoy*, i.e. *judged*, *killed* and *enjoyed*, are pronounced [dʒʌdʒd], [kɪld] and [ɪn'dʒɔɪd]. Phonemically, these pronunciations of the suffix represent /d/.

3. as [t] elsewhere, i.e. when *-ed* is added to a verb stem ending in a strong obstruent (except /t/). Thus, the past tense and past participle forms of the verbs *help*, *dance*, i. e. *helped* and *danced*, are pronounced [helpt] and [dænst]. Phonemically, these pronunciations represent /t/.

/k/ and /g/

The position of the articulatory organs during the pronunciation of /k/ and /g/ is shown in the following diagram:

(3.20)

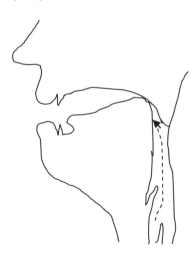

/k/

articulation: from the diagram it is apparent that /k/ is articulated by the back of the tongue forming a complete closure against the velum at the same time as this is raised so no air can escape out through the nose. The air compressed behind this closure is subsequently let out as the tongue is lowered, releasing the air in an abrupt and quick way as is characteristic of plosives. Given this articulatory description and its strong energy, /k/ can be defined as a **strong velar**

plosive where velar describes the place of articulation of /k/. As a strong obstruent consonant, /k/ is not only fortis but also always voiceless, i.e. articulated with an open glottis, as well as it has a shortening effect on the preceding sound as described in § 3.4.2 above.

variation: /k/ has the following variant pronunciations:

1. aspirated, specifically strongly aspirated in stressed initial position before vowels as in *key, cold, precaution*; less aspirated in other positions (see § 3.4.2 above)
2. unaspirated after syllable-initial /s/ as in *skid, skull*
3. inaudibly released when followed by another stop as in *lack courage, act, sack Joe* and optionally in utterance final *Hi Jack!* (see §3.4.3 above)
4. without a closing phase when preceded by another velar stop as in *make cakes, big crisis* (see § 3.4.3 above)
5. nasally released as in *bacon, shake them* ([ˈʃeɪkm̩]) (see § 3.4.3 above)
6. reinforced or replaced by a glottal stop particularly wordfinally; the glottal stop, [ʔ] (see § 3.2 above), may completely supplant /k/ in e.g. *fuck* so it is pronounced [fʌʔ] or reinforce it so the pronunciation is [fʌʔk]; glottal replacement/reinforcement is not as common in American English as in English English, and as a variant pronunciation in American English much more common of /t/ than of /k/

spelling: /k/ is regularly spelled *c* or *cc* before *a, o, u* and *c* before a consonant letter as in *catch, curl, copy, account, cry*; other common spellings are *ck* and *k* as in *lack, acknowledge, skull, skirt. ch* may also represent /k/ which is typical of Greek words such as *chaos, chemistry* and when *ch* is followed by a consonant letter as in *Christmas, technology*, or initially after *s* as in *school, schedule*. Finally *q*, or in a few words *que* or *cqu*, is used for /k/ as is apparent from *quite, technique, liquor, lacquer* [ˈlækər]. Historical /k/ is no longer pronounced syllable-initially before *n* as in *know, knee*, nor pronounced in a few exceptional words like *muscle, indict* [ɪnˈdaɪt], *Connecticut* where the spelling *c* + consonant letter would otherwise lead us to expect /k/.

/g/
articulation: /g/ is articulated in the same way as /k/ except that /g/ is weak and not strong, so /g/ is defined as a **weak, velar plosive** where velar describes the place of articulation of /g/. As a weak obstruent consonant, /g/ is lenis and partially or fully voiced depending on context as described in § 3.4.2 above.

variation: /g/ has the following variant pronunciations:

1. voiced, partially voiced or voiceless depending on context so that it is fully voiced between voiced sounds as in *bigger*, partially voiced or voiceless in initial and final positions as in *hog, got*
2. inaudibly released when followed by another stop as in *big girl, hug Janet, log-book* or optionally in utterance-final *hand me the mug!*
3. without a closing phase when preceded by another velar stop as in *big gorilla*
4. nasally released as in *wagon, tugging* if these are not pronounced with a vowel between /g/ and the final nasal, i.e. ['wægən], ['tʌgɪn]

spelling: /g/ is regularly spelled *g* or *gg* as in *girl, logging, fig*. Other renderings are *gh* and *gu* as in *ghost, guess*. /g/ is silent before /n/ and /m/ in the same syllable: *gnome, gnat, foreign, phlegm* [flem].

3.5.3 Summing up the individual stops

The following points should be noted about the individual stops:

- Manner of articulation aside, the stops can be organised in 4 pairs according to shared place of articulation
- The affricates /tʃ/ and /dʒ/ are alveopalatal stops. They have no important free or bound allophones apart from /dʒ/ varying in degree of voicing
- The plosives /p/ and /b/ are bilabial stops. Apart from unreleased allophones, /p/ and /b/ have nasally released variant pronunciations. /p/ also varies in degree of aspiration and /b/ in degree of voicing
- The plosives /t/ and /d/ are alveolar stops. Apart from unreleased allophones, /t/ and /d/ have three important variant pronunciations, viz. nasally and laterally released variants and, optionally, the characteristic American flapped pronunciations. /t/ also varies in degree of aspiration and /d/ in the degree of voicing
- The plosives /k/ and /g/ are velar stops. Apart from unreleased allophones, /k/ and /g/ have nasally released variant pronunciations. /k/ also varies in degree of aspiration and /g/ in degree of voicing.

3.6 Classes of obstruents in NAERD – fricatives

There are two main classes of obstruents in NAERD as is apparent from (3.4): stops and fricatives. § 3.5 above dealt with stops in detail describing the manner, energy and place of this obstruent type. The remaining sections of this chapter will be devoted to the description of fricatives. Unlike stops, fricatives are never articulated with a complete closure. Instead fricatives (except /h/) are produced with a narrow constriction in the oral cavity, at the same time as a raised velum closes off the nasal cavity. Thus just like the articulation of stops may be illustrated in a diagram with two horizontal lines representing active and passive articulators (see diagrams in (3.6) and (3.7) above), the articulatory properties of fricatives may be represented as in (3.21):

(3.21)

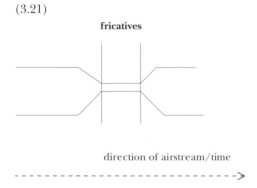

fricatives

direction of airstream/time

Because fricatives involve narrow constriction but not closure, the two horizontal lines in (3.21) do not meet but only approach each other and form a stricture of close approximation for the time span represented between the vertical lines.

3.6.1 Sibilant and non-sibilant fricatives

Just like stops are divided into two groups, stops and affricates, according to the way they are released (see § 3.4.1 above), fricatives are divided into sibilants and non-sibilants according to how noisy they are, sibilants being more noisy than non-sibilants. **Sibilants** include /s, z, ʃ, ʒ/ and they are fricatives produced such that the outgoing airstream is concentrated along the middle of the tongue. This concentration of air follows from /s, z, ʃ, ʒ/ being articulated with a grooved tongue with raised sides. Such a grooved tongue shape concentrates air in the middle, and when the out-going air flows along this groove and hits the back of the upper front teeth, the result is a distinctly hissing noise. This noise is referred to as sibilance and a consonant characterised by this noise is consequently referred to as a sibilant.

Non-sibilants, by contrast, which include /f, v, θ, ð, h/, lack sibilance because during their articulation the outgoing air is dispersed over the entire stricture and not concentrated in a relatively small area as in the sibilants. In /f/ and /v/ this stricture area is between the lower lip and the upper teeth (see § 3.7.1 below) and in /θ/ and /ð/ (see § 3.7.1 below) it is between the front of the tongue and the upper teeth, whilst in /h/ it is the entire vocal tract (see § 3.7.1 below). The absence of concentrated energy makes /f, v, θ, ð, h/ much less noisy and they are therefore classified as non-sibilant.

3.6.2 Strong versus weak

Whilst the distinction between sibilant and non-sibilant divides the fricatives into two relatively neat noise-based classes, the distinction between strong and weak cuts across these classes (except for /h/ which does not fit into this system) just like it cuts across the classes of affricates and plosives among the stops. Except for aspiration, which is only characteristic of voiceless stops in English, the strong-weak properties relevant for stops are also relevant for fricatives, so that the strong-weak distinction in fricatives depends on the following more or less constant properties:

- **force of articulation** referring to muscular energy, duration of stricture and noise. Fricatives in which these properties are prominent are fortis; fricatives in which these properties are less prominent are lenis
- **voicing** referring to whether the vocal cords vibrate or fail to vibrate. Fricatives which in some positions exhibit full or partial vocal cord vibration are voiced; fricatives which never involve vocal cord vibration are voiceless
- **length of the preceding sound** referring to whether the length of the preceding sound, especially a vowel, is or is not affected by a following fricative

On the basis of these properties, /f, θ, s, ʃ/ are classified as strong fricatives as they are fortis, voiceless and with a shortening effect on a preceding sound, whereas /v, ð, z, ʒ/ are classified as weak fricatives, because they are lenis and partially or fully voiced as well as lacking a shortening effect on a preceding sound. The following diagram sums up the fricative classes outlined so far. The horizontal line shows how the strong-weak distinction cuts across the sibilant-non-sibilant classification (/h/ is bracketed because although classifiable as a non-sibilant, it does not fit into the strong-weak system):

(3.22)

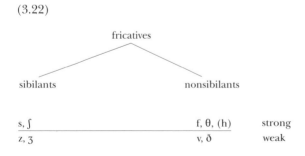

The extent to which force of articulation, voicing and length of the preceding sound contribute to the distinction between strong and weak depends on the position that the fricatives occupy within the syllable. As in stops, three positions are relevant in this connection, viz. initial, medial between voiced sounds and final position. The contribution of the three properties in these three positions may be illustrated by the following word pairs:

(3.23)

initial	fan	thigh	sue	Shaw
	van	thy	zoo	–
medial	rifle	Martha	facing	pressure
	rival	father	phasing	pleasure
final	life	sheath	rice	push
	live	sheathe	rise	rouge

Force of articulation. In all positions, strong /f, θ, s, ʃ/ are fortis, whereas /v, ð, z, ʒ/ are lenis in all positions.

Voicing. In initial, medial and final positions, strong /f, θ, s, ʃ/ are always voiceless. The voicing of weak /v, ð, z, ʒ/, on the other hand, varies. Initially and medially /v, ð, z, ʒ/ are fully voiced, but when they occur in final position they are either voiceless or partially voiced so that when it occurs, voicing is found in that part of the weak fricative which adjoins a contiguous voiced sound. Thus weak fricatives are not fully voiced finally contrary to the popular perception of many both native and not least non-native speakers and their teachers.

Length of the preceding sound. Strong /f, θ, s, ʃ/ shorten the length of the preceding sound, weak /v, ð, z, ʒ/ do not shorten the length of the preceding sound. This characteristic and for non-native speakers often difficult feature of English plays an important part in distinguishing between members of word pairs like *life – live, use* (noun) – *use* (verb), *wreath – wreathe*, in which the second member of these pairs has a distinctly longer [aɪ], [u] and [i] which are followed by a weak fricative than in the first members of these pairs which contain a strong fricative.

No single property then serves to distinguish strong from weak fricatives. Instead an interplay of properties upholds the distinction and their relative contribution depends on where the fricatives occur within the syllable. The following diagram summarises the main points about the contribution of the properties force, voicing and length of the preceding sound:

(3.24)

f θ s ʃ / v ð z ʒ	initial	medial	final
force	fortis / lenis	fortis / lenis	fortis / lenis
voicing	voiceless / voiced	voiceless / voiced	voiceless / voiced voiceless
length		shorten preceding sound	shorten preceding sound

where in each box the information listed above the diagonal lines describes the properties of strong fricatives, and the information listed below the diagonal lines describes the properties of weak fricatives in the three positions, initial, medial and final.

3.6.3 Summing up the manner and energy of fricatives

Before we proceed with a description of each individual fricative, a summary of the manner and energy properties of fricatives is in order:

- Fricatives belong to the class of obstruent consonants; obstruent consonants are characterised by complete closure or close approximation of the articulators
- Fricatives is the class of obstruents articulated with a stricture of close approximation
- Depending on the amount of concentrated energy in the stricture of close approximation, fricatives are divided into noisy sibilants and less noisy non-sibilants
- /s, z, ʃ, ʒ/ are articulated with a high degree of concentrated energy and therefore classified as sibilants
- /f, v, θ, ð, h/ are articulated with a smaller degree of concentrated energy and therefore classified as non-sibilants
- Fricatives, like stops, are classified as strong or weak. /f, s, θ, ʃ/ are strong, /v, z, ð, ʒ/ are weak
- Strong fricatives are fortis, voiceless and shorten the length of the preceding sound, weak fricatives are lenis, partially or fully voiced and do not shorten the length of the preceding sound.

3.7 The individual fricatives

With the manner and energy properties of fricatives established, it is now possible and appropriate to turn to a description of each NAERD fricative individually. Following the description of the individual stops, the description of each fricative will concentrate on the following points:

1. articulation of the fricative with special emphasis on place of articulation specified in a diagram showing the position of the articulatory organs
2. variation, i.e. important free and bound allophones of each fricative
3. spelling, i.e. the typical orthographic renderings of each fricative

3.7.1 The sibilants

Sibilants, as outlined above, are noisy fricatives whose distinctive noise is a result of a grooved tongue shape concentrating energy along the middle of the tongue. The four sibilants, /s/, /z/, /ʃ/, /ʒ/, make up two pairs, the members of which are articulated in the same place. /s/ and /z/ constitute one pair, /ʃ/ and /ʒ/ the other pair.

/s/ and /z/

The position of the articulatory organs during the articulation of the sibilants /s/ and /z/ is shown in the following diagram:

(3.25)

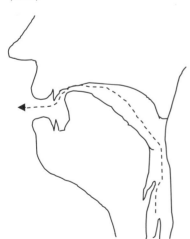

/s/

articulation: from the diagram in (3.25), it is apparent that /s/ is articulated by the tip or front of the tongue forming a stricture of close approximation at the alveolar ridge, at the same time as the velum is raised closing off the nasal cavity. The alveolar stricture is formed with raised tongue sides forming a distinct groove along the middle of the tongue. This tongue configuration concentrates energy along the middle of the tongue so that when the air escapes out through the mouth, /s/ is articulated with a distinctive sibilant noise. Given its manner and energy of articulation (cf. § 3.6.2 above), /s/ can then be classified as a **strong, alveolar sibilant fricative** where alveolar describes the place of articulation of /s/. As a strong obstruent consonant, /s/ is not only always fortis but also always voiceless, i.e. articulated with an open glottis, as well as one which shortens the length of the preceding sound, as described in § 3.6.2 above.

variation: /s/ has no important variant pronunciations

spelling: /s/ is regularly spelled *s*, as in *seen, basic, gas, sense, house*, the latter two before silent *e. ss* is also used as in *miss, lesson*, but note that *ss* may also represent /z/, as mentioned under /z/-spellings below. A third regular spelling is *c, cc* or *sc* when *c* occurs before one of *e, i, y* as in *city center, cycle, accept, scene, disciple* [dɪ'saɪpl]. It is a notorious problem that *s* stands for both /s/ and /z/. *s* normally represents /s/ in *-lse, -nse, -rse* as in *else, dense, endorse* and when it occurs after a vowel and before a strong obstruent, cf. *haste*. But between vowel letters *s* sometimes stands for /s/, sometimes for /z/: *basis, promising* with /s/ and *easy, poison* with /z/ and no rule applies here. *x* also represents /s/ but /s/ in combination with /k/, i.e. /ks/. /ks/ is spelled *x* wordfinally, cf. *sex, tax*, or word-medially when /ks/ are followed by another consonant phoneme or the preceding vowel has primary or secondary stress (see Ch. 6 below): *expect* [ɪk'spekt], *exhale* and *vixen* ['vɪksən], *exercise, execution* [ˌeksɪ'kjuʃn], *exocentric*. Silent *s* is found in French loan words or words influenced by French. *island, debris, corps* [kɔr], *Illinois* illustrate this; notice also the name of the state *Arkansas* ['ɑrknsɔr] (as opposed to the pronunciation of the name of the river: [ɑr'kænzəs]).

/s/ is also spelled *-(e)s* when this is i) the inflectional suffix on nouns indicating plural (*the two boys*) or the genitive case (*the boy's bicycle*) or ii) the inflectional suffix on verbs indicating 3rd person singular present tense indicative (*the boy speaks English*). In fact, the inflectional suffix *-(e)s*, whatever its grammatical function (plural, genitive or tense marker) represents three different phoneme/phoneme combinations, only one of which is /s/. What *-(e)s* should be identified with phonemically appears from the following rules describing the three possible pronunciations of the suffix *-(e)s*. The suffix is pronounced:

1. as [ɪz] or [əz] when it is added to a stem ending in one of the following obstruents: /tʃ, dʒ, s, z,ʃ, ʒ/. Thus, for example, *Kerry misjudges Bush's choices*, with stems ending in /dʒ, ʃ, s/ (*misjudge, Bush, choice*), may be pronounced either [ˈkerɪ mɪsˈjʌdʒɪz ˈbuʃɪz ˈtʃɔɪsɪz] or [ˈkerɪ mɪsˈjʌdʒəz ˈbuʃəz ˈtʃɔɪsəz]. Phonemically, these pronunciations of the suffix represent /ɪz/ or /əz/.

2. as [z] when it is added to a stem ending in a weak obstruent (except /dʒ/, /z/ and /ʒ/) a sonorant consonant or a vowel. Thus, for example, *Kerry succeeds if he follows Bill's plans*, with stems ending in /d, oʊ, l, n/ (*succeed, follow, Bill, plan*), will be pronounced [ˈkerɪ səkˈsidz ɪf hɪ ˈfɔloʊz ˈbɪlz ˈplænz]. Phonemically, these pronunciations of the suffix all represent /z/.

3. as [s] elsewhere, i.e. when it is added to a stem ending in a strong obstruent (except /s, ʃ, tʃ/). Thus, for example, *Kerry likes his wife's mock-ups*, with stems ending in /k, f, p/ (*like, wife, mock-up*) will be pronounced [ˈkerɪ ˈlaɪks hɪz ˈwaɪfs ˈmɑkʌps]. Phonemically, these pronunciations of the suffix all represent /s/.

/z/

articulation: /z/ is articulated in the same way as /s/ except that /z/ is weak and not strong like /s/. Thus given its manner and energy of articulation (cf. § 3.6.2 above), /z/ is classified as a **weak, alveolar sibilant fricative** where alveolar describes the place of articulation of /z/. As a weak obstruent consonant, /z/ is lenis and partially or fully voiced depending on context (cf. § 3.6.2 above).

variation: the voicing of /z/ varies so that it is fully voiced initially and medially as in *zero, zoo, using, ouzo*, partially voiced or voiceless in final position *choose, ooze*. Otherwise it has no important variant pronunciations.

spelling: /z/ is regularly spelled *z* or *zz* as in *zero, hazy, dazzle*. Except for a few foreign loans like *Nazi, pizza*, *z* nearly always (see under /ʒ/-spellings below) represents /z/. As mentioned under /s/-spellings, /z/ is also spelled *s* and *ss*. The latter is not very common but found in a few frequent words: *scissors, possess, dessert*. Rendering /z/ as *s* is very common in the middle of a word. Whether *s* represents /z/ or /s/ in this environment depends on the neighbouring letters. Between a vowel and consonant, *s* stands for /z/ if the consonant letter represents a weak obstruent or a sonorant, cf. *wisdom, husband, haslet*; between a consonant and a vowel letter *s* stands for /z/ if the consonant letter represents a weak obstruent or a sonorant, except if it is one of /l, r, n/, cf. *clumsy, observe* with /z/, but *else, dense, endorse, gipsy* with /s/. Between vowel letters, *s* stands for both /s/ and /z/, so *rising, choosing* with /z/, *oasis, greasy* with /s/. No rule applies in this environment and each instance must be noted individually. Just like *x* may stand for /ks/, *x* is also a way of spelling /gz/ but only word-medially. Whilst spelling /ks/ as *x* between vowels is only possible when the preceding vowel is stressed, *x*-spellings of /gz/ between vowels presuppose that the following vowel is stressed. Thus *exaggerate, exact, exist, example,* for example, have /gz/. Sometimes words whose stress pattern predicts /gz/, rather than /ks/, have /ks/ because of influence from underived forms: thus, *taxation,* for example, has /ks/ and not /gz/, as expected, because *tax* has /ks/.

/ʃ/ and /ʒ/

The position of the articulatory organs during the production of /ʃ/ and /ʒ/ is shown in the following diagram:

(3.26)

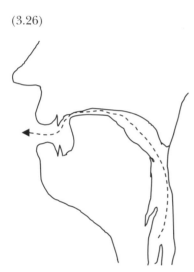

/ʃ/

articulation: from the diagram in (3.26), it is apparent that /ʃ/ is articulated by the blade of the tongue forming a stricture of close approximation just behind the alveolar ridge, at the same time as the velum is raised closing off the nasal cavity. As in /s/ and /z/, the stricture is formed with raised tongue sides creating a groove along the middle of the tongue and with this tongue configuration air escapes out through the mouth. Although it creates a sibilant noise, this groove along the middle of the tongue is not so distinct as in /s/ and /z/. Therefore /ʃ/ is produced with a not quite so distinctly hissing noise as are /s/ and /z/. Thus given its manner and energy properties (cf. § 3.6.2 above), /ʃ/ can be classified as a **strong alveopalatal sibilant fricative** where alveopalatal describes the place of articulation of /ʃ/, i.e. that its stricture is in the postalveolar-prepalatal area. As a strong obstruent consonant, /ʃ/ is not only always fortis but also always voiceless, i.e. articulated with an open glottis, as described in § 3.6.2 above. As a fortis obstruent, it also shortens the length of the preceding sound. Some speakers produce this fricative with a raised tongue tip, some with a lowered tongue tip.

variation: /ʃ/ has no important variant pronunciations.

spelling: /ʃ/ is regularly spelled *sh* as in *shade, shoe, cash, fish*; less frequent is *ch* which is mostly found in recent loans from French: *machine, champagne, moustache*. *sch* is also a possible rendering mostly in words borrowed from German: *schmuck, schwa*, but not in *schedule* which represents /sk/ in American English. Notice that *s* is sometimes a possibility word-initially: *sugar, sure, Sean*. Word-medially, other spellings than *sh* and *ch* abound. Firstly, /ʃ/ is spelled *s* and *ss*. *s* represents /ʃ/ either between a vowel and *ia* or *ian*, cf. *Asia, Polynesian* (in this context /ʒ/ competes with /ʃ/) or between the letters *l, r, n* and *ion, ial, ure*: *expulsion, controversial, suspension*. *ss* represents /ʃ/ before *ion, ia, ian, ure*: *impression, Russian, pressure*. Secondly, /ʃ/ is spelled *t* before the letter *i* plus another vowel letter provided *i* belongs to an unstressed syllable within a word: *nation, partial, superstitious*. Thirdly, /ʃ/ is spelled *c* or *sc* before the vowel letters *e* or *i* plus another vowel letter provided *e* or *i* belongs to an unstressed syllable within a word: *special, delicious, herbaceous, luscious*; in words of this type /ʃ/ sometimes competes with /s/. *appreciate*, for example, is sometimes pronounced [ə'priʃieɪt] and sometimes [ə'prisieɪt]. Finally, note that *x* in *luxury* stands for /kʃ/ or /gz/.

/ʒ/
articulation: /ʒ/ is articulated in the same way as /ʃ/ except that /ʒ/ is weak and not strong like /ʃ/. Thus given its manner and energy properties (cf. § 3.6.2 above), /ʒ/ may be classified as a **weak alveopalatal sibilant fricative** where alveopalatal describes the place of articulation of /ʒ/, i.e. that its stricture is in the postalveolar-prepalatal area. As a weak obstruent consonant, /ʒ/ is lenis and is partially or fully voiced depending on context.

variation: the voicing of /ʒ/ varies so that it is fully voiced medially between voiced sounds, as in *leisure, casual*, partially voiced or voiceless in final position as in *beige, rouge* (note that /ʒ/ does not occur in initial position in native words). Otherwise /ʒ/ has no important variant pronunciations.

spelling: /ʒ/ is regularly spelled *s* between a vowel letter and *ion, ual, ure* as in *vision, usual, pleasure* and *s* between *r* and *ion, ia, ian*, cf. *submersion, Persia, Persian* (in the latter three other varieties of English usually have /ʃ/). Wordfinally, /ʒ/ is regularly spelled *ge* as in *garage* [gə'rɑʒ] (if this word is not pronounced with what phonemically is /dʒ/), *rouge, beige*. Note that *z*-spellings are also found: *sei-*

zure, glazier [ˈɡleɪʒər], the latter usually pronounced [ˈɡleɪzɪə] in English English.

3.7.2 The non-sibilant fricatives.

Unlike sibilants, non-sibilants lack distinctive frictional noise. Articulatorily, non-sibilants are produced with a stricture of close approximation which disperses the outgoing energy over a wide area rather than concentrating it in a relatively narrow space as in the sibilants. The wider dispersal of energy in non-sibilants is what makes them less noisy. There are five non-sibilant fricatives in NAERD: /f/ and /v/ make up one pair, /θ/ and /ð/ another, whilst /h/ is the odd man out.

/f/ and /v/

The position of the articulatory organs during the production of /f/ and /v/ is shown in the following diagram:

(3.27)

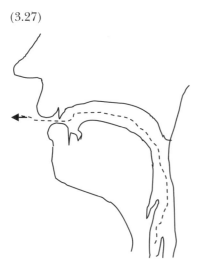

/f/

articulation: from the diagram in (3.27), it is apparent that /f/ is articulated by the outer part of the lower lip forming a stricture of close approximation with the lower and back part of the upper teeth. The air escapes out over the entire contact area of this stricture, causing not so distinct friction as in sibilants. At the same time as this stricture is formed, the velum is raised closing off the nasal cavity. Given the manner and energy properties of /f/ (cf. § 3.6.2 above), /f/ can then be classified as a **strong, labiodental non-sibilant fricative** where labiodental describes the place of articulation of /f/, i.e. that the contact area between active and passive articulators is the lower lip and the upper teeth. As a

strong obstruent consonant, /f/ is not only fortis and always voiceless, i.e. articulated with an open glottis, but it also shortens the length of the preceding
sound, as described in § 3.6.2 above.

variation: /f/ has no important variant pronunciations

spelling: /f/ is regularly spelled *f, ff* and *ph* as in *father, foot, stuff, snuffing, photo,
graph. ph*-spellings occur in words of classical origin. In some native English
words, /f/ is spelled *gh* medially and finally as in, for example, *laughing, tough.*

/v/

articulation: /v/ is articulated in the same way as /f/ except that /v/ is weak
and not strong like/f/. Given its manner and energy properties (cf. § 3.6.2
above), /v/ may then be classified as a **weak labiodental non-sibilant fricative**
where labiodental describes the place of articulation of /v/, i.e. that the contact
area between active and passive articulators is the lower lip and the upper teeth.
As a weak obstruent consonant, /v/ is lenis and partially or fully voiced depending on context.

variation: the voicing of /v/ varies so that it is fully voiced initially and medially
between voiced sounds as in *veil, valid, civic, living*, partially voiced or voiceless in
final position as in *live, dove*. Otherwise /v/ has no important variant pronunciations.

spelling: /v/ is regularly spelled *v* as in *vine, vivid, live*. Occasionally, /v/ is
spelled *vv* or *ph* as in *skivvy, Stephen*. Notice the spelling *f* in the word *of* pronounced [ʌv/əv].

/θ/ and /ð/

The position of the articulatory organs during the production of /θ/ and /ð/ is
shown in the following diagram:

(3.28)

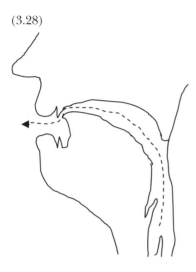

/θ/

Articulation: from (3.28) it is apparent that /θ/ is articulated by the tip and the blade forming a stricture of close approximation with the upper teeth. The air escapes out over the entire contact area of this stricture causing a not so distinct friction as in sibilants. At the same time, the velum is raised closing off the nasal cavity. Given the manner and energy properties outlined in § 3.6.2 above, /θ/ may be classified as a **strong, dental non-sibilant fricative** where dental specifies the place of articulation of /θ/. As a strong obstruent consonant, /θ/ is not only fortis and always voiceless, i.e. articulated with an open glottis, but it also shortens the length of the preceding sound, as described above in § 3.6.2.

variation: apart from auditorily similar interdental pronunciations, /θ/ has no important variant pronunciations. In AAVE (see Ch.1 above), /θ/ is frequently replaced with /f/ or /t/ medially and finally so that *Bethlehem* is pronounced ['beflǝhǝm] and *month* is pronounced [mʌnf] or [mʌnt]. Similar replacements are also heard in English English Cockney. The susceptibility of /θ/ (and in fact /ð/) to substitutions of this kind is perhaps explicable in terms of its overall low frequency of occurrence in languages and its articulatory complexity, something which is supported by /θ/ being a difficult obstruent for foreign learners to learn to master.

spelling: /θ/ is spelled *th* as in *thought, theme, bath*, unless *t* and *h* belong to separate syllables (cf. *anthill*). Notice that *th* also represents /ð/ and that *th* in a few instances represent /t/ as in, for example *thyme, Thomson, Anthony*.

/ð/

articulation: /ð/ is articulated in the same way as /θ/ except that /ð/ is weak and not strong. Given its manner and energy properties (cf. § 3.6.2 above), /ð/ may then be classified as a **weak, dental non-sibilant fricative** where dental specifies the place of articulation of /ð/. As a weak obstruent consonant, /ð/ is lenis and is partially or fully voiced depending on context.

variation: the voicing of /ð/ varies so that it is fully voiced initially and medially between voiced sounds as in *these, those, gather, bathing,* partially voiced or voiceless in final position as in *bathe, scythe.* In AAVE, /ð/ is frequently replaced with either /d/ or /v/ so that *these* may be pronounced [diz] and *smooth, mother* may be pronounced [smuv] and [ˈmʌvər]. A similar process occurs in English English Cockney and, as in the case of /θ/, /ð/'s susceptibility to substitution is explicable in terms of its general low frequency of occurrence in languages and its articulatory complexity, the latter property manifested by the problems it poses to foreign learners.

spelling: /ð/ is spelled *th*, initially only in grammatical words (see Ch. 5) like, for example, *the, that, than, those, there.* Medially and finally, /ð/ is spelled *th* in lexical and grammatical words alike: *father, feather, whether, with, bathe, breathe.*

/h/

articulation: the articulation of /h/ is not shown in a diagram because, unlike other fricative consonants, /h/ has no characteristic constriction in the vocal tract except that the velum is raised to close off the nasal cavity. When /h/ is produced alone, the air is simply expelled out through the mouth, and the sound which is heard is due to a slight constriction in the glottis and the passing of air out through the mouth. Because of the slight glottal constriction, /h/ is classified as a **voiceless glottal non-sibilant fricative**. The strong-weak distinction does not apply to /h/. Therefore /h/ is described as voiceless here. Its failure to enter into the strong-weak system has also meant that /h/ often is classified as an approximant. The absence of voicing makes this interpretation less obvious in the present context.

variation: there are as many variants of /h/ as there are sounds which may follow it (/h/ does not occur in final position). This means that the tongue and lip positions of /h/ depend on the following sound: in *huge* [hjudʒ] it is the tongue and lip positions of /j/, in *heard* [hɜrd] it is the tongue and lip positions of /ɜr/. Between vowels as in *a habit, behind* /h/ is not always voiceless. In this position, the vocal cords are very often slightly apart but vibrating loosely. This is known as **breathy voice** and notated [ɦ]. Finally, /h/ may not be pronounced at all at the beginning of unstressed grammatical words. Thus in *give him his beer* or *take her home*, *him*, *his* and *her* often lack /h/.

spelling: /h/ is typically spelled single *h* as in *hill, hollow, ahead, aha*. It is also possible to render /h/ as *wh*, cf. *whose, whore, whole*, but note that *wh* also stand for /w/. /h/ is not pronounced in some French loan words as in, for example, *hour, honest, herb*. *h* occurs in a number of digraphs: *th* (=/θ/ or /ð/), *gh* (=/g/ or /f/), *sh* (=/ʃ/), *ch* (=/tʃ/, /ʃ/ or /k/).

3.7.3 Summing up the individual fricatives

The following points should be noted about the individual fricatives:

- Manner of articulation aside, the fricatives can be organised in 4 pairs according to shared place of articulation, plus /h/ as the odd member out
- The sibilants /ʃ/ and /ʒ/ are alveopalatal fricatives. They have no important free or bound allophones apart from /ʒ/ varying in degree of voicing
- The sibilants /s/ and /z/ are alveolar fricatives. They have no important free or bound allophones apart from /z/ varying in degree of voicing
- The non-sibilants /θ/ and /ð/ are dental fricatives. Apart from /ð/ varying in the degree of voicing they have no important free or bound allophones
- The non-sibilants /f/ and /v/ are labiodental fricatives. Apart from /v/ varying in degree of voicing, they have no important free or bound allophones
- /h/, the odd member out, is categorised as a glottal fricative. It has no important free or bound allophones.

3.8 Summarising the obstruent consonants of NAERD

Obstruent consonants are characterised by oral constriction either such that the articulators make a complete closure or form a narrow stricture of close approximation. Corresponding to these two stricture types, obstruents are divided into stops and fricatives. Stops fall into two groups: affricates and plosives, the former releasing the compressed air gradually and the latter releasing the compressed air abruptly. Fricatives, similarly, consist of two subtypes: sibilants and non-sibilants, the former being articulated with considerably more noise than the latter. Both stops and fricatives (except /h/) make up a neat system of strong and weak obstruent consonants such that the strong members are fortis, voiceless, sometimes aspirated and with a shortening effect on the preceding sound, whereas the weak obstruent consonants are lenis, partially or fully voiced and without a shortening effect on the preceding sound. The obstruent consonants in NAERD are dispersed over a range of passive places of articulation, extending from the lips to the glottis. The following diagram, (3.29), summarises the main categories of obstruents and specifies the place of articulation of each obstruent. Strong obstruents are printed in thick type.

(3.29)

```
                          obstruents
                         /          \
                   stops              fricatives
                  /     \            /          \
           affricates  plosives   sibilants   non-sibilants
```

	affricates	plosives	sibilants	non-sibilants
Bilabial		**p** b		
Labio-dental				**f** v
Dental				**θ** ð
Alveolar		**t** d	**s** z	
Alveopalatal	**tʃ** dʒ		**ʃ** ʒ	
Velar		**k** g		
Glottal				h

Further reading
Comprehensive introductions to the organs of speech can be found in Laver 1994, Ladefoged 2001 and in numerous other textbooks dealing with phonetics and phonology. The description of obstruents follows classic accounts as presented in Roach 2001, Ladefoged 2001, Gimson 1962 Giegerich 1993. Bauer et al. 1980 is also a very detailed account dealing specifically with American English. Wells 1982 discusses variant pronunciations in American English such as the flap. Wells 2000 should also be consulted.

CHAPTER 4

Sonorant consonants in American English

4.1 Types of sonorant consonants

Whereas obstruents are those voiced or voiceless consonants which are articulated with complete closure or narrow constriction, sonorants are those voiced consonant sounds that never involve complete closure or narrow constriction. Instead sonorants are articulated with a stricture of open approximation and thus always produced with a free air passage, allowing the air to pass out freely either through the mouth or through the nose depending on which sonorant type is articulated. As sounds produced with free air passage, sonorants border on vowels and are therefore typically described as the most vowel-like consonant type. But although they also involve free air passage (see Ch. 5 below), sonorants differ from vowels, as well as from obstruents, in their phonological behaviour. Unlike sonorants, vowels may constitute the central element of both stressed and unstressed syllables, while sonorants never make up the syllabic peak of stressed syllables and only some sonorants, but not all, can form the peak of unstressed syllables. Acoustically, sonorants differ from obstruents by having a periodic wave pattern, something they share with vowels, but in the latter this pattern is more regular and lacks energy reduction. In sum, sonorants then differ from obstruents by being articulated with a stricture of open approximation and by involving acoustic periodicity, and from vowels by not being able to form the peak of stressed syllables and having some energy reduction. Consequently, the term sonorant will here be used to refer to those consonant sounds articulated with **free oral or nasal air passage,** at the same time as they are acoustically periodic, which **cannot form the syllabic peaks of stressed syllables**. The diagram in (4.1) summarises the distinction between the three sound types, obstruent, sonorant and vowel.

It is apparent from the preceding paragraph that sonorants do not make up a homogenous class. Some sonorants are articulated with an open nasal passage only and some with the air passing out of the mouth only. Those sonorants which are articulated with an open nasal passage, i.e. with a lowered velum, at the same time as there is no oral passage so the air escapes out through the nose are termed **nasals**. There are three nasals in NAERD: /m/, /n/ and /ŋ/, differing in the place of articulation of the oral closure (see § 4.2.1 below). The remaining sonorants, /l/, /r/, /j/ and /w/, are oral sounds. As sonorants they

(4.1)

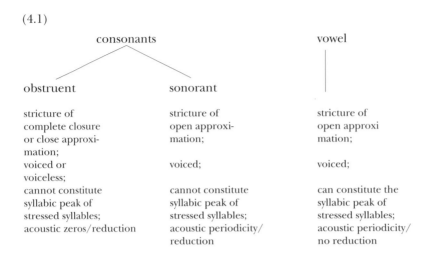

consonants   vowel

obstruent   sonorant

stricture of   stricture of   stricture of
complete closure   open approxi-   open approxi
or close approxi-   mation;   mation;
mation;
voiced or   voiced;   voiced;
voiceless;
cannot constitute   cannot constitute   can constitute the
syllabic peak of   syllabic peak of   syllabic peak of
stressed syllables;   stressed syllables;   stressed syllables;
acoustic zeros/reduction   acoustic periodicity/   acoustic periodicity/
                             reduction   no reduction

are characterised articulatorily by free air passage, but air passes out in different ways in these four consonants. In the case of /r/, /j/, and /w/, the active and passive articulators form a stricture of open approximation and the air passes out along the middle of the tongue. As this articulation of open approximation is very similar to that of vowels, /r/, /j/, /w/ are termed **semivowels** or **approximants** and they differ among one another in where there is the narrowest contact between active and passive articulators, i.e. in place of articulation (see § 4.2.2, 3 & 4). In /l/, on the other hand, the air passes out typically along the sides of the tongue and not along the middle of the tongue, because there is contact between tongue tip and alveolar ridge centrally. As another term for 'at/from/along the sides' is lateral, this sonorant is called a **lateral**. The three sonorant classes are shown below (cf. (3.5) in Ch. 3):

(4.2)

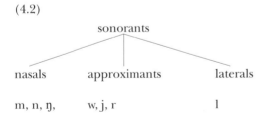

sonorants

nasals   approximants   laterals

m, n, ŋ,   w, j, r   l

Before each sonorant is considered in more detail, the following main points should be noted about the sonorants:

- sonorants are always voiced sounds
- sonorants are the most vowel-like consonants and as such produced with a stricture of open approximation unlike obstruents
- sonorants differ from vowels phonologically in that they do not constitute the peak of stressed syllables
- sonorants share with obstruent consonants the ability not to form the peak of stressed syllables
- the air passage of sonorants may be nasal only or oral only; when oral it is either tongue-central or tongue-lateral
- Acoustically, sonorants show periodicity and low reduction of energy, but not as low as in that of vowels.

4.2 The individual sonorants

Following the procedure used in Ch. 3, this section will describe each sonorant individually and as in Ch. 3 the description will concentrate on **articulation**, **variation** and **spelling**. Since the status of /r/ is special, if not unique, in English, this consonant will receive more attention than the other sonorant consonants. Therefore a separate section will discuss in greater detail such issues as its history, its distribution (geographical and phonological) and its socially-based fluctuation.

4.2.1 The nasals

In terms of manner of articulation, nasals can be defined as those sounds which are articulated by lowering the velum, at the same time as the oral cavity is closed so the air passes out through the nose only. True nasals allow nasal passage only. But it is also possible to produce sounds with both oral and nasal air passage. These sounds are **nasalised** sounds and they are not phonemic (contrastive) in NAERD (or other varieties of English), but exist as variants of some vowels when these occur next to nasals. Thus /æ/ in *can* is frequently pronounced nasalised in American English: [kãn].

/m/

articulation: as is apparent from (4.3), /m/ is articulated by the lower and upper lips forming a closure, at the same time as the vocal cords vibrate and a lowered velum allows the air to escape out through the nose. Since the closure is formed at the lips, the place of articulation of /m/ is bilabial and /m/ is therefore classified as a **bilabial nasal sonorant**.

articulation variation: when followed by *f, v*, the place of articulation of /m/ may become labiodental like that of /f/ and /v/: *same fuel, same value*. A partially devoiced /m/ may occur after /s/ or /ʃ/ as in *smear, schmuck*. Syllabic /m/

(4.3)

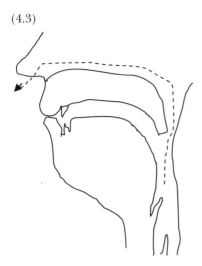

occurs in, for example, *open, happen* when these words are pronounced with a final bilabial nasal: [ˈoʊpm̩] [ˈhæpm̩].

spelling: /m/ is regularly spelled *m* or *mm* as in *middle, mother, hammer, Mum, velum, gram.* Note that *mnemonic* has no /m/.

/n/

(4.4)

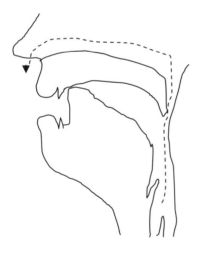

articulation: as is apparent from (4.4), /n/ is articulated by the tip and/or the blade of the tongue forming a closure at the alveolar ridge, at the same time as the vocal cords vibrate and the velum is lowered so the air escapes out through the nose. Since the mouth is blocked at the alveolar ridge, the place of articulation of /n/ is alveolar and /n/ is therefore classified as an **alveolar nasal sonorant**.

variation: /n/'s place of articulation may vary depending on the preceding or following consonant. /n/ is dental when followed by dental /θ/ and /ð/ as in *tenth* and *men that die*, and postalveolar and retroflex when preceded by postalveolar and retroflex /r/: *learn, churn*. A partially devoiced /n/ may occur after /s/, particularly in a stressed syllable as in *snow, sneer*. Syllabic /n/ occurs in, for example, *christen, listen*: ['krɪsn̩, 'lɪsn̩].

spelling: /n/ is regularly spelled *n* and *nn*: *name, no, thin, tan, funny, thinner*. Note that not.all *n*'s represent /n/, as is apparent from the comments on /ŋ/-spellings below. In the combination *mn* word-finally *n* is silent as in, for example, *autumn, damn, condemn*.

(4.5)

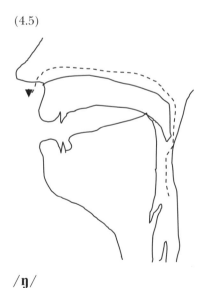

/ŋ/

articulation: as is apparent from (4.5), /ŋ/ is articulated by the back of the tongue forming a closure against the soft palate or velum, at the same time as the vocal cords vibrate and the nasal passage is open so the air escapes out through the nose. As the air is blocked by the tongue raised against the velum, the place of articulation of /ŋ/ is velar and /ŋ/ is therefore classified as a **velar nasal sonorant**.

variation: the place of articulation of /ŋ/ varies depending on the preceding sound. After front vowels, the place of articulation of /ŋ/ is pushed forward approaching palatal as in *ring, length, gang*; after back vowels it is further back as in *among, song*. Otherwise it has no important variant pronunciations.

spelling: /ŋ/ is always spelled *n* in combination with one or more letters representing /k/ or /g/. Regularly, *nk* represent /ŋ/ plus /k/ as in *sink* [sɪŋk] and *rank* [ræŋk]. *ng* typically stand for either /ŋ/ word-finally or /ŋ/ plus /g/ word-medially as in *rang* [ræŋ], *long* [lɔŋ] and *finger* [ˈfɪŋgər], *younger* [ˈjʌŋgər]. As *c, ch, q* and *x* may represent /k/, *n* in combination with one of these /k/-renderings also represents /ŋ/ plus /k/: *uncle* [ˈʌŋkl̩], *anchor* [ˈæŋkər], *banquet* [ˈbæŋkwət], *anxious* [ˈæŋkʃəs].

4.2.2 The approximant /r/

The status of /r/ in English is quite unique since by describing the distribution of this consonant in **postvocalic** position, it is possible to divide varieties of English into two main types. Those varieties in which /r/ is always pronounced after a vowel and before a consonant as in *card, sort* and word-finally after a vowel and before a tone-group boundary (| or || cf. Ch. 8 below), as in *far* and *car* in the strings *He has gone too far! Is it in the car?*, are termed **rhotic** or **r-full** varieties, and those in which /r/ is not pronounced in these positions are termed **non-rhotic** or **r-less** varieties. This difference in distribution of /r/ leads to the following division of English varieties:

rhotic: most American varieties, Scottish English, Irish English, some South-Western English varieties
non-rhotic: most varieties of English English including RP, South African English, the English of Australia and New Zealand

Rhoticity is typically said to be a diagnostic feature of American English. It is characteristic of NAERD, the variety chosen as reference dialect here, which as far as consonants are concerned covers most of North America. However, non-rhotic American varieties exist, most notably in Eastern New England and in the South around Charleston, Savannah, Atlanta and on the Gulf coast in New Orleans, but some New Yorkers are also non-rhotic. Originally, all varieties of English were rhotic as attested by the spelling. Within a time span of approximately 300 years (1600-1900), *r* in the positions mentioned above, i.e. postvocalicly, was lost in south-eastern English English, the forerunner of English English RP. Thus some of the first settlers arriving in North America specifically in the North East in the first of the four great waves (see Ch. 1) may have been non-rhotic, but most settlers, including the majority of those arriving in the first wave, are generally thought to have been rhotic. So present-day non-rhoticity in eastern New England is not likely to be a direct result of settlers' importation of an *r*-less pronunciation. Instead those who kept close contact with 'the old motherland' sometimes adopted a non-rhotic pronunciation, as *r*-loss became a prestige feature of south-eastern English English. The speakers who maintained close contact with England after the settlement came from Eastern New England and the lowland coastal South. Therefore these areas to this day have non-rhotic speakers. AAVE, with its strong southern links, is also normally described as non-rhotic. Elsewhere rhoticity prevailed, partly because this was the pronunciation of settlers in general, and partly because those who settled further inland maintained little or no contact with non-rhotic England and therefore kept their postvocalic *r*'s. As illustrated by the situation in New York City, rhoticity is spreading in the US. New York City originally was rhotic, but under the influence of New England speech New York English became non-rhotic. Within the past 50 years or so, New Yorkers have returned to using a rhotic pronunciation, which is a prestige feature of present-day American English and used by the majority of American English speakers.

   Although American English in general is considered rhotic, a few words about non-rhotic varieties are in order. As pointed out above, in a non-rhotic variety /r/ is not pronounced before consonants and finally before a tone-group boundary (*card, car*). But when it is followed by a vowel, /r/ in non-rhotic varieties is not only always pronounced in instances like *rice, roar, luring, roaring* but also potentially found in strings like the following (representing English English RP):

(4.6)

the car in the garage	[ðə ˈkɑːr ɪn ðə gəˈrɑːʒ]
four of them	[ˈfɔːr əv ðəm]
the chair in the hall	[ðə ˈtʃeər ɪn ðə ˈhɔːl]
better off	[ˈbetər ɒf]
they fear eating	[ðeɪ ˈfɪər ˈiːtɪŋ]

In other words, in non-rhotic varieties it is possible to pronounce a postvocalic /r/ if the following sound is a vowel also when there is a word boundary – but no tone group boundary – between these two vowels. This rule is known as **linking-*r*** and applies to /r/ between any one of the vowels /ɜː, ɑː, ɔː, ə/ and a following vowel. Linking-*r* is part of a more general phenomenon known as ***r*-sandhi** (from Sanskrit *sam* 'together' and *dhi* 'put'), covering not only linking-*r* but also the insertion of /r/ as in for example:

(4.7)

law and order	[ˈlɔːr ən ˈɔːdə]
the idea of	[ði aɪˈdɪər əv]
the Stella Artois event	[ðə ˈstelər ɑːˈtwɑːr ɪˈvent]

in which /r/ is inserted under the same conditions as linking-r without having occurred in this position historically and thus not present in the orthography.

This insertion of /r/ is known as **intrusive-r** and since it occurs in the same environment as linking-*r*, intrusive-*r* is generally considered to have arisen by analogy with linking-*r*. Intrusive-*r* and linking-*r*, i.e. *r*-sandhi, are characteristic, if not diagnostic, of English English RP. Although only found in non-rhotic varieties, intrusive-*r* and linking-*r* are not as common in American English non-rhotic varieties as in RP. The non-rhotic variety of the South has neither linking nor intrusive-*r*. Nor has AAVE with its southern roots, whereas non-rhotic Eastern New England English exhibits some fluctuation: typically, speakers in Eastern New England use both linking-*r* and intrusive-*r* but the latter mostly in informal contexts. Among non-rhotic New Yorkers, a similar situation obtains, so Eastern New England and New York English most closely resemble English English RP in respect of the distribution of /r/. But although non-rhotic American varieties exist, it is probably correct to say that within the next 50 years or so there will be very few if any non-rhotic Americans left. The national norm of /r/-pronouncing is spreading, as evidenced by the return of postvocalic r in New York City, and since there is every indication that this development continues, all *r*-less pockets may well have disappeared by the end of the 21st century so that American English by this time will be fully rhotic.

The distinction rhotic/non-rhotic also affects the vowel system. As is discussed in § 5.2.3 below (see also Ch. 10), in rhotic varieties the presence of postvocalic r reduces the number of vowel contrasts before /r/. Conversely, non-rhotic varieties typically have vowel phonemes which rhotic varieties lack, in particular centring diphthongs whose second element is /ə/, a residue of the lost /r/. Thus English English RP, for example, as well as American non-rhotic varieties, will have diphthongs in the following words, whereas rhotic NAERD will have monophthongs plus /r/:

(4.8)

	RP	NAERD
fear	[fɪə]	[fɪr]
care	[keə]	[ker]
sure	[ʃʊə]	[ʃʊr]

The interplay of /r/ and vowels in rhotic NAERD will not be discussed further here. Instead one final aspect of rhoticity should be observed. In American English rhotic varieties, postvocalic *r* 'colours' the preceding vowel so that it is either partially retroflex (/r/ is retroflex as will be discussed presently) or fully retroflex. Partial colouring or **rhotacisation** affects the vowels given in (4.8) plus /ɑ, ɔ, aʊ, aɪ/ as in *tar, tore, tower, tyre*. Full colouring, or rhotacisation, affects only the central vowels /ɜ/ and /ə/ as in *nurse, bird* and the second vowels of *better* and *actor*. Full rhotacisation entails that /ɜ/ and /ə/ and the following /r/ fuse into one phonetic rhotacised sound, one ***r*-coloured** vowel. Consequently, the phonetic representation of *r*-coloured /ɜ/ and /ə/ in, for example, *bird* and *better* is often [bɜˑd] and [ˈbeDə˞] instead of [bɜrd] and [ˈbeDər]. The former is preferred throughout this book when the emphasis is on pronunciation and the latter when the emphasis is on phonemic system (phonology).

As an approximant sonorant, /r/ is articulated with a stricture of open approximation. This means that the articulators only approach but do not touch each other centrally or laterally in the mouth during its articulation. But it remains to be seen how /r/ is distinct from /l/, /j/ and /w/, the other members of the class of approximants. One property has already been mentioned, namely that /r/ is retroflex. What retroflex stands for and what other articulatory properties characterise /r/ will appear from the following description of its articulation, variation and spelling.

/r/

(4.9)

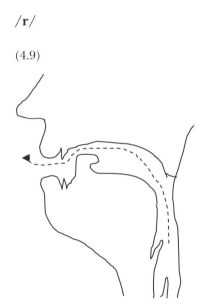

articulation: as is apparent from the diagram in (4.9), /r/ is articulated by the tongue tip pointing backwards toward the postalveolar region without touching the roof of the mouth. With this tongue shape, which is the source of the term **retroflex**, the air passes out through the mouth at the same time as the vocal cords vibrate and a raised velum closes off the nasal cavity. Behind the tongue tip the tongue is slightly hollow centrally and its sides raised against the upper molars. Because the tongue points toward the intersection between the alveolar ridge and the hard palate, /r/ is classified as a **postalveolar, retroflex approximant** where postalveolar refers to the place of articulation of /r/.

variation: there is considerable variation in the tongue shape when /r/ is pronounced. The articulatory description given above is typical of /r/ before vowels, unless /r/ is also preceded by a vowel. Elsewhere, including intervocalic position, /r/ is typically articulated without a raised tongue tip and instead the tongue is bunched backwards and upwards in the mouth against the upper molars. The *r*-colouring of vowels, i.e. rhotacisation, typically involves this bunched tongue shape. The length of *r*-colouring varies also, so fully *r*-coloured vowels as in *bird*, *better* are much longer than partially *r*-coloured vowels as in *lord* and *card*. Initially, /r/ is normally pronounced with some lip rounding. Otherwise, lip rounding depends on the adjacent vowel so some lip rounding occurs in *sure* and no or very little lip rounding occurs in *shear*.

  /r/ is classified as a sonorant consonant and as such regarded as inherently voiced. But /r/ may lose both sonorancy and voicing. When /r/ forms a syllable-initial cluster with either /t/ or /d/ and the syllable is stressed, /r/ is desonorised to a fricative as in *dry* and *try*, [dɹaɪ] and [tɹaɪ]. After /p, t, k/ and sometimes after other strong obstruents in stressed syllables, /r/ is also devoiced. So in *try* /r/ not only becomes a fricative but is also devoiced, [tɹ̥aɪ], whereas in *cry* /r/ is merely devoiced, [kɹ̥aɪ].

spelling: /r/ is always spelled *r* one way or the other. Regularly, the spelling is *r* or *rr* as in *rise, reverent, dirt, far* and *sorry, ferry, Carr. rh* and, rarely, *rrh* are also possible /r/-renderings: *rhotic, rhytm, catarrh*. Finally, the combination *wr* also represents /r/ unless *w* and *r* belong to separate syllables: compare *rewrite, wrong, wrath* with *showroom*.

4.2.3 The approximants /j/ and /w/

As sonorant consonants, /j/ and /w/ are articulated with a stricture of open approximation. In the case of /j/, this stricture corresponds to the tongue position used to articulate the vowel /ɪ/ and in the case of /w/ this stricture corresponds to the tongue position and lip protrusion used to articulate the vowel /ʊ/. However, /j/ and /w/ differ from /ɪ/ and /ʊ/ as sonorants differ from vowels. /j/ and /w/ are non-syllabic and /ɪ/ and /ʊ/ are syllabic, syllabicity being the property which distinguishes vowels from the most-vowel like consonants, the sonorants. The close affinity between, on the one hand, /j/ and /ɪ/ and, on the other, /w/ and /ʊ/ explains why /j/ and /w/ are often termed semivowels.

/j/

A few points about /j/ are in order before its articulation and variant pronunciations are considered. It is a characteristic feature of American English (not just NAERD) that /j/ has a more restricted distribution than in other varieties of English. Typically, /j/ does not occur after dental and alveolar obstruents and sonorants in American English, unless the syllable is unstressed. Thus in (4.10a) no /j/ occurs whilst in (4.10b), which is the English English RP pronunciation, /j/ is pronounced:

(4.10)

	a.	American English	b.	English English RP
tune		[tun]		[tjuːn]
duke		[duk]		[djuːk]
sue		[su]		[sjuː]
enthusiastic		[ɪnθuzi'æstɪk]		[ɪnθjuːzi'æstɪk]
new		[nu]		[njuː]
lurid		['lurɪd]		['ljuːrɪd]

By contrast /j/ occurs in words like *undulate* [ʌndju'leɪt], *Matthew* ['mæθju], *billion* ['bɪljən], *tenure* ['tenjʊr] in both varieties alike since /j/ in such words, and in many others, stands in unstressed syllables. Similarly, /j/ in all varieties never occurs syllable-finally.

Sometimes /j/ crops up unexpectedly syllable-initially. Just like /r/ in some non-rhotic varieties may be inserted (see description of intrusive-*r* above) after an open or a half-open vowel and before another vowel, i.e. intervocalicly, as in *the idea* [r] *of, law* [r] *and order*, it is possible to insert /j/ also intervocalicly when the first vowel is a half-close or close front vowel. Such an **intrusive-*j*** may occur in *I am* [aɪ 'jæm], *I can see it* [aɪ kən 'si jɪt]. A similar *w*-insertion occurs intervocalicly after a half-close or close back vowel (see § 5.2.2 below). Interestingly, in the varieties that have intrusive-*r*, intrusive-*j* (and intrusive-*w*) appear in the context where intrusive-*r* is not found and vice versa.

articulation: as is apparent from (4.11), /j/ is articulated by the front of the tongue being raised towards the hard palate to a position corresponding to that of /i/ or /ɪ/, at the same time as the vocal cords vibrate and a raised velum closes off the nasal cavity. Since /j/ is always followed by a vowel, the tongue position of /j/ glides from the position shown in (4.11) to the position of the following vowel. For example, in *you*, [ju], the tongue moves from a front half-close to a back close position. Thus, when it occurs, /j/ is not unlike the first element of a diphthong (see § 5.2.2 below), but the diphthong it occurs in has a strong second element, a so-called rising diphthong, unlike vowel + vowel diphthongs such as, for example, /aɪ/ and /aʊ/, whose first element in NAERD is

(4.11)

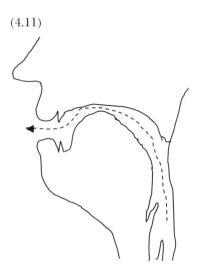

the stronger, so-called falling diphthongs. Since it is articulated by raising the front of the tongue against the hard palate, /j/ is described as a **palatal approximant sonorant** where palatal describes the place of articulation of /j/.

variation: the extent to which the front tongue is raised in /j/ varies depending on context. Before /i/ and /ɪ/ the tongue position is much closer than before all other vowels. Before /i/ the tongue position is so close that it sometimes results in palatal friction. Like other sonorants, /j/ is devoiced partially or fully after strong obstruents, including /h/, particularly in stressed syllables. Thus in stressed *puke, few, huge*, for example, /j/ is devoiced: [pj̥uk], [fj̥u], [hj̥udʒ].

spelling: /j/ is regularly spelled *y* as in *Yankee, Yale, yet, you, beyond*. Sometimes it is spelled *i* or *ie* as in *onion, convenient* [ˈʌnjən] [kənˈvinjənt]. /j/ is rarely spelled *j*, but *j*-renderings do occur: *jod, hallelujah*. Note that the letter *j* typically represents /dʒ/.

/**w**/
Like /j/, /w/ does not occur syllable-finally. It is always followed by a vowel but may be preceded by a consonant including dental and alveolar ones, and this pattern of distribution applies to all varieties of English alike. As mentioned above, **intrusive-*w*** is possible in an intervocalic context after a close or half-close back vowel. Thus, intrusive-*w* may be found in strings like the following: *how are you?* [haʊ ˈwɑr jʊ], *two are enough* [ˈtu wɑr ɪˈnʌf]. The complementary distribution, in the non-rhotic varieties that have intrusive-*r*, of intrusive-*j/w* on the one hand and intrusive-*r* on the other, highlights the appropriateness of classifying /r/, /j/ and /w/ as approximants.

(4.12)

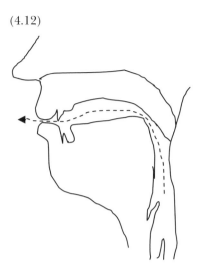

articulation: as is apparent from (4.12), the articulation of /w/ involves two strictures of open approximation. First, the lips are protruded and rounded and, second, the back of the tongue is raised against the velum to a position corresponding to that of /ʊ/ or /u/. Simultaneous with this double articulation, the velum is raised so that the nasal cavity is closed off. Since /w/ is always followed by a vowel, the tongue glides from the position shown in (4.16) toward the position of the following vowel. For example, in *weep*, [wip], the tongue glides from a back half-close to a front close position. Thus /w/, like /j/, is not unlike the first element of a diphthong, but the diphthong is a rising diphthong with a prominent second element unlike vowel + vowel diphthongs, like /aɪ/ and /aʊ/, which have prominent first elements. Since it is articulated with two strictures of open approximation, /w/ is described as a **labio-velar approximant sonorant** where labio-velar describes the double place of articulation of /w/.

variation: /w/'s lip rounding varies, in particular before /u/ the lips are more rounded than before other vowels, in fact so much that friction may be the result. Like other sonorants, /w/ is devoiced partially or fully after strong obstruents particularly in stressed syllables. Thus in stressed *twice, quite, thwart*, for example, /w/ is devoiced: [tw̥aɪs], [kw̥aɪt], [θw̥ɔrt].

Like /j/, /w/ is also devoiced after /h/ for those speakers who pronounce words spelled with *wh* as if they consist of the phoneme combination /wh/. These speakers, and there are many of them, distinguish between *which* and *witch*, *whale* and *wail*, for example, by pronouncing the first member of these pairs [hw̥-] and the second member [w̥-].

spelling: /w/ is regularly spelled *w* and *wh* for those speakers who do not pronounce this combination [hʍ] as in *water, work, sweat, away, what, white, whop*. /w/ is also spelled *u* as in *persuade, language, quite*. In vowel + *w* combinations of the same syllable, vowel + *w* represent a vowel phoneme since /w/ only occurs before a vowel: *few, law, sow*. /w/ is also not pronounced in the syllable-initial combination *wr* as in *wrong, writing, wreck*. Similarly, no /w/ is found in *whole* and *who* (and other forms involving *who*). Notice, finally, the two exceptions: *two, answer*.

4.2.4 The lateral /l/

Whilst /r/ is unique in that its postvocalic distribution divides English varieties into two main types, rhotic and non-rhotic, /l/ is unique by articulatorily involving open approximation and closure at the same time, an articulatory property created by the flexibility of the tongue. (4.13) shows the articulatory properties of /l/.

(4.13)

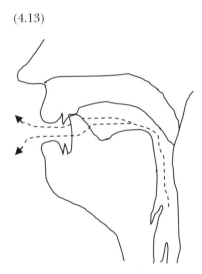

articulation: as is apparent from the diagram in (4.13), /l/ is articulated by the tongue tip forming a closure at the alveolar ridge, and the sides of the tongue are lowered so that air can escape out through the mouth along these sides, at the same time as the vocal cords vibrate and a raised velum closes off the nasal cavity. Behind the raised tongue tip the back of the tongue is bunched up towards the velum. This tongue shape results in American English /l/ being generally perceived as darker than /l/'s in other varieties. Since another term for 'at or along the sides' is lateral, /l/ is called a **lateral** sonorant, in particular a **bilateral** because air flows along the two passage ways on either side of the tongue. Thus /l/ is classified as an **alveolar, lateral sonorant** where alveolar specifies the place of articulation of /l/.

variation: the shape of the back of the tongue varies. Some American speakers always pronounce /l/ with some degree of a bunched up back tongue. This variant of /l/ is known as **dark-***l* and notated [ɫ]. But /l/ may also be pronounced without a bunched up back tongue. This variant is known as **clear-***l* (or light-*l*) which is notated [lⱼ]. Dark-*l* is always found in the following environments:

(4.14)

dark-*l* occurs when: /l/ is followed by a consonant, *told, help*

                         /l/ is word-final, *fall, hill*

                         /l/ is syllabic, *cattle, shuttle*

Dark-*l* is also found before central and back vowels (see Ch. 5 below). In this environment, the tongue is typically less bunched up and consequently pronounced with a less dark resonance:

(4.15)

dark-*l* occurs when: /l/ is followed by central vowels, *lust, learn*

                         /l/ is followed by back vowels, *lose, low, law, large*

Before front vowels, some American speakers pronounce /l/ dark, but with a less bunched up tongue than before central and back vowels and hence with a not so dark resonance as before central and back vowels. Thus sometimes

(4.16)

dark-*l* occurs when: /l/ is followed by front vowels, *lease, letter, lamb*

Those American speakers who have clear-*l* typically use it in the last mentioned environment and most typically only before half-close or close front vowels (*lit, lease*). In other varieties of English, except Irish English, which has only clear-*l*, dark-*l* is only found in the environment of a following consonant, finally and when /l/ is syllabic, whereas clear-*l* occurs elsewhere. Thus in English English RP, for example, the distribution of clear-and dark-*l*'s is as follows

(4.17)

dark-*l* occurs in RP when: /l/ is followed by a consonant except /j/, *told, help*

                           /l/ is word-final, *fall, hill*

                           /l/ is syllabic, *cattle, shuttle*

clear-*l* occurs in RP when: /l/ is followed by any vowel or /j/, *limb, luck, lord, lucid*

In the phonological system of those speakers who use both *l*'s, clear-*l* and dark-*l* are in complementary distribution. Clear-*l* occurs exactly in those environments where dark-*l* does not occur and vice versa. As outlined in Ch. 2 above, variants with this distribution are bound allophones, so [ɫ] and [lʲ] are bound allophones of /l/.

In addition to clear-and dark-*l*'s, /l/ has two other important variants. The first concerns laterality. Sometimes the articulation is not bilateral as described above, but instead /l/ is articulated by the air passing out along only one side of the tongue, the other side being blocked by the tongue. Because it has only one passage way, this variant of l/ is described as **monolateral**. The second variant occurs when /l/ is preceded by a strong obstruent and this strong obstruent and /l/ constitute the initial cluster of a stressed syllable as in, for example, *clue, acclaim, plot, apply*. /l/ in this position is devoiced as a result of the preceding strong obstruent. This devoicing of /l/ is parallel to the devoicing of /r/ found in the same environment.

spelling: /l/ is spelled *l* or *ll* as in *lame, magnolia, until, dwelling, tall*. /l/ is often silent when it occurs between the letters *a* and *f, k* or *m*: *calf, stalk, salmon*. Notice also silent /l/ in *could, should* and *would*.

4.2.5 Summing up the individual sonorants
The following points should be noted about the individual sonorants:
- NAERD has three nasal sonorants. /m/ is bilabial, /n/ is alveolar and /ŋ/ is velar, but the place of articulation of the nasals varies somewhat depending on the contiguous sound. /m/, /n/ and /ŋ/ may all be syllabic, and /m/ and /n/ may have devoiced variants after /s/
- NAERD has three approximant sonorants. /r/ is postalveolar and retroflex, /j/ is palatal and /w/ is labio-velar
- In NAERD /r/ is pronounced in postvocalic position, and NAERD is therefore termed a rhotic variety of English. Varieties which do not have postvocalic /r/ are termed non-rhotic
- /j/ is the non-syllabic congener of the vowel /ɪ/, and it does not occur after dental and alveolar consonants in NAERD. The most important variant pronunciation is devoiced /j/ after strong obstruents
- /w/ is the non-syllabic congener of the vowel /ʊ/. The most important variant pronunciation is devoiced /w/ after strong obstruents
- The lateral /l/ is unique in that it involves contact between tongue and alveolar ridge at the same times as air passes out along one or both sides of the tongue
- Most Americans pronounce /l/ with the back of the tongue bunched up. This variant pronunciation is termed dark-*l*. The degree to which the tongue is bunched up varies depending on the contiguous sound. In some contexts, some American speakers pronounce /l/ without a bunched up tongue. This variant pronunciation is termed clear-*l*. The only other important variant pronunciation is devoiced /l/ after strong obstruents.

4.3 Syllabic consonants

It is apparent from the description of each sonorant above that some sonorants have syllabic variants. The ability to form a syllable is typically associated with vowels and in English only vowels can constitute the peak or central and indispensable element of stressed syllables (see Ch. 6 below for a discussion of syllable structure). When a consonant constitutes the peak of a syllable, i.e. is syllabic, this syllable is unstressed and the consonant alone makes up this syllable. In English such a syllabic consonant is almost always one of the 4 sonorants, /m/, /n/, /ŋ/ and /l/.

The conditions under which syllabification of /m/, /n/, /ŋ/ and /l/ occurs are identical. For one of these sonorants to take over the role of syllabic peak, the following conditions have to be met: i) that the syllable is unstressed, as just mentioned, and ii) that a vowel, typically /ə/, preceding the sonorant is lost. Very often the speech style in which the process of consonant syllabification occurs is informal conversation, but this is not a necessary condition. Syllabic /m/, /n/ and /ŋ/ occur in the following instances:

> /**m**/ is typically syllabic in, for example, *bottom, let them, open* when pronounced ['bɑtm̩], ['letm̩] ['oʊpm̩] (the diacritic [̩] indicates syllabic consonant). It is possible in slow deliberate speech to pronounce these words with /ə/ before the nasals: ['bɑtəm], ['let θəm → 'leDəm], ['oʊpən → 'oʊpm̩] (for the change of /n/ → /m/ see Ch. 9 below). When /ə/ is lost, which is a frequent process in unstressed syllables, /m/ is left as the sole member of the second syllable and consequently becomes syllabic. As a result *bottom, let them, open* are pronounced as indicated at the beginning of this paragraph. There are also cases where /m/ probably always is syllabic as in, for example, *chasm* ['kæzm̩]. In those instances where the preceding stop and /m/ are homorganic, as in *happen*, the stop is nasally released (see Ch. 3 above).

> /**n**/ is typically syllabic in, for example, *cotton, sudden, christen* when pronounced ['kɑtn̩], ['sʌdn̩], ['krɪsn̩]. It is possible in slow deliberate speech to pronounce these words with /ə/ before the nasals: ['kɑtən], ['sʌdən], ['krɪsən]. When /ə/ is lost, which is a frequent process in unstressed syllables, /n/ is left as the sole member of the second syllable and consequently becomes syllabic. The result is that *cotton, sudden, christen* are pronounced as listed at the beginning of this paragraph. In those instances where the consonant before the syllabic /n/ is a homorganic stop as in, for example, *sudden*, the stop is released nasally (see Ch. 3 above).

> /**ŋ**/ is typically syllabic in, for example, *bacon, Morgan* when pronounced ['beɪkŋ̍], ['mɔrgŋ̍]. Again, as in the case of /m/ and /n/, it is also possible

in slow deliberate speech to pronounce these words with a /ə/ before the nasals: ['beɪkən](/n/ → /ŋ/ after the loss of /ə/, see Ch. 9 below), ['mɔrgən](/n/ → /ŋ/ after the loss of /ə/). When /ə/ is lost, which is a frequent process in unstressed syllables, and /n/ has changed to /ŋ/, the latter becomes the sole member of the second syllable and bearer of syllabicity. As a result, *bacon* and *Morgan* are pronounced as listed at the beginning of this paragraph. The stop preceding /ŋ/, since it is homorganic with /ŋ/, is nasally released.

The syllabification of /l/ is found in instances like the following:

/**l**/ is typically syllabic in, for example, *cattle, middle, hazel* when pronounced ['kætl̩], ['mɪdl̩], ['heɪzl̩]. Again, as in the case of the nasals, it is possible in slow deliberate speech to pronounce these words with /ə/ before the lateral i.e.: ['kætəl], ['mɪdəl], ['heɪzəl], although these pronunciations are rare and exist perhaps only as theoretical possibilities. When /ə/ is lost, as is common in unstressed syllables, /l/ is left as the sole member of the second syllable of these words and consequently becomes syllabic. The result is the pronunciations listed at the beginning of this paragraph. The outgoing airstream of the homorganic obstruent consonant preceding /l/ is lateral.

/r/ is also often mentioned as a potential syllabic sonorant in American English, sometimes even of stressed syllables. Thus the second syllable of *father, armour*, for example, will be said to have syllabic /r/ as indicated by the transcriptions ['faðr̩], ['ɑrmr̩]. But unlike other potentially syllabic sonorants, syllabic /r/ does not alternate with a pronunciation involving schwa plus /r/. As discussed briefly above in connection with *r*-variation, this is to do with /r/ fusing in unstressed syllables with a preceding /ə/. This rhotacisation or *r*-colouring of /ə/ can be interpreted as a syllabic /r/ rather than as a vowel which is *r*-coloured. Here the *r*-colouring interpretation is preferred and the phonetic transcription of *father* and *armour* is therefore ['faðɚ], ['ɑrmɚ]. Similarly, potentially stressed words like *bird* and *nurse* (as content words they are likely to receive sentence stress, see Ch. 5 below) are also not assumed to have syllabic /r/. In the present context, their phonetic transcription is not [brd], [nrs], but instead they are assumed to have *r*-coloured /ɜ/ and are consequently represented [bɜd], [nɜs]. The latter is the most obvious solution in a context where /ɜ/ is considered to be a member of the inventory of vowel phonemes (which is not entirely unproblematic as discussed briefly in Ch. 2 above). When *bird* and *nurse* are interpreted as [bɜd], [nɜs], *father* and *armour* with /ə/ + /r/ are also interpreted as ['faðɚ], ['ɑrmɚ] to avoid inconsistency.

As a final comment on syllabic consonants, it should be observed that ob-struents, in particular fricatives, sometimes can become syllabic so that conso-nant types produced with stricture and not open approximation may bear syl-labicity. Consider the following string and the two transcriptions of it (a. and b.):

(4.18)

> *I suppose they suspect me of the crime*

a. [aɪ səˈpoʊz ðeɪ səˈspekt mɪ əv ðə ˈkraɪm]
b. [aɪ sˈpoʊz ðeɪ sˈpekt mɪ əv ðə ˈkraɪm]

The a.-version could be called the unmarked pronunciation of this string. The b.-version is characteristic of relatively fast conversational speech style. They dif-fer in the way the first syllable of *suppose* and the first syllable of *suspect* are pro-nounced (and in other ways not relevant here). Both syllables are unstressed and both contain /ə/. As often happens in unstressed syllables, /ə/ is lost and the consonant left to itself has to take over the role of syllabic element. In this case this consonant is not a sonorant with vowel-like characteristics. The conso-nant that takes over the role of syllabic element is an obstruent, in particular the strong fricative /s/. In the absence of a sonorant, a fricative can then become a syllabic peak provided the syllable is unstressed. This is to be expected given the sonority hierarchy (see Ch. 6 below), as fricatives are next in line as the third most sonorant sound type after vowels and sonorant consonants.

4.4 Summarising the sonorant consonants of NAERD

It is characteristic of sonorant consonants that they are voiced sounds produced with a stricture of open approximation which aligns them with an acoustically periodic wave structure. The stricture of open approximation is either oral or nasal. Corresponding to these two possible air passage ways, the sonorants are grouped into, on the one hand, nasals and, on the other, approximants and laterals. In nasals the velum is lowered and the mouth is closed so air only es-capes out through the nose. Approximants and laterals are oral and differ in the way the oral stricture of open approximation is formed. In approximants the air passes out of the mouth over the entire width of the tongue, whilst the lateral is characterised by the tongue tip closing the air passage centrally in the mouth, at the same time as air can escape out of the mouth along one or, typically, both sides of the tongue. As sounds which are articulated with a stricture of open ap-proximation, sonorants are the most vowel-like consonants. But sonorants differ from vowels in that they cannot form the peak of a stressed syllable. They can take on the role of syllabic peaks in unstressed syllables, and do so regularly, but in the present interpretation only vowels constitute the peak of stressed sylla-bles. The diagram in (4.19) summarises the main categories of sonorants in NAERD and specifies the place of articulation of each sonorant.

(4.19)

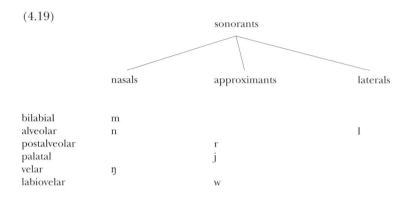

	nasals	approximants	laterals
bilabial	m		
alveolar	n		l
postalveolar		r	
palatal		j	
velar	ŋ		
labiovelar		w	

Further reading
Comprehensive introductions to sonorant consonants can be found in Laver 1994, Ladefoged 2001, Gimson 1962, Giegerich 1993. Bauer et al. 1980 deal specifically with American English. Special treatments of /r/ and rhoticity can be found in Wells 1982. See also Wolfram and Schilling-Estes 1998 and Algeo 2001. Aitchinson 1991 summaries nicely the fluctuation as a result of prestige in the pronunciation of /r/ in some forms of North American English. A recent account of the distribution of /r/ in North America can be found in Labov et al. 2006.

CHAPTER 5

Vowels in American English

5.1 How to describe vowels

It is apparent from Ch. 4 that vowels, the third major sound type and the topic of this chapter, cannot be defined solely in articulatory terms. The problem is that an articulatory definition of vowels does not uniquely distinguish vowels from all sonorants. More specifically, if they are defined solely as those always voiced sounds produced without a major oral obstruction or without any direct contact between active and passive articulators, vowels cannot be distinguished from those sonorant consonants which are produced with a stricture of open approximation in the mouth such as the approximant sonorants /j, w, r/. Therefore a definition of vowels must invoke not only articulatory but also functional (phonological) as well as acoustic properties. Functionally, vowels differ from (approximant) sonorants in their ability to constitute the peak or central element of stressed syllables, something sonorants cannot do. Sonorants are able to form the syllabic peak of unstressed syllables, even obstruents may serve this function under certain conditions, but only vowels can constitute the peak of stressed syllables. Acoustically, vowels exhibit no energy reduction and periodicity, whereas sonorants, although also periodic, are characterised by some energy reduction. Thus vowels are not only those sounds which are produced **without a major obstruction in the mouth**, and which **lack direct contact between active and passive articulators**, but they are also the only periodic sounds without energy reduction which simultaneously can form **the peak of stressed syllables**. Whereas the latter ability of vowels is very concrete and easy to describe and one which will be drawn on in the following, it is not so easy to describe the articulatory properties of vowels. The absence of directly determinable contact between active and passive articulators complicates the description. Nevertheless, vowels can be described and classified just as consonants can be described and classified, but the methodology has to take into account the more fluid articulatory properties of vowels.

The established and common way in which to describe vowels is to use a reference frame known as the **cardinal vowels**. The cardinal vowels, which were posited by the British phonetician, Daniel Jones (1881-1968), are a set of artificial vowels which Jones recorded and which have been used extensively since their proposal by phoneticians around the world. Recognising that it was necessary to have some fixed points in the otherwise fluid continuum that vowel qualities represent, Jones pronounced first the lowest and most retracted vowel possible without producing a pharyngeal consonant and without rounding his lips. This vowel is very similar to the sound produced by patients when doctors ask to look at their throats and is notated [ɑ]. Then Jones produced the most forward vowel quality possible using the front part of the tongue without producing the palatal approximant sonorant consonant /j/ and with the lips spread. This resulted in a vowel which is quite similar to the vowel found in the word *seen* and is written [i]. After he had produced these two auditority and articulatorily defined vowels, representing auditory and articulatory extremes, Jones produced three vowels using [i] as his point of departure so that these vowels sounded as if the distance between them was the same. This resulted in the vowels which he represented as [e], [ɛ] and [a]. Subsequently, Jones, taking [ɑ] as his point of departure, pronounced three vowels again in such a way that it sounded as if the distance between them was the same, at the same time as he added lip rounding. This resulted in the vowels he represented as [ɔ], [o] and [u]. He charted these vowels in a scheme, the cardinal vowel scheme, and numbered them as shown in (5.1):

(5.1)

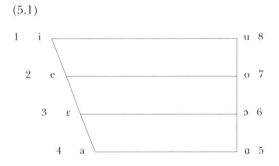

[i], [e], [ɛ] and [a] are what is referred to as **front vowels**. Articulatorily, these vowels are produced with the front part of the tongue, but in such a way that the tongue height is slightly lower for [e] than for [i] and again lower for [ɛ] than for [e] and yet lower for [a] than for [ɛ]. Among the front vowels, the auditory difference is then matched by an articulatory difference, and this is shown in the chart by placing [i] at the top of the diagram, [e] at a step lower in the diagram and so on.

[u], [o], [ɔ] and [ɑ] constitute the class of **back vowels**. Although produced with the back part of the tongue, these vowels are not matched articulatorily by a gradual difference in tongue height in the same way as the front vowels. Nonetheless, they are charted in the vowel scheme at different levels just like the

front vowels because both acoustic and phonological evidence in addition to auditory facts support such a representation.

The cardinal vowel scheme then explicitly shows two properties. Firstly, it shows the location or place of articulation of a vowel. This appears from the placement of a vowel along the horizontal axis. A vowel in the left hand side of the scheme is a **front** vowel, a vowel placed in the right hand side is a **back** vowel and a vowel placed in the area between front and back is a **central** vowel. Secondly, the scheme shows the height of a vowel. This appears from the placement of the vowel along the vertical axis. A vowel on or near the top horizontal line is a **close** vowel, a vowel on or near the second horizontal line from the top is a **half close** vowel, a vowel placed on or near the second horizontal line from the bottom is a **half open** vowel, and a vowel placed on or near the bottom horizontal line is an **open** vowel. Implicitly, the cardinal vowel scheme contends that all the back vowels except [ɑ] are produced with lip rounding (in fact increasing lip rounding as we approach [u]) and that [ɑ] and all the front vowels are produced without lip rounding. This does not mean that front vowels and open back vowels are always unrounded and back vowels higher than open ones are always rounded. It merely means that those Jones pronounced and charted as shown in (5.1) are associated with lip rounding in this way. He termed these the **primary cardinal vowels** because lip rounding is typically distributed in this way in the world's languages. The secondary cardinal vowels, which Jones pronounced and recorded subsequently, have lip rounding distributed reversely, i.e. rounded front vowels and unrounded back vowels.

In the following description, the NAERD vowels will be described in terms of the cardinal vowel system. Each vowel will be placed and described in relation to the nearest cardinal vowel(s). For example, the vowel [i], as found in the word *seen*, will be described as very close to but not quite identical with cardinal vowel (1). This classification will be shown in a vowel box based on the cardinal vowel scheme in (5.1), but in a box which is simpler, lacking the slanting left-hand vertical line which signifies a relatively greater acoustic distance between front vowels than between back vowels which are arranged along a right-angled line:

(5.2)

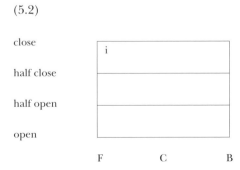

By plotting it in this way, the vowel in *seen* is described as an **unrounded**, **close front vowel**.

The cardinal vowels have been used extensively by phoneticians since they were proposed as a frame of reference, in terms of which any vowel system may be described. It enables phoneticians to communicate about the **quality** of a vowel in any language, known or unknown, where quality refers to the totality of properties describing place, height and lip position of a vowel. The cardinal vowel scheme is pedagogically very helpful allowing a learner of a new language not only to acquire a good pronunciation of the new language by comparing the new vowels with the cardinal vowels (found at the web-address http://hctv. humnet.ucla.edu/departments/linguistics/VowelsandConsonants/), but also by helping the learner to get a clear and easily understandable overview of the vowel system of the language to be learned. The following description of vowels will be based on the cardinal vowel system. As such, the description incorporates articulatory, auditory and acoustic properties. In fact, it is mostly auditory, only [i] and [ɑ] can be described articulatorily as well as auditorily, so when a vowel is described as back or front or as close or open they are descriptions of how vowels sound relative to one another rather than references to precise tongue positions and articulation in general.

5.2 Subclasses of vowels

From the preceding discussion of the cardinal vowels, it is clear that vowels may be classified as front vowels, back vowels, close vowels, open vowels and so on. But back vowels, close vowels etc. are fairly narrow classes. There exists also a broader classification of vowels which cuts across these narrow classes. Before we look at such narrow classes, it is necessary first to consider this broader sub-classification. This subclassification can be of two kinds: a phonological one concerning distribution and a phonetic one concerning stability.

5.2.1 Checked and free vowels

The first broad subclassification, the phonological one, subclassifies vowels according to **distribution**. This subclassification is also sometimes referred to as one of **vowel length**. Subdividing vowels according to distribution results in two classes: **free vowels** (sometimes referred to as long vowels) and **checked vowels** (sometimes referred to as short vowels). Of the vowels established in Ch.1 as phonemic in NAERD, the following are free:

(5.3)

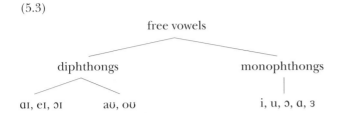

and the remaining monophthongs are checked:

(5.4)

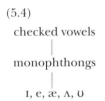

Free vowels are characterised by being able to occur in so-called open syllables like the following, all of which are well-formed:

(5.5)

a.   *buy*   [b a ɪ]   *bow*   [b a ʊ]   **b.**   *pee*   [p i]
         bay   [b e ɪ]   *bow*   [b o ʊ]   *shoe*   [ʃ u]
         boy   [b ɔ ɪ]   *Shaw*   [ʃ ɔ]
                                                                  Shah   [ʃ ɑ]
                                                                  sir   [sɜˑ]

Syllables like those in (5.5) which are not closed by a consonant are termed open syllables, and only free vowels can occur in open syllables when these are stressed (in connected speech the monosyllabic words in (5.5) will typically receive sentence stress, see Ch. 8). By contrast, checked vowels cannot occur in open syllables. Instead checked vowels require that at least one consonant follows the vowel for the syllables to be well-formed, provided these syllables are stressed. Thus the words in (5.6a) are well-formed syllables because they are closed by a consonant, but those in (5.6b) in which the final consonants have been removed are ill-formed:

(5.6)

a. *hid*   [h ɪ d]   *hut*   [h ʌ t]   *hood*   [h ʊ d]
    head [h e d]
    had   [h æ d]

b. **hi*   [*h ɪ]   **hu*   [*h ʌ]   **hoo*   [*h ʊ]
    *hea [*h e]
    *ha   [*h æ]

From (5.6) and (5.5a), it can be inferred that a stressed syllable in NAERD should at least contain either a vowel plus a consonant, one of the free monophthongs or the two vowel elements of a diphthong. If syllables are assumed to have three constituents, **onset**, **peak** and **rhyme** (see Ch. 6 below) where the onset is the consonant(s) preceding the central indispensable peak (always a vowel in stressed syllables) and the rhyme is the peak plus following consonant(s), then a stressed syllable in NAERD minimally has this structure:

(5.7)

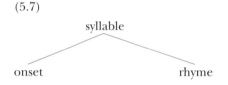

That is, for a syllable to be well-formed the rhyme must minimally contain two elements. Clearly this basic general structure is fulfilled both by e.g. *buy* and *hid*, because *buy* has two vocalic elements in it and *hid* has one vowel followed by one consonant. But the general structure of (5.7) is also fulfilled by the words in (5.5b), those words with free monophthongs in them. Since, like the diphthongs in (5.5a), they also do not require (but can have) a following consonant for the syllables they occur in to be well-formed, they equally fulfil the general structure because they underlyingly consist of two vocalic elements or two vowels. Obviously, these vocalic elements are not two different vowel elements like the elements of the diphthongs. Instead they are identical elements. Thus the three (monosyllabic) words *shy, shoe* and *hit* fulfil the general structure as shown below:

(5.8)

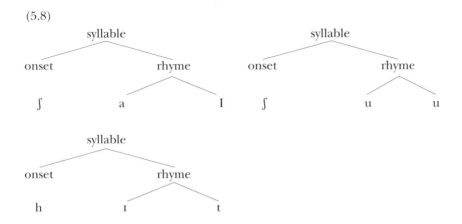

On the basis of syllable structure, it is thus possible to describe all the free vowels as consisting of two vocalic elements: either two non-identical elements whose pronunciation involves a glide from the first to the second (diphthongs), or two identical elements whose pronunciation is stable (free monophthongs). Checked vowels, on the other hand, consist of just one stable vocalic element.

The division into checked and free vowels is to do with the distribution of vowels. As mentioned earlier, this division is sometimes referred to as one of **vowel length** or **vowel quantity**, so that all the free vowels are defined as long vowels and all the checked vowels are defined as short vowels. The present description has preferred the first division because it is not so obvious in NAERD, as in other varieties of English (English English RP for example), that the free vowels are longer than the checked vowels when compared in identical environments. This does not mean that the length of NAERD vowels does not vary. As is apparent from the discussion of the difference between strong and weak obstruents, the length of NAERD vowels plays an important part in signalling strong or weak obstruent. The point made there was that the length of a vowel depends on the following type of consonant. The system of vowel length dependent on the following environment is slightly more complex than shortened vowel before strong obstruent and non-shortened vowel before weak obstruent. The length is also different if no sound follows or a sonorant follows. This more refined system was irrelevant for obstruent distinctions. But it is important in a discussion of vowels, as it reflects a variation typical of this sound type.

If, as is common in representations of monophthongal vowel length, [:] represents full length, [.] intermediate length and no dot signals considerable shortening, then this difference in pronunciation of vowels appears from the following sets of words:

(5.9)

bee	bead	beam	beat		awe	awed	all	ought
[biː]	[biːd]	[bi.m]	[bit]		[ɔː]	[ɔːd]	[ɔ.l]	[ɔt]

pry	prize	prime	price		low	load	loan	loaf
[praɪː]	[praɪːz]	[praɪ.m]	[praɪs]		[loʊː]	[loʊːd]	[loʊ.n]	[loʊf]

(5.9) specifies not only that vowels before strong obstruents are shorter than before weak obstruents (in fact they are about twice as long before weak obstruents), but also that before sonorants vowels are longer than vowels before strong obstruents but not as long as vowels before weak obstruents. Moreover, (5.9) stresses that vowels before weak obstruents have the same length as vowels which occur in open syllables. That vowels have the same length before weak obstruents as in open syllables supports the contention that strong obstruents shorten the preceding vowel rather than weak obstruents lengthen the preceding vowel. As it is conditioned by the following consonant, the variation in vowel length represented in (5.9) evidently is allophonic. This means that each NAERD vowel can at least have two and up to three length allophones. This variation frequently poses considerable problems to non-native speakers of English learning English.

5.2.2 Monophthongs and diphthongs

The second broad subclassification divides the vowels according to **stability** and results in two sub-classes, **monophthongs** and **diphthongs**. Monophthongs belong to the sub-class of **stable** vowels, a stable vowel being a vowel which is articulated with the same tongue position throughout its articulation and, thus, is perceived as having the same quality throughout its articulation. Diphthongs, the other class, belong to the sub-class of **unstable** vowels. By unstable is meant that a diphthong is articulated such that the tongue begins at one position and then moves more or less smoothly to a second position. Diphthongs are therefore perceived as gliding from one to another vowel quality, and in NAERD the first is the more prominent and the second a weaker off-glide. The division into monophthongs and diphthongs is shown below:

(5.10)

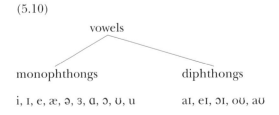

monophthongs   diphthongs

i, ɪ, e, æ, ə, з, ɑ, ɔ, ʊ, u   aɪ, eɪ, ɔɪ, oʊ, aʊ

The subclassification into monophthongs and diphthongs does not coincide with the distinction between checked and free. All diphthongs are free vowels, but among the monophthongs only the stable /i, ɜ, ɑ, ɔ, u/ belong to the class of free vowels. That the two subclassifications do not coincide is also not surprising. The subclassification into checked and free is phonological/distributional and the subclassification into diphthong and monophthong is articulatory/phonetic.

5.2.3 Classification according to place and height

Having established the broad classes of vowels, it is now time to look at the narrower classes. Let us first consider the classification that refers to which part of the horizontal dimension of the vowel scheme is used in the classification of a vowel, i.e. the classification which concerns what is traditionally referred to as place of articulation.

Classifying vowels according to where they are placed along this dimension, which in part reflects whether the front, middle or back part of the tongue is used, leads to the following subdivision of the monophthongs:

(5.11)

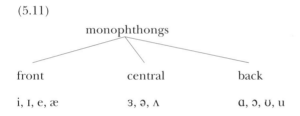

Front vowels are those vowels which are auditorily associated with cardinal vowels 1-4 and which are perceived to differ from one another by fairly regular steps of height. In terms of production, the front part of the tongue is regularly involved, where front means that part of the tongue which lies below the hard palate, but excluding the tip and the blade, which lie down below the front teeth. The auditory difference of height is matched by the front of the tongue being highest with /i/ and lowest with /æ/ and /ɪ/ and /e/ representing intermediate steps. Back vowels, on the other hand, are those vowels which are auditorily associated with cardinal vowels 5-8. Although traditionally said to be articulated with the back of the tongue, the tongue shape and position of /ʊ/ is not the same and lower than that used for /u/; nor is it the same but higher than the tongue shape used for /ɔ/ and so on. Instead the shape and position of the tongue vary considerable with these vowels and it does not assume four fairly homogenous stepwise positions as it does when /i, ɪ, e, æ/ are pronounced. Nonetheless, all of /ɑ, ɔ, ʊ, u/ are classified as back vowels and described as representing regular steps on a scale of height, because they are auditorily perceived in this way, and because they interact with one another in a way which indicates that they form a group with such a scalar structure (see Ch. 9 for discussion). Central vowels, lastly, are neither front nor back. Instead they belong to a group of vowels which acts as an intermediate step between front and back vowels. Their intermediate status is partly apparent from the fact that the central part of the tongue constitutes the highest point of articulation when they are produced, and members of central vowels can act as targets when front vowels are retracted and back vowels fronted.

The other narrow subclassification is shown in (5.12). It involves the vertical dimension, rather than the points on the horizontal dimension of the vowel diagram (cf. (5.1)), and refers to the relative height of the tongue. More specifically, it leads to the following classes:

(5.12)

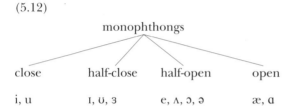

In principle, close vowels are produced with a high tongue position, half-close vowels with a somewhat lower tongue position, half-open vowels with a yet more open tongue position and open vowels with an open or low tongue position. But as just observed, this subclassification according to height works best for front vowels, but is less appropriate as a description of back vowels, because the height position of these does not match that of the front vowels and because the back vowels vary considerably in their degree of backness and height. Nevertheless, this system as reflected in the cardinal vowel scheme is maintained for all vowels, because it makes good sense auditorily as well as in the way vowels interact across the front-back boundary. Typically, /i/ and /u/, /ɪ/ and /ʊ/ and /e/ and /ɔ/ interact and form small pairs of classes, classes which according to the vowel scheme have the same height. Interestingly, rotations, also known as chain shifts (see Ch. 9), among front vowels, which are articulatorily equidistant, are matched by identical rotations among back vowels which lack articulatory homogeneity, a correlation which argues for treating both front and back vowels in the same way in the descriptive system. (5.13) illustrates how different tongue parts are used to produce front vowels and back vowels and how the tongue height varies in close, half-close, half-open and open vowels (the different jaw positions that go with these different tongue positions are ignored here; only three positions are shown for back vowels):

(5.13)

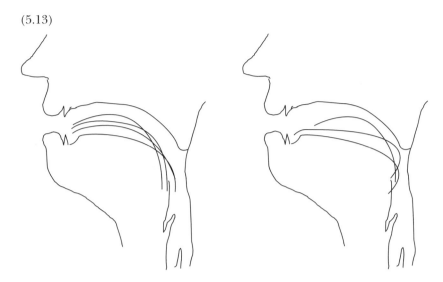

Finally, it is possible to subclassify the monophthongs according to lip rounding:

(5.14)

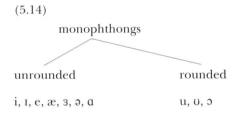

        monophthongs

unrounded   rounded

i, ɪ, e, æ, ɜ, ə, ɑ   u, ʊ, ɔ

The unrounded ones are produced with spread lips, the rounded ones with protruded and rounded lips. Among the rounded vowels, height and rounding are inter-related: the more close a back vowel is, the more rounded it is.

The classification according to the three parameters, place, height and lip rounding, is also applicable to the diphthongs. But as they consist of two vowels, clearly both elements must be described in terms of the three parameters. Firstly, the diphthongs are classified according to the second less prominent offglide. One group of diphthongs glides towards /ɪ/; since /ɪ/ is a front and half-close vowel this group is termed **front-closing** diphthongs. Another group of diphthongs glides towards /ʊ/; since /ʊ/ is a back and half-close vowel, this group is termed **back-closing** diphthongs. NAERD has only these two diphthong types, but there exist other types in other varieties of English. The general classification according to the second off-glide is summarised in (5.15):

(5.15)

Below the most prominent first element of the diphthongs will be described in terms of the three parameters, place, height and lip rounding. As in the description of the monophthongs, this will be done by placing the first elements inside the vowel box shown in (5.2), at the same time as the direction of the off-glide will be shown by associating the most prominent vowel elements with an arrow indicating the direction of the off-glide. Diphthongs whose first element is the most prominent, as in NAERD, are termed **falling diphthongs**. A diphthong showing the reverse pattern, i.e. with a prominent second element, is called a rising diphthong. For the possible occurrence of this diphthong type in NAERD, see Ch. 4 on /j/ above.

5.2.4 Vowels before /r/

It appeared from Ch. 2 and Ch. 4 above that vowels in NAERD interact more closely with /r/ than with other sounds simply because /r/ is pronounced in positions where other accents of English fail to have an /r/. This close interaction is not only apparent from the way that specifically /ə/ and /ɜ/ merge with a following /r/, i.e. how /ə/ and /ɜ/ become *r*-coloured, but it is also clear from the fact that specifically /ɜ/ occurs only in the environment of a following /r/. But the close interaction or influence that a following /r/ has on a preceding vowel is manifest in yet another way. /r/ also restricts the number of vowels that can contrast meaning before it. This section describes in more detail exactly how many – or how few vowels – contrast before /r/ in NAERD.

That NAERD has fewer vowel contrasts before /r/ may be illustrated in the following way which shows how vowel contrasts merge:

(5.16)

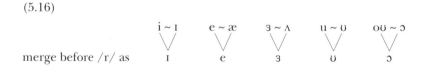

These losses of contrast or neutralisations call for the following comments:

> **/i/ ~ /ɪ/**: /i/ and /ɪ/ do not contrast before /r/ in most accents of English. The absence of this contrast in NAERD leads to *mirror* and *nearer* being perfect rhymes, both appearing with [ɪr].

/e/ ~ /æ/: The loss of the /e/ ~ /æ/ contrast means that *merry, Mary, marry* are homophones, all pronounced ['merɪ]. This pronunciation is very different from e.g. English English RP (as well as some forms of Eastern and Southern American English, see Ch. 10) which, as shown in (5.17), has three distinct vowels in *merry, Mary, marry*:

(5.17)

	merry	Mary	marry
NAERD	[-e-]	[-e-]	[-e-]
RP	[-e-]	[-eə-]	[-æ-]

/ɜ/ ~ /ʌ/: the absence of this contrast entails that in NAERD *furry* rhymes with *curry* and *hurry*, all of which have [ɜ]. In most other varieties, including RP and some forms of Eastern and Southern American English, only the latter two rhyme, both having [ʌ], while *furry* is pronounced with [ɜ].

/oʊ/ ~ /ɔ/: before /r/ /oʊ/ is always realised as a monophthong. In other environments, this monophthong is the vowel written [o] which is a back vowel but closer than [ɔ]. Thus it is better to say that the contrast /o/ ~ /ɔ/ rather than the contrast /oʊ/ ~ /ɔ/ is neutralised before /r/. The stability of this neutralisation varies somewhat according to geographical area. When it occurs, neutralisation results in *hoarse* and *horse* and *mourning* and *morning* becoming homophonous. They are then usually pronounced with the vowel [ɔ], but a pronunciation with the closer quality [o] is also a potential realisation.

/u/ ~ /ʊ/: like /i:/ and /ɪ/, /u:/ and /ʊ/ do not contrast before /r/ in most accents of English. In NAERD the absence of this contrast leads to *you're* and *your* being pronounced alike, both having [ʊr] (in English English RP they appear as [ʊə]/ [ɔ:]).

The loss of vowel contrasts before /r/ is a characteristic feature of American English and of NAERD in particular. Thus one more subclass of vowels in NAERD is the class listed in (5.18):

(5.18)
vowels which occur before /r/: ɪ, e, ɜ, ʊ, ɔ

5.3 Ongoing vowel changes in American English

Before we leave this general classification of NAERD vowels and turn to a description of the individual vowels, it is necessary to draw attention to two major vowel changes affecting American English pronunciation in these years. These changes are The Northern Cities Shift and The Southern Vowel Shift, two changes which were discussed briefly above in connection with the demarcation of NAERD (see Ch. 1 and Ch. 10 for a more detailed discussion). NAERD is defined as the American English variety which, among other features, is left unaffected by these two vowel changes. It is then perhaps not obvious why it is necessary to discuss The Northern Cities Shift and The Southern Vowel Shift, if NAERD is not a variety of North American English which shows traces of these vowel rotations. But the Northern Cities Shift and The Southern Vowel Shift are important because they concern a very large number of American speakers. Those cities of the inland north, for example, where The Northern Cities Shift is found, number approximately 34 million people, just like the South is not exactly a small secluded area within The United States. Knowledge of both vowel shifts will then help account for present-day fluctuation in NAERD, as inter-dialect influence is inevitable, and also makes it easier to foresee as well as explain the direction of future changes within the NAERD vowel system.

5.3.1. The Northern Cities Shift

The Northern Cities Shift (NCS hereafter) affects only monophthongs, both checked and free monophthongs. As the name suggests, NCS is a uniform development of the Inland North (see Ch. 10), most especially a development found in many large cities surrounding the great lakes, such as Chicago, Detroit and Buffalo. Following the work of the ANAE (see Ch. 1), NCS can be summarised as shown in the following diagram:

(5.19)

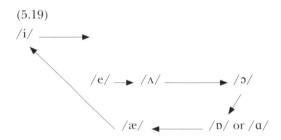

NCS is a chain process (see Ch. 9 below) in which the monophthongs change their phonetic realisations either as a result of being forced to move out of the way by another monophthong or as a result of filling slots vacated by other monophthongs. It is supposed to have started with the shift of /æ/ which moves in the direction of /i/. The empty slot resulting from the vacation of /æ/ fronts

/ɒ///ɑ/ (/ɒ/ is a rounded variant of /ɑ/), upon which /ɔ/ is lowered to fill the slot vacated by /ɒ///ɑ/ (note that in the North, unlike in NAERD, /ɔ/ and /ɒ/ are assumed to be contrastive as in *dawn* and *don*). Subsequently, /e/ is retracted towards /ʌ/ which responds by shifting back to the position formerly occupied by /ɔ/. Lastly, /i/ moves backward as a reaction to the raising of /æ/. As is characteristic of chain shifts, one change triggers a wholesale change of the monophthong system of the North resulting in an output system very different from input system. Thus, for example, as a result of NCS the vowel of *man* is heard with the second vowel of *idea*, the vowel of *steady* is pronounced like the vowel of *study*, *cawed* is heard as *cod*, and the vowel of *lock* or *pop* is pronounced with the vowel of *bat*.

5.3.2 The Southern Vowel Shift

Unlike NCS, the Southern Vowel Shift (SVS hereafter, see Ch.10 for further discussion) is a rotation that affects monophthongs and diphthongs alike within the area which on the map in (1.3) of Ch. 1 is referred to as the South. Following the work of ANAE, SVS can be summarised as in the diagram shown below, which leaves out the changes occurring before /r/:

(5.20)

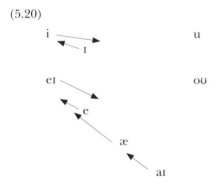

The monophthongisation of /aɪ/ is assumed to have started the rotation. The slot vacated by /aɪ/ is then filled by the lowering of /eɪ/ and the general lowering is joined by /i/. Subsequently, all of /æ/, /e/ and /ɪ/ rise towards the vacated slots developing inglides simultaneously (the characteristic southern diphthongisation). Finally, /u/ and /oʊ/ become fronted. As in NCS, the mechanism of SVS is that of a chain process, whereby the vacation of one slot in the phonological vowel system triggers a wholesale restructuring of the system when vowels are pushed out of the way or the empty slots are filled by other members of the system. The results of SVS are, for example, that the vowel of *hide* is pronounced like the vowel of *had* (monophthongisation), the vowel of *slade* is pronounced like the vowel of *slide* and the vowel of *bed* is pronounced like the vowel of *bid* and the vowel of *kid* is heard as the vowel *keyed*.

As is apparent from Ch. 1, the existence of both NCS and SVS plays a significant part in the process delimiting the reference dialect, NAERD, which with regard to the pronunciation of vowels is partly defined negatively by not showing signs of either of these two chain shifts. But their inclusion here is not only justified because they establish the southern and northern boundaries of Northern and Southern dialects. Another justification for their inclusion is the influence they exert or are likely to exert on NAERD.

5.3.3 Summing up the vowel description

As a preamble to the following description of each individual vowel of NAERD, the following general points about vowel description should be noted:

- Vowels are described in terms of a reference frame known as the cardinal vowel system. In this system, vowels are described in terms of place and height, which reflect a mixture of articulatory, acoustic and auditory properties
- Vowels are also described in terms of a third parameter, lip rounding, which may be absent or present in a vowel
- According to place, vowels may be divided into front vowels, central vowels and back vowels
- According to height, vowels may be divided into close vowels, half-close vowels, half-open vowels and open vowels
- According to distribution, vowels are divided into free vowels and checked vowels. Free vowels can occur in both open and closed stressed syllables, checked vowels can only occur in stressed syllables if these are closed by at least one consonant
- According to stability, vowels are divided into monophthongs and diphthongs. Monophthongs are stable vowels, diphthongs are unstable vowels
- Diphthongs involve bivocalic pronunciations with a glide from the first more prominent element towards the second less prominent off-glide
- According to the second and the less prominent off-glide, diphthongs are divided into front-closing and back-closing diphthongs.

5.4 The individual vowels

Following established practice in English vowel description, the individual vowels will be described in classes. These classes are the result of dividing vowels according to the categories length/distribution, stability and diphthongal off-glide as described above in this chapter. Firstly, a division according to length/distribution splits vowels into two classes: checked monophthongs (A), and free vowels

(B, C and D). Secondly, a division according to stability splits the free vowels into free monophthongs (B) and diphthongs (C and D) (note that all checked vowels are stable). Finally, a division on the basis of off-glide results in two subclasses of diphthongs, viz. front-raising diphthongs (C) and back-closing diphthongs (D). These divisions and the resulting subsystems are summarised in (5.21):

(5.21)

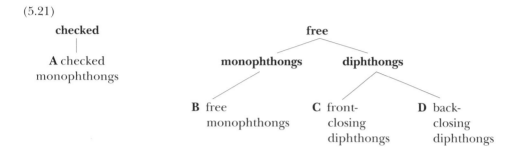

The vowels organised in subsystems A-D all share the property that they are potential occupants of stressed syllables. For this reason /ə/, the first vowel of e.g. *above*, is not included in any of these classes, as it does not occur in stressed syllables. Instead /ə/ will be discussed in the last section of this chapter, which deals with the vowels of unstressed syllables.

5.4.1 Subsystem A – checked vowels
Distributionally, subsystem A comprises a class of vowels which cannot occur in open stressed syllables. They are all stable and fairly short and hence often referred to as short monophthongs, but apart from these shared properties they constitute a heterogeneous class. The heterogeneity appears from the following diagram in which the checked vowels have been plotted to indicate their individual place and height properties:

(5.22)

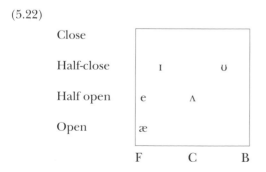

Given the properties expressed in the vowel box, the distinctive features (cf. Ch. 2) of the five checked vowels are as follows:

(5.23)

/ɪ/: half-close, unrounded front vowel
/e/: half-open, unrounded front vowel
/æ/: open, unrounded front vowel
/ʌ/: half-open, unrounded central vowel
/ʊ/: half-close, rounded back vowel

/ɪ/, sometimes called 'checked *i*', is the vowel of such words as *kit, pimp, rid*, as well as the vowel of the unstressed syllables of *Spanish, many, city*. In unstressed word-final position, /ɪ/ is often pronounced with a closer quality approaching the quality of free /i/. Inflectional (unstressed) endings in words like *pitted, taxes* may also vary so they are pronounced either with [ɪ] or [ə]. Before /r/, /ɪ/ contrasts with fewer vowels than in other environments as described in § 5.2.3. The length of /ɪ/ varies also so that it is longest before a weak obstruent, shorter before a sonorant and shortest before a strong obstruent. Outside NAERD, the distinction between /ɪ/ and /e/ is often neutralised before /m/ and /n/ and realised as /ɪ/, so both *pin* and *pen* are pronounced with this vowel. This merging is quite widespread in Southern and spreading to other areas. As can be seen from the previous examples, /ɪ/ is normally spelled *i* or *y*. Notice the unusual spellings in e.g. *b*̲*usy*, *w*̲*omen*, *E*̲*ngland* and in the second syllables of *missile, hostile* which may be pronounced with [ɪ].

/e/ is the vowel of such words as *dress, ten, tell, head*. Before /r/, /e/ contrasts with fewer vowels than in other environments as described in § 5.2.3, see in particular (5.17), which shows how non-high front vowel contrasts found in other varieties of English are not maintained by NAERD speakers. The length of /e/ varies too so that it is longest before a weak obstruent, shorter before a sonorant and shortest before a strong obstruent. Outside NAERD, /e/ undergoes change both in the North and in the South. In the North, as a result of NCS, /e/ is retracted, leading in the most advanced form to the positions of /e/ and /æ/ being reversed, since /æ/ at the same time as a result of NCS is fronted and raised. In the same way, in the most advanced form of NSC, /e/ and /ɔ/, are rearranged along the same high-low line of the vowel space, because /e/ is retracted and /ɔ/ is fronted. These changes involving /e/ are diagnostically important in the North. SVS also affects /e/, but in a different way, raising it and sometimes developing an inglide leading to, for example, *bed* being pronounced as *bid*. These northern and southern changes should be noted as they can help explain deviation from the standard /e/-pronunciation within NAERD. As can be seen from the previous examples, /e/ is normally spelled *e* or *ea*. Notice the unusual spellings in e.g. *b*̲*ury*, *s*̲*ays*, *s*̲*aid*, *a*̲*ny*, *l*̲*eopard*.

/æ/, sometimes called 'ash' (or flat *a*), is the vowel of such words as *trap*, *trash*, *can*, *had*. In about 150 native words, NAERD (and most other North American varieties except the dialect of Eastern New England) has /æ/ where non-American varieties have /a/ or /ɑ/. Thus *bath*, *staff*, *class*, *dance*, for example, typically have /æ/, but /ɑ/ or /a/ outside North America. Before /r/, /æ/ contrasts with fewer vowels than in other environments as described in § 5.2.3. The length of /æ/ varies too so that it is longest before a weak obstruent, shorter before a sonorant and shortest before a strong obstruent. Before a nasal, /æ/ is not only commonly nasalised but also particularly susceptible to raising and diphthongisation. Specifically in the North, this raising/diphthongisation affects all /æ/-vowels, not just /æ/ before nasals. In the North, this raising/diphthongisation constitutes the first stage of NCS and entails that not only *man*, *hammer*, but also *happen*, *bath*, *half* are pronounced [iə] (see also Ch. 10). In the South, as a result of SVS, /æ/ is raised and sometimes diphthongised to something like [e] so *bad* sounds like *bed*. /æ/ is also the result of the the SVS monophthongisation of /aɪ/. The latter leads to *side* sounding like *sad*. These characteristic northern and southern features should be noted as they can help explain deviation from the standard /æ/-pronunciation within NAERD. In the East, specifically in New York City and the Mid-Atlantic states, /æ/ is split into /æ:/ and /æ/, the former occurring specifically in the context of a following /m, n, f, θ, s/, as described in Ch. 10 below. /æ/ is regularly spelled *a*.

/ʌ/, sometimes called 'wedge', is the vowel of such words as *strut*, *sun*, *come*, *love*, *country*, *tug*. Before /r/, /ʌ/ contrasts with fewer vowels as described in §5.2.3. The lack of contrasts before /r/ means that words like *hurry*, *curry*, *furry* rhyme in NAERD, as they all have /ɜ/, unlike in many non-American varieties, including English English RP, which has /ʌ/ in *hurry* and *curry* but /ɜ/ in *furry*. Notice that a pattern with /ʌ/ in all these words is also found and is characteristic of some varieties of Scottish English. The length of /ʌ/ varies so that it is longest before a weak obstruent, shorter before a sonorant and shortest before a strong obstruent. Outside NAERD, /ʌ/ is affected by NCS in the North, being partly the target of the retraction of /e/ as well as moving in the direction of /ɔ/. This NCS variation should be noted as it will help explain deviation from the standard /ʌ/-pronunciation within NAERD. Historically, /ʌ/ derives from Middle English short /u/ or shortened /u:/. Spellings reflecting these vowels will then represent present-day /ʌ/ such as *u*, *ou* (see the words above). The frequent and etymologically confusing *o*-spelling for /ʌ/, as in, for example, *love*, *son*, *come*, is the result of spelling Old English /u/ as *o* when contiguous to minim letters like *m*, *n*, *v*. Notice the unusual spelling in *flood*, *blood*.

/ʊ/, sometimes called 'checked *u*', is the vowel of such words as *foot*, *push*, *would*, *stood* and the only rounded member of subsystem A. Before /r/, /ʊ/ contrasts with fewer vowels as described in § 5.2.3. In unstressed final position, it is often pronounced with a closer quality approaching the quality of free /u/. The length of /ʊ/ varies so that it is longest before a weak obstruent, shorter before a sonorant and shortest before a strong obstruent. /ʊ/ is neither affected by NCS nor SVS. It is regularly spelled with *u, oo*; unusual spellings are found in the frequent words *would, could, should* and in *w͟oman, b͟osom*.

5.4.3 Subsystem B – free monophthongs

Distributionally, subsystem B comprises a class of vowels which can occur in open, stressed syllables. Because they are all stable and do not have to be checked by a consonant, they are often referred to as free monophthongs (in other varieties of English as long monophthongs), but apart from these shared properties they constitute a heterogeneous class. The heterogeneity appears from the following diagram in which the subsystem B vowels have been plotted to indicate their individual place and height characteristics:

(5.24)

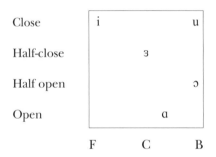

Given the properties expressed by the vowel box, the distinctive features of the free monophthongs are as follows:

(5.25)

/i/:	**close unrounded front vowel**
/ɜ/:	**half-close unrounded central vowel**
/u/:	**close rounded back vowel**
/ɔ/:	**half-open rounded back vowel**
/ɑ/:	**open unrounded back vowel**

/i/, sometimes called 'free i', is the vowel of such words as *fleece, sleet, seem, feed, key*. Before /r/, /i/ contrasts with fewer vowels as described in §5.2.3. Finally and before vowels, unstressed /i/ is in free variation with /ɪ/ as in *taxi, city* and *react, radio*. /i/ is moreover often diphthongised and realised as [ɪi]. The length of /i/ varies also so that it is longest before a weak obstruent, shorter before a sonorant and shortest before a strong obstruent. Outside NAERD, /i/ is lowered and retracted in the South as a result of SVS. /i/ is regularly spelled *ee* or *ea*, but other spellings abound, cf. *field, she, p͟eople, key, am͟oeba*.

/ɜ/, sometimes called 'reversed epsilon', is the vowel of such words as *nurse, perk, girl, turd, fur.* Arguably, /ɜ/ is not a true free vowel. Except in the word *colonel*, it is always followed by /r/, but since i) in non-rhotic varieties it is categorised as free, and ii) in rhotic American English varieties like NAERD it fuses with /r/ phonetically, the latter transcribed [ɝ], it is defensible to consider /ɜ/ a free vowel. As described above in § 5.2.3, /ɜ/ is the only central vowel which occurs before /r/ in NAERD. Thus, unlike in non-rhotic varieties, the pronunciation of *hurry, curry* with [-ʌr-] is not found in NAERD. The length of /ɜ/ varies too, so that it is longest when no consonant follows /r/, shorter when a weak obstruent follows /r/, shorter again when /r/ is followed by a sonorant and shortest when /r/ is followed by a strong obstruent. /ɜ/ is neither affected by NCS nor SVS and therefore pronounced fairly homogeneously in North America. /ɜ/ is spelled *ir, ur, er*, as in the words listed above, as well as *our* (*courage*) and *ear* (*earth*).

/u/, sometimes called 'free *u*', is the vowel of such words as *goose, shoot, school, food, shoe.* In the most of North America, /u/ is now a fronted back vowel with a quality approaching [ʉ] (high central rounded vowel). SVS is a possible source of this fronting which fronts /u/ so much that the South has the most fronted realisation of /u/ in North America. In NAERD it is less fronted, whilst the North and Eastern New England exhibit the most conservative and retracted realisations of /u/. Before /r/, /u/ contrasts with fewer vowels as described in § 5.2.3. In unstressed final position, /u/ is sometimes realised as [ʊ]. The length of /u/ varies so that it is longest word-finally, shorter before a weak obstruent, shorter again before a sonorant and shortest before a strong obstruent. /u/ is regularly spelled *oo*, but *o, oe, ou* are also found as in *lose, shoe, through*. Other renderings are *u, ue, ui* as in *tune, sue, suit.* Notice the unusual spellings in *lewd, beauty, manoeuvre.*

/ɔ/, sometimes called 'open o', is the vowel of such words as *loss, thought, crawl, north, force, cause, awe.* Before /r/, /ɔ/ contrasts with fewer vowels and is often realised with a closer quality as described in § 5.2.3. The length of /ɔ/ varies according to position so that it is longest word-finally, shorter before a weak obstruent, shorter again before a sonorant and shortest before a strong obstruent. The overall most important property of /ɔ/ is its participation in the low back merger. In NAERD, (and Canada and Eastern New England) the /ɒ/ – /ɔ/ contrast as in *don – dawn* and *cot – caught* has been suspended. Instead such pairs have just /ɔ/ or to an increasing extent /ɑ/ except before /r/. Outside NAERD the /ɒ/ – /ɔ/ contrast is maintained, as it is in many other varieties of English, including English English RP, where *don – dawn* and *cot – caught* are minimal pairs. The result of the low back merger and the increasing phonological reorganisation of /ɔ/ as /ɑ/ is that *don, dawn, khan* rhyme, all being pronounced with [ɑ]. Assuming the most extensive use of [ɑ], a phonemic distribution like the following then holds for many NAERD speakers:

(5.26)

	NAERD	RP
on, John, hot, Scotch	/ɑ/	/ɒ/
lawn, thought	/ɑ/	/ɔ:/
farm, car, palm	/ɑ/	/ɑ:/
more, floor, soar, war	/ɔ/	/ɔ/

As a result of these mergers, /ɑ/ in NAERD then does the work of three vowel phonemes in, say, RP. The low back merger is not complete among all NAERD speakers. Nor are all non-NAERD speakers excluded from the low back merger. Many Canadian speakers also exhibit this merger, just as it is common in Eastern New England. But the north is not influenced by this merger, NCS affecting /ɔ/ so that the vowel of *cawed* sounds like the vowel of *cod* whose vowel again is fronted so it sounds like the vowel of *cad*, changes which rule out the low back merger. Similarly, changes in the South and the East presuppose a phonemic contrast among the low back vowels with a possible realisation of /ɔ/ as [au] in the South and as [ʊə] in the East (see discussions in Ch.10). /ɔ/ is regularly spelled *au, ou, aw* as in *caught, thought, awe*. Notice also *a*-spellings before /l/ and /w/ and that *o, oa,* and *oo* are also used (cf. *broad, floor*).

/ɑ/, sometimes referred to as 'unhatted a', is the vowel of such words as *palm, start, lager, shah*. The length of /ɑ/ varies according to context so that it is longest word-finally, shorter before a weak obstruent, shorter again before a sonorant and shortest before a strong obstruent. As described under /ɔ/, /ɑ/ is involved in an extensive merging process whereby the low back vowels /ɔ/, /ɒ/ merge either in /ɔ/ or to an increasing extent in /ɑ/. This means that /ɑ/ does the work of sometimes three vowel phonemes in other English varieties, but there is still extensive alternation between [ɑ] and [ɔ] in many words. The unrounded quality of /ɑ/ which, as a result of these mergers is found in many NAERD words, is a characteristic property of NAERD (but not of this variety exclusively). As a result of the potential merging of low back vowels in /ɑ/, this vowel is spelled both *o* and *a*. *o*-spellings include, for example, *stop, Scotch, posh, common, log, sorry*; *a*-spellings are *father, ma, car*.

5.4.3 Subsystem C – front-closing diphthongs
Distributionally, subsystem C comprises a set of free vowels which can occur in open stressed syllables. As diphthongs they are unstable vowels gliding from the nucleus, the first element of the diphthong, towards front-closing [ɪ]. The place/height qualities of the first element of these diphthongs as well as the direction of the glide are indicated in the following diagram, showing all subsystem C vowels:

(5.27)

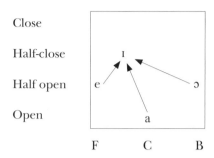

Close

Half-close

Half open

Open

F   C   B

Given the properties expressed by this vowel box, the front-closing diphthongs can be described in terms of the following distinctive properties:

(5.28)

/eɪ/:   **starting from the position between an unrounded half-close and a half-open front vowel, the tongue glides towards the position of front half-close /ɪ/.**

/aɪ/:   **starting from the position of an unrounded slightly retracted open central vowel, the tongue glides towards the position of front half-close /ɪ/**

/ɔɪ/:   **starting from the position of a rounded half-open back vowel, the tongue glides towards the position of half-close front /ɪ/.**

/eɪ/ is the vowel of such words as *face, mail, chain, bade, day*. The length of /eɪ/ varies according to context. It is longest word-finally, shorter before a weak obstruent, shorter again before a sonorant consonant and shortest before a strong obstruent. /eɪ/ is sometimes realised as the monophthong [e]. The degree of monophthongisation depends on length: the shorter the less monophthongised. Outside NAERD, /eɪ/ in the South as a result of SVS can become the lowest vowel in the vowel system overlapping with /aɪ/ which is monophthongised to /æ/. This lowering means that *slade* is heard as *slide*. So far little effect of this change is heard outside the South, but it is a development that could leak northwards. /eɪ/ is regularly spelled *a* in open syllables in disyllabic words (*gate, bade*) and *ai* and *ay*. Notice the spellings in *they, veil*, and *steak, great* and the unusual rendering in *gauge*.

   /aɪ/ is the vowel of such words as *price, prime, kind, hide, lie*. The length of /aɪ/ varies according to context so that it is longest word-finally, shorter before a weak obstruent, shorter again before a sonorant consonant and shortest before a strong obstruent. The front-back position of the nucleus varies somewhat. In the North, the starting position is front of centre, changing to back of centre as we move southwards (in /aʊ/ these relations are reversed). It is a characteristic feature of SVS that /aɪ/ is monophthongised to a lengthened /æ/ so that *hide* is pronounced like *had*. In areas where southern influence is strong monophthongal realisation is therefore heard. /aɪ/ is regularly spelled *i* in open syllables in disyllabic words (*mine, kite*) and *y* (*fly, my*). Note the spellings in such words as the following: *aisle, buy, choir, eye, light, might, height, dye*.

/ɔɪ/ is the vowel of such words as *choice, foil, coin, void, toy*. The length of /ɔɪ/ varies according to context so that it is longest word-finally, shorter before a weak obstruent, shorter again before a sonorant consonant and shortest before a strong obstruent. The degree of opening of /ɔ/, the nucleus of this diphthong, varies somewhat so that it may be in-between a raised open, rounded back vowel and a lowered, half-close rounded back vowel. Apart from this variation, /ɔɪ/ is pronounced fairly homogeneously within North America. /ɔɪ/ is spelled *oi* and *oy*.

5.4.4 Subsystem D – back-closing diphthongs

Distributionally, subsystem D comprises a set of free vowels which can occur in open stressed syllables. As diphthongs they are unstable vowels gliding from the nucleus, the first element of the diphthong, towards back-closing [ʊ]. The place/heigt qualities of the first element of these diphthongs as well as the direction of the glide are indicated in the following diagram, showing the two subsystem D vowels:

(5.29)

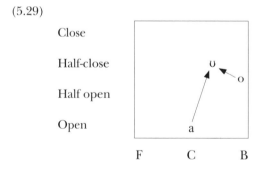

Close			
Half-close		ʊ	
Half open			o
Open		a	
	F	C	B

Given the properties expressed by this vowel box, the two back-closing diphthongs can be defined as follows:

(5.30)

/aʊ/:   **starting from the position of an open unrounded central vowel, the position of the tongue glides towards the position of half-close back /ʊ/**

/oʊ/:   **starting from the position between half-open and half-close, a rounded somewhat fronted back vowel glides towards the position of half-close /ʊ/.**

/**aʊ**/ is the vowel of such words as *mouth, found, foul, cows, now.* The length of /aʊ/ varies according to context so that it is longest word-finally, shorter before a weak obstruent, shorter again before a sonorant consonant, and shortest before a strong obstruent. The front-back position of the nucleus varies somewhat. In the North, the starting position of this vowel is typically back of centre changing to front of centre as we move southwards (in /aɪ/ these relations are reversed). /aʊ/ is regularly spelled *ou, ow.* Note that when *bow, row* and *sow* represent /aʊ/ they differ in meaning from *bow, row* and *sow* with /oʊ/.

/**oʊ**/ is the vowel of such words as *goat, loan, soul, load, low.* The length of /oʊ/ varies according to context so that it is longest word-finally, shorter before a weak obstruent, shorter again before a sonorant obstruent and shortest before a strong obstruent. Before /r/, /oʊ/ contrasts with fewer vowels than in other contexts, as described in § 5.2.3. /oʊ/ is sometimes realised as a monophthong ([o]) depending on length: the shorter the less monophthongised. It is assumed here that /oʊ/ is a back vowel, but actually it varies considerably in North America. In the West it is back as it is in the North, including Canada, and the East. Elsewhere, /oʊ/ is fronted, as it is in the South. The contended rounded backish nucleus of /oʊ/ in NAERD is quite distinct from the English English RP pronunciation of this vowel which has a fronted unrounded nucleus (written /əʊ/ phonemically). /oʊ/ may be spelled in several ways almost always involving *o* or *o* plus another vowel symbol or *w,* as in the following words: *no, old, soap, soul, know, foe.* Note the unusual spellings in *sew, beau, brooch* and that *bow, row* and *sow* can also have /oʊ/.

5.4.5 Summing up the individual vowels

The following points sum up the main properties of the individual vowels in NAERD; for a schematic overview see diagram at the end of this chapter:

- The vowels in NAERD are divided into 4 subsystems: checked monophthongs, free monophthongs, front-closing diphthongs and back-closing diphthongs.
- Subsystem A, checked monophthongs, has 5 members. /ɪ, e, æ/ are front, /ʌ/ is central and /ʊ/ is back; in addition /ɪ, ʊ/ are half-close, /e, ʌ/ half-open and /æ/ open. Apart from their non-occurrence in open stressed syllables, the most important feature of subsystem A vowels is their restricted occurrence before /r/.
- Subsystem B, free monophthongs, has 5 members. /i/ is front, /ɜ/ is central, /u, ɔ, ɑ/ are back; in addition /i, u/ are close, /ɜ/ half-close, /ɔ/ half-open and /ɑ/ open. As free vowels, they are able to occur in both open and closed syllables.
- In final unstressed syllables /i/ and /u/ vary freely with /ɪ/ and /ʊ/ respectively.

- /ɔ/ and /ɑ/ participate in merging processes. /ɔ/ is the result of the merging of /ɒ/ and /ɔ/, and frequently /ɔ/ and /ɑ/ merge in /ɑ/. Unrounded /ɑ/ is often listed as a characteristic American feature.
- Subsystem C, front-closing diphthongs, has 3 members all gliding towards /ɪ/. /aɪ/ has a central open starting point, /eɪ/ a front half-open starting point and /ɔɪ/ a back half-open starting point. As free vowels, they are able to occur in both open and closed syllables. One variant pronunciation should be noticed: /eɪ/ is sometimes realised as the monophthong [e].
- Subsystem D, back-closing diphthongs, has 2 members both gliding towards /ʊ/. /aʊ/ has a central open starting point, /oʊ/ has a starting point midway between half-open and half-close. As free vowels, they are able to occur in both open and closed syllables. The most important variant pronunciation is fronted /oʊ/.

5.5 Vowels in unstressed syllables

So far the discussion of vowels has focused on those vowels which can contrast meaning in stressed syllables. But it goes without saying that vowels also occur in unstressed syllables. The reason that vowels in these two environments have not been treated under one is that in NAERD, as well as in English in general, vowels in unstressed syllables behave differently from those of stressed syllables by showing fewer contrasts and by being susceptible to considerable reduction of distinctness in this environment. This section deals with how vowels behave in unstressed syllables, starting with those of content words, words with lexical (denotative) meaning. § 5.5.2 then deals with how vowels behave in unstressed forms of form words, words which typically lack lexical (denotative) meaning.

5.5.1 Unstressed syllables of content words

Let us first establish what is meant by stressed and unstressed syllables. Anticipating the discussion of Ch. 7 and Ch. 8, stress refers to the property which in the word *tutorial* and in the string *Jonathan carefully avoided publicity* brings out or emphasises the second syllable of *tutorial* and the first syllable of *Jonathan*, the first syllable of *carefully*, the second syllable of *avoided* and the second syllable of *publicity*. The properties that make these syllables more distinct are i) greater muscular effort, ii) longer duration, iii) pitch variation and iv) distinct as opposed to blurred vowel quality. When stress is characterised by these properties, stressed syllables are characterised by having these properties, but not necessarily all properties at any time (see Ch. 7 for further discussion). Stress in a polysyllabic word like *tutorial* is referred to as **word stress** and stress occurring in connected speech and assigned to monosyllabic and polysyllabic words alike, as in the string *Jonathan carefully avoided publicity*, is referred to as **sentence stress**. In connected speech sentence stress typically coincides with word stress.

When stressed syllables are said to exhibit the four properties mentioned above, unstressed syllables must lack these properties. But since lack of pitch, lack of muscular effort and lack of muscular energy are not so easy to measure, the non-distinct or blurred vowel quality becomes the most obvious and distinctive property of unstressed syllables. How this lack of distinctness is manifested can be seen by considering the following transcriptions of *tutorial* and *Jonathan carefully avoided publicity*, in which stress is marked by a raised vertical stroke before the stressed syllable and each syllable within polysyllabic words is followed by a horizontal stroke:

(5.27)

tutorial
[tʊ-ˈtɔ-rɪ-əl]

Jonathan would carefully avoid publicity
[ˈdʒɑ-nə-θən wʊd ˈker-fʊ-lɪ əˈvɔɪd pəb-ˈlɪ-sɪ- Dɪ]

In these transcriptions the vowels of the unstressed syllables, the syllables not marked by a raised vertical stroke, display a recurrent pattern, namely that they contain one of /ʊ/, /ɪ/ or /ə/, notably /ə/. Articulatorily, /ə/ is neither front nor back and neither open nor close. In other words, /ə/, or 'schwa' as it is usually called, is right in the middle of the cardinal vowel scheme. As such it differs from most other NAERD vowels which are peripheral occurring close to the outer limits of the cardinal vowel scheme with the exception of two vowels, viz. /ʊ/, /ɪ/. Like schwa, /ʊ/, /ɪ/ are also centralised, not so centralised as schwa, but still centralised: /ʊ/ back centralised and half-close and /ɪ/ front centralised and half-close. /ʊ/, /ɪ/ and /ə/ are shown in (5.28):

(5.28)

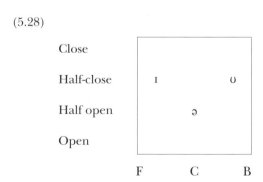

/ə/ is frequently described as the sound of hesitation, the potential sound produced before a speaker decides on a particular articulatory target. When it is the
sound uttered before clear distinctive articulation is initiated, /ə/ is also likely to
be the sound produced when no clear distinction is necessary. This makes it an
obvious target of reduction. The predominance of /ʊ/, /ɪ/ and /ə/ in unstressed
syllables is then no coincidence. When lack of stress entails non-distinctness,
these three vowels are likely to pop up in this environment. But of /ʊ/, /ɪ/ and
/ə/, schwa occurs far more often than /ʊ/ and /ɪ/. In fact, very often unstressed
syllables with /ʊ/ and /ɪ/ have alternative pronunciations with /ə/. That /ə/
can be an alternative to both /ʊ/ and /ɪ/ is illustrated by the following words:

(5.29)

equality   [ɪˈkwɔlɪDɪ] or [əˈkwɔləDɪ]   ɪ   →   ə
tutorial   [tʊˈtɔrɪəl] or [təˈtɔrɪəl]   ʊ   →   ə

The potential replacement of /ʊ/ and /ɪ/ by /ə/, as illustrated in (5.29), is
generally viewed as a weakening process towards less distinction. This view is
supported by the fact that the process sometimes continues and results in the
loss of /ə/. That it makes sense to regard it as a weakening process is also supported by the fact that it can be regarded as part of a process which starts with a
distinct (peripheral) vowel, so that /ɪ/ → /ə/ and /ʊ/ → /ə/ are parts of the
more general /i/ → /ɪ/ → /ə/ and /u/ → /ʊ/ → /ə/ developments. That /ɪ/
and /ʊ/ are possible reduction products of /i/ and /u/ respectively is apparent
from vowel alternations appearing in, for example, word derivations. Compare,
for example, *equality* with *equal* and *tutorial* with *tutor*.

(5.30)

equal   [ˈikwəl]   *equality*   [ɪˈkwɔlɪDɪ]   i → ɪ
tutor   [ˈtuDə]   *tutorial*   [tʊˈtɔrɪəl]   u → ʊ

The vowel of the first syllable of the underived forms, *equal* and *tutor*, are distinct
peripheral vowels. In the derived forms, *equality* and *tutorial*, distinct, peripheral
/i/ and /u/ have changed (they do not always change) to /ɪ/ and /ʊ/. This
alternation is to do with stress. In the underived forms, *equal* and *tutor*, the first
syllable is stressed and in the derived forms, *equality* and *tutorial*, stress has shifted
to the second syllable, so the absence of initial stress in *equality* and *tutorial* opens
up for the potential reduction of /i/ and /u/ to /ɪ/ and /ʊ/ and the further
reduction to /ə/ as illustrated in (5.29).
  The reduction of /i/ and /u/, when the shift of stress permits it to take place,
typically follows the track via /ɪ/ and /ʊ/ respectively and then to /ə/. But /i/

and /u/ (and /ɪ/ and /ʊ/) are not the only vowels susceptible to reduction in unstressed syllables. Other vowels (monophthongs as well as diphthongs) can participate in this process, but for other vowels reduction in unstressed syllables normally involves an alternation with /ə/ directly. Consider the following examples involving derivation:

(5.31)

bellum	[ˈbeləm]	belligerent	[bəˈlɪdʒərənt]	e → ə
fallacy	[ˈfæləsi]	fallacious	[fəˈleɪʃəs]	æ → ə
person	[ˈpɜsən]	personify	[pəˈsɑnɪfaɪ	ɜ → ə
public	[ˈpʌblɪk]	publicity	[pəbˈlɪsɪDɪ]	ʌ → ə
artist	[ˈɑrtɪst]	artistic	[ərˈtɪstɪk]	ɑ → ə
portrait	[ˈpɔrtrət]	portray	[pəˈtreɪ]	ɔ → ə
postpone	[poʊstˈpoʊn]	postposition	[poʊstpəˈzɪʃən]	oʊ → ə
famous	[ˈfeɪməs]	infamous	[ˈɪnfəməs]	eɪ → ə
admire	[ædˈmaɪɚ]	admiration	[ædməˈreɪʃn]	aɪ → ə

in which the shift of stress in the words in the second column leads to reduction of a distinct vowel quality to /ə/.

The same reduction process is found in the second syllable of new words formed by combining two or more individual words as in, for example, the lexicalisations below which, following the main stress rule (see Ch. 7), receive stress on the first syllable:

(5.32)

postman	[ˈpoʊstmən]	compare	man	[mæn]
cupboard	[ˈkʌbəd]	compare	board	[bɔrd]
nonsense	[ˈnɑnsəns]	compare	sense	[sens]
vineyard	[ˈvɪnjəd]	compare	yard	[jɑrd]

But reduction of distinct peripheral vowels to specifically /ə/, although extensive in connection with word derivations and lexicalisations, is equally characteristic of a set of words which appear under the name of form words or grammatical words. As the name suggests, these are words that have little lexical meaning but instead serve a grammatical function. When these words occur in unstressed position in connected speech, their vowels are highly susceptible to reduction.

5.5.2 Reduction in form words in connected speech

It is necessary first to establish what is meant by **form words** and **content words**. As mentioned earlier, form words lack clear lexical meaning. Thus typically, form words are listed in a dictionary without a denotative definition of their meaning. Instead their meaning appears from the way they are used, from the context in which they occur, and form words are therefore grammatical rather than lexical. (5.33) lists the classes of words, each with an inexhaustive list of examples, which are categorised as form words:

(5.33)

conjunctions: *that, if, and, but, as* etc.
prepositions: *in, from, to, into, at* etc.
auxiliary verbs: *can, may, will, is, am, have, had, could, should* etc.
pronouns: *it, he, them, us, you, that* etc.
determiners: *a, an, the, some, such* etc.

As words with a denotative definition, content words, by contrast, include the following:

(5.34)

nouns: *boy, dog ceiling, idea, matter, misunderstanding* etc.
verbs: *change, sing, perform, ride, understand* etc.
adjectives: *small, happy, minimal, punctual, acrimonious* etc.
adverbs: *soon, fast, better, temporarily, obviously*

Form words are assumed to have a strong form and a weak form. The **strong form** is the form occurring when the word is stressed and, as in stressed syllables of content words, the vowel of the strong form of a form word can be any vowel, peripheral or non-peripheral, except /ə/. The **weak form** is the form occurring when the word is unstressed. As in the unstressed syllables of content words, the vowel of the weak form can be /ə/, indeed typically is /ə/, and if the vowel is not /ə/ it is very often one of /ɪ/ or /ʊ/. Weak forms are moreover likely to undergo further reduction in the form of vowel loss, specifically /ə/ loss. As mentioned above, loss of /ə/ is also found in the unstressed syllables of content words and is thus a general property of the weakening process affecting unstressed vowels.

The occurrence of strong and weak forms is to do with the stress system of English, including NAERD. The stress system of connected speech is such (see Ch. 7 below) that in the **unmarked** case content words receive stress and form words receive no stress. Thus in an unmarked pronunciation of the following strings, stress will be distributed as indicated by the raised stress marks (a lot of phonetic detail not relevant here is left out):

(5.35)

I would have liked to have seen it one day at a new exhibition
[aɪ wʊd həv ˈlaɪkt tə həv ˈsin ɪt ˈwʌn ˈdeɪ əD ə ˈnu eksəˈbɪʃn]

As an introduction to the first scene Jimmy has decided to close the bar
[əz ən ɪntrəˈdʌkʃn tə ðə ˈfɜst ˈsin ˈdʒɪmɪ həz dɪˈsaɪDəd tə ˈkloʊz ðə ˈbɑr]

(5.35) highlights the system that the content words receive stress, whereas the form words fail to become stressed. Thus the nouns *day, exhibition* in the first string are stressed, as are the lexical verbs *liked, seen* and the adjective *new* and the numeral *one*. Similarly, in the second string, the nouns *introduction, scene, Jimmy, bar*, the lexical verbs *decided* and *close* and the adjective *last* all receive stress as members of the class of content words. By contrast, the remaining words in both strings are unstressed: *would, have* and *has* because they are auxiliary verbs, *I* and *it* because they are pronouns, *to* and *at* because they are prepositions, *a, an* and *the* because they are articles and *as* because it functions as a conjunction.

The pattern illustrated by (5.35) is characteristic of an unmarked pronunciation. But content words may be unstressed just as form words may receive stress. Although regarded here as marked, both situations occur frequently. Suppression of stress in the former occurs when several content words follow one another in close succession. Stress assignment to the latter occurs, for example, in contexts of contrast, when special emphasis is required or when the grammatical structure demands it. Stressed form words result in **strong forms** of form words and as defined above the strong form of a form word can have any vowel except /ə/ – very typically one of the peripheral vowels. (5.36) provides examples of strong forms:

(5.36)

i)   A: *Didn't you say you would like to meet her?*
         [...   wəd   ... hɚ]
ii) B: *No, I said him not her and I said might and not would!*
         [...   ˈhɝ   ... ˈwud]

iii)   *They did not look at this manuscript*
         [...   ət   ...]
iv)   *The manuscript has not been looked at*
         [...   ... æt]

In the first pair, the form words *would* and *her* are unstressed in i) and as expected the forms of these words contain /ə/. In the second utterance, ii), *would* and *her* receive stress to emphasise contrast and because they are stressed the vowels change from /ə/ to /ɜ/ and /u/ respectively. In the second pair in (5.36), the preposition *at* in iii) is followed by its prepositional complement, *this manuscript*, but in iv) *at* is left stranded after a passive transformation has shifted *this manuscript* to the front of the utterance. In utterance-final position, *at* maintains its distinct vowel quality because final position is the position of focus or new information (see Ch. 8 below).

The weak form of a form word can be one with /ə/ or one with another non-distinct vowel. It can also be a single consonant or rarely two consonants, and frequently all possibilities are potential weak realisations of one form word. When the weak form is a single consonant, this one consonant is either a syllabic sonorant or strong /s/ or weak /z/. In forms whose initial consonant is /h/, there always exist an alternative without /h/, which is frequently lost in unstressed position (see Ch. 3 above), but initial consonant loss also affects other consonants than /h/. Below follows a list of the various weak forms that some of the most common form words can assume. For comparison the strong form is listed first:

(5.37)

	strong form	**weak form**
a, an (indef. artic.)	[eɪ], [æn]	[ə], [ən], [n]
the (def. artic.)	[ði]	[ðɪ], [ðə]
her (poss. determ.)	[hɝ]	[hə], [ə]
his (poss. determ.)	[hɪz]	[hɪz], [ɪz]
your (poss. determ.)	[jʊr]	[jər]
some (indef. determ.)	[sʌm]	[səm], [sm̩]
she (pers. pron.)	[ʃi]	[ʃɪ]
he (pers. pron.)	[hi]	[hɪ] [ɪ]
him (pers. pron.)	[hɪm]	[hɪm], [ɪm]
you (pers. pron.)	[ju]	[jʊ], [jə]
we (pers. pron.)	[wi]	[wɪ]
us (pers. pron.)	[ʌs]	[əs]
them (pers. pron.)	[ðem]	[ðm̩]
at (prep.)	[æt]	[ət]
from (prep.)	[frɑm], [frʌm]	[frəm]
of (prep.)	[ʌv], [ɑv]	[əv]
am (aux.)	[æm]	[əm], [m]
is (aux.)	[ɪz]	[ɪz], [z], [s]
are (aux.)	[ɑr]	[ər], [r]
was (aux.)	[wʌz], [wɑz]	[wəz]
were (aux.)	[wɝ]	[wɚ]
has (aux.)	[hæz]	[həz], [əz], [z], [s]
had (aux.)	[hæd]	[həd], [əd], [d]
have (aux.)	[hæv]	[həv], [əv], [v]
do (aux.)	[du]	[dʊ], [də]
does (aux.)	[dʌz]	[dəz]
will (modal aux.)	[wɪl]	[wəl], [əl], [l]
can (modal aux.)	[kæn]	[kən], [kn̩]
must (modal aux.)	[mʌst]	[məst], [məs]
would (modal aux.)	[wʊd]	[wəd], [əd], [d]
could (modal aux.)	[kʊd]	[kəd]
should (modal aux.)	[ʃʊd]	[ʃəd]

and (conj.)	[ænd]	[ənd], [ən], [n]
as (conj.)	[æz]	[əz]
or (conj.)	[ɔr]	[ər]
but (conj.)	[bʌt]	[bət]
that (conj. or rel. pron.)	no strong form	[ðət]
than (conj.)	[ðæn]	[ðən]

A few comments are in order as regards those auxiliaries whose weak forms can be single consonants. These auxiliaries fall into two groups. The first group consists of *are, am, have, had, will* and *would*. It is characteristic of these auxiliaries that they are realised as single consonants ([r], [m], [v], [d], [l], [d]) when they follow a word ending in a vowel as shown by the *a*-examples below, whilst the full and unreduced forms are found when they follow words ending in consonants or themselves are utterance-initial, as shown by the *b*-examples:

(5.38)

a.	*I'm tired*	[aɪ**m** ˈtaɪrd]
b.	*Am I tired?*	[**æm** aɪ ˈtaɪrd]
a.	*You're tired*	[jʊ**r** ˈtaɪrd]
b.	*What are you tired of?*	[ˈwʌD **ɑr** jʊ ˈtaɪrd əv]
a.	*I've seen it*	[aɪ**v** ˈsin ɪt]
b.	*What have you seen?*	[ˈwʌt **hæv** jʊ ˈsin]
a.	*I had seen it*	[aɪ**d** ˈsin ɪt]
b	*The post had arrived*	[ðə ˈbed **həD** əˈraɪvd]
a.	*I'll tell you*	[aɪ**l** ˈtel jʊ]
b.	*The man will tell you*	[ðə ˈmæn **wɪl** ˈtel jʊ]
a.	*He'd do it*	[hi**d** ˈdu ɪt]
b.	*The man would do it*	[ðə ˈmæn **wʊd** ˈdu ɪt]

The second group of auxiliaries whose weak forms may be realised as single consonants consists of *is* and *has*. When pronounced as single consonants, *is* and *has* may be realised partly as [s] and partly as [z]. Just like the distribution of the inflectional *s*-ending (see discussion of /s/ in Ch. 3), [s] occurs after strong obstruents, except /s, ʃ, tʃ/, and [z] occurs after weak obstruents, except /z, ʒ, dʒ/, and after sonorants and vowels:

(5.39)

Jack's leaving	[ˈdʒæks ˈlivɪŋ]
Jack's got it	[ˈdʒæks ˈgɑD ɪt]
The dog's running	[ðə ˈdɑgz ˈrʌnɪŋ]
The dog's got it	[ðə ˈdɑgz ˈgɑD ɪt]
Earl's leaving	[ˈɝlz ˈlivɪŋ]
Earl's got it	[ˈɝlz ˈgɑD ɪt]
Mona's running	[ˈmoʊnəz ˈrʌnɪŋ]
Mona's got it	[ˈmoʊnəz ˈgɑD ɪt]

After /s, ʃ, tʃ/ and /z, ʒ, dʒ/, *is* and *has,* just like the inflectional *s*-ending, assume a different form than in the other environments. After these sibilant obstruents, the weak forms of *is* and *has* are not realised as single consonants, but consist of a vowel plus [z]: *is* is pronounced [ɪz] and *has* is pronounced [əz]:

(5.40)

George's running	[ˈdʒɔrdʒɪz ˈrʌnɪŋ]
George's got it	[ˈdʒɔrdʒəz ˈgɑD ɪt]

A small group of words never have weak forms although they belong at least in some of their uses to the class of form words. This group includes, among others, *then, when, or, on, up.* No matter whether these words are stressed or unstressed, they will always be pronounced [ðen], [wen], [ɔr], [ɑn], [ʌp].

5.5.3 Summing up vowels in unstressed syllables
The following list summarises the main points about vowels in unstressed syllables:

- The vowel of an unstressed syllable in NAERD is typically one of the non-peripheral vowels /ɪ/, /ʊ/ or /ə/
- /ə/ is the most frequent vowel occurring in unstressed syllables
- /ə/ is an unrounded central vowel articulated with the tongue raised to a position between half-close and half-open
- /ə/ does not occur in stressed syllables, but in unstressed syllables it can replace all monophthongs and most diphthongs after stress shift
- Replacing other vowels with /ə/, is a weakening process changing a peripheral and distinct vowel to a non-distinct and blurred vowel
- /ɪ/, /ʊ/ and particularly /ə/ occur in a large group of grammatical words without content, the so-called form words, when these are unstressed, just as they occur in the unstressed syllables of content words.

- The weakening process leading to /ə/ is frequently taken one step further so /ə/ is lost. The weak forms of many form words, specifically auxiliary verbs, therefore often consist of a single consonant only.

5.6 Summarising the vowels of NAERD English

Vowels are those voiced and acoustically periodic sounds which are produced without a major oral obstruction and which, with the exception of /ə/, constitute the peak of stressed syllables. As described in this chapter, the vowels of stressed syllables fall into four sub-classes. These subclasses are defined partly on the basis of phonological distribution and partly on the basis of phonetic stability. The phonological definition divides vowels into checked vowels and into free vowels, whereas the phonetic subclassification splits vowels into monophthongs and diphthongs. The members of each subclass are described in terms of the same descriptive system. This system describes two properties. First the place of articulation of the individual members of each sub-class, identifying them as front, central or back, and second the relative height, according to which each member is identified as close, half-lose, half-open or open. Vowels are also classified as rounded or unrounded according to lip position. This binary opposition does not appear directly from the classificatory system, but rounded vowels are written in bold face in the diagram in (5.41), which summarises the classification of the vowels in NAERD:

(5.41)

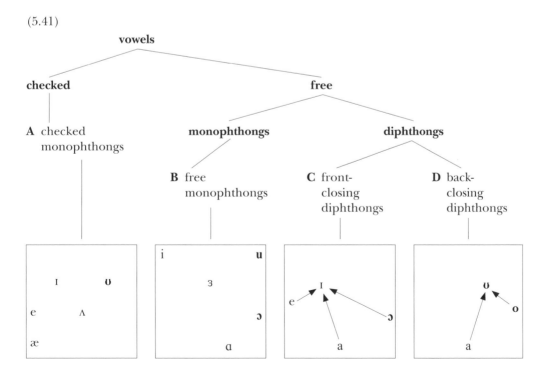

Further reading

Comprehensive introductions to the description of vowels can be found in Laver 1994, Ladefoged 2001, Giegerich 1993, Gimson 1962. Bauer et al. 1980 deal specifically with American English. A very detailed but now somewhat dated account of phonological variation in North American English is found in Wells 1982. The regional variation discussed in this chapter, as well as on-going vowel shifts, can be studied closely by consulting Labov et al. 2006.

PART II

CHAPTER 6

Syllable structure in American English

6.1 Prosodic or suprasegmental phenomena

A string of continuous speech such as the following utterance

(6.1)

Did he have to tell the minister as soon as they had left the church?

involves not only a series of successive consonants and vowels, such as was described in the previous chapters. Such a string is also characterised by a number of properties whose domain is larger than a single consonant or vowel. For example, the sub-string *tell the minister* consists of five entities, each of which organises the vowels and consonants into groups of segments according to a regular pattern. Such entities are called **syllables**, and all of (1) can be shown to be organised into such entities. But the syllables in a string like (6.1), and in all other strings, are not completely identical. Not only do they differ in segmental composition. Some of the syllables are also more prominent or stand out more clearly than other syllables. For example, in *minister* the first syllable is more prominent than the second and the third syllables of this word. This property which accentuates one or more syllables is called **stress** and is also one whose domain is larger than a single consonant or vowel.

Two further properties whose domain is larger than a single consonant or vowel appear when it is recognised that a string like (6.1) is pronounced with a certain rhythmic beat where each beat is marked by the stressed syllables, *have, tell, min* (in *minister*), *soon, left* and *church*. These beats fall at roughly isochronous intervals. That is, they mark stretches of syllables of approximately the same length. Such stretches of syllables are called **feet**. In (6.1) the first foot extends from *have* to *to*, the second from *tell* to *the*, the third from *min* (in *minister*) to *as*, the fourth extends from *soon* to *had*, the fifth from *left* to *the* and the last comprises *church*. Thus just like consonants and vowels are organised into syllables, syllables form groups of syllables in which the first syllable in each group is stressed and where this syllable marks the **rhythm** of NAERD.

But there exist yet larger structural units than the rhythmic groups, the feet, with their constituent syllables. Feet can make up a larger unit which may encompass all of (6.1). This unit is called the **tone group**. The tone group is a unit in which pitch and stress together form the melody or **intonation** of NAERD utterances. For example, it is a regular pattern of the tone group that one and just one syllable is more prominent than any other syllable within the tone group. As a rule, this syllable is the last potentially stressed syllable of the tone group. In (6.1), *church* (in an unmarked pronunciation) would be the most prominent syllable and pitch, specifically a dynamic rising pitch (because (6.1) is a yes/no question), plays a particularly important part in marking *church* as the most prominent. Another important property of the tone group is pitch level. Disregarding *church*, which has a dynamic rising pitch, the syllables in (6.1) are pronounced at approximately the same pitch level which is a little below medium level.

The general term used to refer to such phenomena as syllable, stress, foot, rhythm and intonation, all of which encompass more than one segment at a time, is **suprasegmental** or **prosodic**, and the discipline which describes such phenomena is termed **prosody**. Chapters 6, 7 and 8 of this introduction to NAERD pronunciation are concerned with prosody exclusively. The present chapter deals with syllables. Ch. 7 deals with stress, in particular stress in compound and non-compound words as well as the rhythm of speech, whilst Ch. 8 is devoted to the nature and function of intonation in NAERD and to the presentation of a simplified and less simplified transcription system. Thus the view of NAERD sound structure as hierarchical which was introduced in Ch. 2 with the claim that phonological consonants and vowels are made up of smaller non-successive contrastive features, the distinctive features, will become even more obvious once the properties of prosody have been dealt with in more detail. It will become clear that the phonological segments make up larger chunks, the chunks which are called syllables, which again are organised into groups of syllables, the feet, which subsequently can be grouped together in tone groups. In other words, the phonological hierarchy does not end with the individual consonant or vowel. Larger entities of sound structure also enter into a hierarchy. The entire hierarchy of sound structure is shown in the tree below for the string *soon they had left the church*. This tree thus functions as an appropriate preamble to the topics which will be dealt with in this and the following two chapters, as well as specifying where the dividing line between a segmental and a suprasegmental description should be drawn:

(6.2)

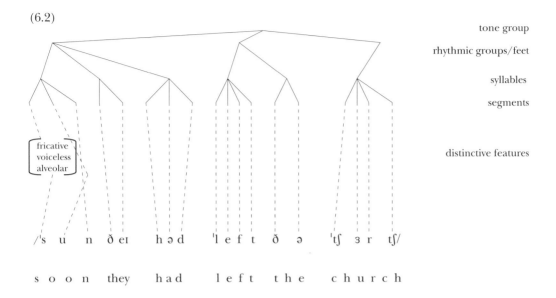

6.2 Introduction to syllable structure

As established already, prosody is concerned with the study of units which encompass more than one consonant or vowel at a time. The **syllable** is the prosodic unit which organises consonants and vowels into sequences of segments. Since consonants and vowels here mean phonological consonant and vowels, the term syllable refers to a **phonological** entity of NAERD. Taking a phonological view of the syllable entails that the syllable is regarded as an entity which not only has a regular internal structure of phonemes, but also that it is an entity which specifies the domain of stress and intonation rules, as well as being instrumental in accounting for the occurrence of allophones, such as the flap or clear and dark *l* (see Ch. 3 & 4). But it should be pointed out that attempts have also been made to define the syllable as a **phonetic** unit by referring to acoustic or auditory properties, but so far it has been difficult to demonstrate any objective physical correlates which make a phonetic definition feasible.

Although its phonetic properties are somewhat elusive, the syllable is usually judged to be a very concrete entity by native speakers. When asked how many syllables, say, the word *dependent* consists of, native speakers normally have no difficulty in deciding that it contains three syllables. It is usually more difficult to place the boundaries between the three syllables. For example, many native speakers will not know for sure whether /p/ in *dependent* belongs to the first or the second syllable, but they will have no difficulty in deciding that the second /n/ does not belong to the third and last syllable of the word.

Among other topics, this chapter will deal with such native-speaker phonological intuitions about the syllable, including syllable boundary placement. But the chapter begins with a description of the structure of the syllable. Knowledge of this structure, in particular that it may consist of up to four subparts, is a prerequisite for understanding other aspects of syllable structure. These other aspects, which will be dealt with subsequently, are i) the organising principle of the syllables, a principle known as the sonority sequencing principle, and ii) the rules governing permissible syllable clusters in NAERD, given the principles of the sonority hierarchy. But, as promised, an outline of the structure of the syllable follows first.

6.3 The structure of the syllable

The English syllable, including that of NAERD, consists of one obligatory element. This element is called the **peak** of the syllable. In monosyllabic words, this obligatory peak is always a vowel as has been pointed out in Ch 5. In the following words /ɔ/, /ɪ/ and /æ/ respectively constitute the peaks:

(6.3)

| swarm | /swɔrm/ | shrink | /ʃrɪŋk/ | clamp | /klæmp/ |

In polysyllabic words, consonants, in particular /m, n, ŋ, l, r/ may also constitute the peak of the syllable (in which case they are marked by the diacritic '¦' below them), but as a rule in unstressed syllables only and on the condition that at least one other syllable in the word has a vocalic peak. Thus in the disyllabic words in (6.4), /n/, /ɔ/ and /l/ respectively constitute the peak of the second syllable:

(6.4)

| cotton | /katn̩ / | bacon | /beɪkŋ̩ / | castle | /kæstl̩ / |

The peak of the syllable is said to be obligatory. This is due to the fact that the existence of a syllable depends on the presence of a peak. For example, if the monosyllabic words in (6.3) had no vowels and hence lacked peaks, the result would be the ill-formed strings, */swrm/, */ʃrŋk/, */klmp/.

That the obligatory peak is nearly always a vowel in English monosyllabic words explains why monosyllabic words consisting of only one segment must have a form as shown in (6.5):

(6.5)

| awe | /ɔ/ | eye | /aɪ/ |

and cannot be made up of a single consonant. Monosyllabic words in NAERD may sometimes be interpreted as consisting of consonants exclusively. For example, *yearn* could be interpreted as /jrn/ with /r/ as the peak of the syllable. In the present description, a word like *yearn* is analysed as having a vowel plus /r/ phonemically and an *r*-coloured vowel phonetically. The obligatory strong *r*-colouring of /ɜ/ (see Ch. 4) is what can lead to /jrn/.

But syllables consist as a rule of more than syllabic peaks. What precedes the peak is referred to as the **onset** and what follows the syllabic peak as the **coda**. In addition, the coda and the syllabic peak make up a fourth constituent. This constituent is called the **rhyme** of the syllable. Using the string *swift*, these syllable constituents can be represented as follows:

(6.6)

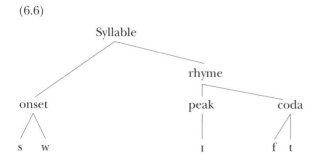

From what has been said so far, it is clear that onset and coda are both optional constituents, but because the peak is always part of the rhyme, the latter, like the peak, is also an obligatory constituent. Thus an English syllable can have any of the following forms:

(6.7)

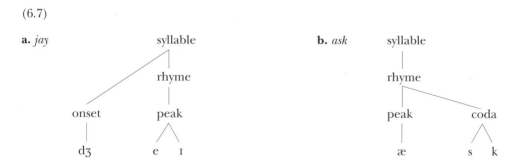

and the syllable structure of the monosyllabic words in (6.5) should, strictly speaking, be as shown below, i.e. they also should have rhymes:

(6.8)

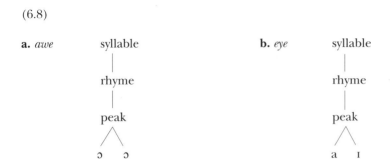

Recall from the general section on vowels (see Ch. 5) that both long vowels and diphthongs are analysed as consisting of two vocalic elements. This analysis reflects the fact that long vowels and diphthongs make up the class of free vowels, a class which is distinct from checked vowels which consist of only one vocalic element and which must be followed by at least one consonant when occurring in a stressed syllable. This property will be referred to presently.

The justification of both the onset and the coda is that these syllable parts constitute domains of the rules which account for permissible syllable-initial clusters and permissible syllable-final clusters (see discussion below). But what is the motivation for recognising the rhyme as a constituent of the syllable? Two motivations will be given here.

The first motivation should be obvious to most readers of English poetry written after the Norman Conquest. In much poetry composed after this date, a repetitive phonetic echo occurs either at the end of metrical lines or sometimes within lines, as when Shelley writes (*Charles The First*):

> *There was no leaf upon the forest bare*
> *No flower upon the ground*
> *And little motion in the air*
> *Except the mill-wheel's sound*

The echo of this stanza involves the matching of identical sequences of phonemes line-finally. In lines 1 and 3 the repeated sequence is in an American pronunciation [er] and in lines 2 and 4 the sequence [aʊnd]. In other words, the echo is achieved by repeating the vowel (in this case stressed) and the consonants after the vowel to the end of the word, whereas the consonants preceding the vowel vary. In syllable structure terms the stretch from vowel to the end of the word is the syllable constituents peak and coda. Peak and coda together make up the constituent referred to as rhyme. So strictly speaking, when two words are said to rhyme, what is involved is that specific syllable subparts are identical. The subpart in question is the constituent referred to as rhyme.

The second motivation for positing a rhyme has to do with the distinction between checked and free vowels alluded to above. It turns out that the rhyme is instrumental in explaining what structure the English syllable minimally must consist of to be well-formed. Consider the following syllable structures:

(6.9)

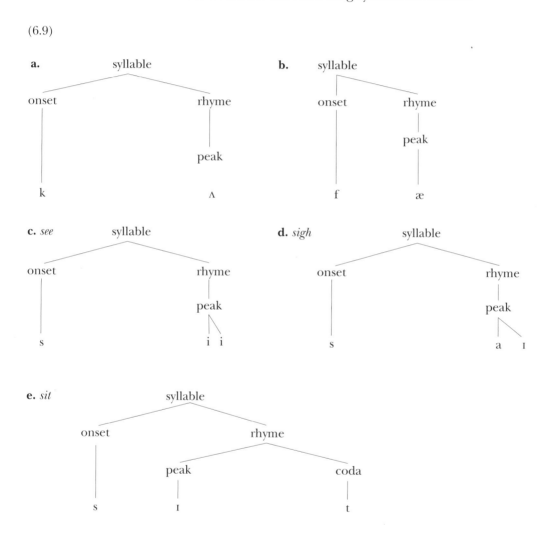

Evidently, **a.** and **b.** in (6.9) are impossible NAERD monosyllabic words (the orthographic representation would be something like *ku* and *fa*). **c.**, **d.** and **e.**, on the other hand, are all attested NAERD monosyllabic words. In other words, a NAERD syllable must minimally comprise either a peak with two segments or minimally a one segment peak plus a one segment coda to be well-formed. The simplest way to express this generalisation is to say that the NAERD syllable minimally has two segments in the rhyme. The familiarity of this constraint should be obvious. It was built into the definition of the difference between checked and free vowels, just alluded to above, which states that a checked vowel requires at least one consonant to close the syllable it occurs in, and that a free vowel occurs in both open and closed syllables, i.e. in syllables which can but need not have a consonant to close them.

6.4 The sonority sequencing principle

Consider now again the monosyllabic words listed in (6.3) above, repeated below:

(6.10)

swarm   /swɔrm/   shrink   /ʃrɪŋk/   clamp   /klæmp/

These words illustrate a recurrent pattern of English and not just NAERD syllable structure: the syllabic peak is flanked by segments which gradually decrease in **sonority**. This is illustrated in (6.11) for *clamp*, where sonority is represented along the vertical axis and time along the horizontal axis:

(6.11)

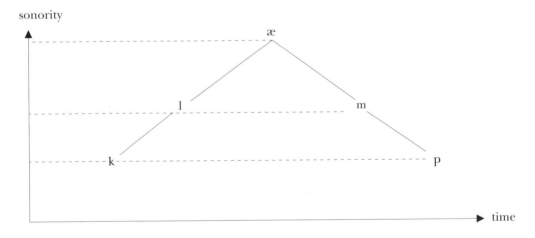

Sonority reflects several properties: i) the **relative loudness** of a segment, ii) the **relative openness** of the vocal tract and iii) the relative amount of **acoustic periodicity** characteristic of the segment. The louder, the more open and the more periodic, the more sonorous a segment is. From (6.11) it is clear that /æ/ is the most sonorant, /l/ and /m/ less sonorant and /k/ and /p/ the least sonorant segments in *clamp*. In fact, all NAERD (and all English) consonants and vowels can be ranked according to their degree of sonority. This ranking is shown in (6.12). The hierarchy which results from this ranking is termed the **sonority hierarchy:**

(6.12)

Voiceless stops are then the least sonorous sound types, and open vowels are the most sonorous sound types of this continuum.

All of the monosyllabic words in (6.10) observe the principle that the syllabic nucleus is flanked by sounds of gradually decreasing sonority. This principle is called the **sonority sequencing principle**. This is the principle governing English syllable structure in general (and syllable structure universally probably), as will be discussed in the following section.

6.5 Permissible onsets and codas in NAERD

Although the sonority sequencing principle is the overall determining factor for the construction of onsets and codas in NAERD, not all clusters obeying this principle are actually permissible onsets and codas. Nor do all permissible onsets and codas actually obey the sonority sequencing principle. This section outlines what constitutes permissible onsets and codas in NAERD and provides general rules for the clusters which violate the sonority sequencing principle, as well as rules for the clusters which do not violate the sonority sequencing principle but which are nonetheless illegitimate. Onset rules are considered first.

6.5.1 Onsets

Let us first consider the rules for **bi-consonantal** onset clusters in NAERD. Disregarding for the moment combinations of /s/ plus another obstruent, the rules for bi-consonant onsets may be summarised as shown in (6.13a), in which the first consonant in such clusters is represented along the vertical axis and the second consonant along the horizontal axis (observe that combinations of /tʃ/ or /dʒ/ plus another consonant are not included, as such never occur in NAERD):

(6.13)

a.

	w	j	r	l	m	n
p	-	+	+	+	-	-
t	+	-	+	-	-	-
k	+	+	+	+	-	-
b	-	+	+	+	-	-
d	+	-	+	-	-	-
g	+	+	+	+	-	-
f	-	+	+	+	-	-
θ	+	-	+	-	-	-
ʃ	-	-	+	-	-	-

b.

	w	j	r	l
		pew	pray	play
	twit		try	
	quite	cube	cry	clay
		bugle	bright	black
	dwell		dry	
	Gwen	ambi-guity	grow	glow
		fume	from	flow
	thwart		throw	
			shrine	

In other words, the first line of (6.13a) reads: /pw-/, /pm-/ and /pn-/ are not possible onset clusters (indicated by minuses), but /pj-/, /pr-/ and /pl-/ are well-formed bi-consonantal onsets in NAERD (indicated by pluses). The correctness of the pluses can be verified by consulting the examples listed in (6.13b) and the correctness of the minuses by attempting to find examples with the purportedly unattested bi-consonantal onsets.

What are the rules that allow these onsets then? As a start, it should be observed that the sonority sequencing principle accounts for all the permissible clusters listed in (6.13): they all display increasing sonority. But as the observant reader will have noticed, the non-permissible ones also obey the sonority sequencing principle. Why are they not found then? A subset of them is not found for articulatory reasons. One group, viz. */pm-/, */pn-/ and */ʃm-/, */ʃn-/, because they contain two successive oral constrictions (stop plus stop or fricative plus stop), and another group, viz. */pw-/, */tl-/ and */ʃj-/ and */θl-/, because they contain two successive segments with the same or almost the same place of articulation. The remaining illegal combinations, viz. /t/, /d/, /s/ and

/θ/ plus /j/, are non-permissible in American English only (in stressed syllables), i.e. they are not found in this kind of English, but other accents such as
RP allow them, a state of affairs which in Ch. 1. above was regarded as one of the
diagnostic features of NAERD and American English in general.

In (6.13) onsets with /s/ were deliberately excluded, since /s/ behaves differently. Let us now consider onsets with /s/. /s/ not only has a wider distribution
in two-consonant onsets, but it may also occur as the first segment in three-consonant onsets. (6.14a) lists two-consonant onsets with /s/ and (6.14b) three-
consonant onsets with /s/, in which /s/ is the first segment:

(6.14)

a.

	w	j	r	l	m	n	p	t	k
s	+	-	-	+	+	+	+	+	+
	sweet			sly	smoke	snow	spy	sty	sky

b.

	w	j	r	l	m	n
sp	-	+	+	+	-	-
st	-	-	+	-	-	-
sk	+	+	+	-	-	-

	spume	spray	splash
		straw	
square	skua	screw	

(6.14a) highlights three properties of two-consonant onsets with /s/ in. Firstly,
that /sw/, /sl/, /sm/ and /sn/ are all permissible onsets in accordance with the
sonority sequencing principle. Secondly, (6.14a) highlights that /s/ does not
combine with /j/ and /r/ in onsets, despite such clusters obeying the sonority
sequencing principle. The absence of /sj/ matches the absence of /tj/, /dj/
and /θj/, that is, the absence of /sj/ is a consequence of the special distribution
of /j/ characteristic of American English only. The absence of /sr/ can be explained as a compensation for the unexpected occurrence of /ʃr/, which is the
only permissible cluster that an alveopalatal obstruent enters into in NAERD, as
can be seen from (6.13). Thirdly, (6.14a) highlights the fact that /s/ can form a
cluster with /p/, /t/ or /k/. These clusters cannot be explained in terms of any
regularity mentioned so far and most certainly not in terms of the sonority sequencing principle which they violate. This is illustrated in (6.15) for the word
start:

(6.15)

sonority

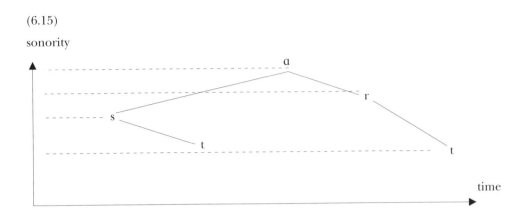

time

which clearly shows that the peak is not preceded by an onset of gradually increasing sonority.

The sonority sequencing principle thus plays an important role in the construction of two-consonant onsets with /s/ as the first element, except in the case of /sp/, /st/, /sk/-clusters. But /sp/, /st/, /sk/-clusters are in fact part of a regular pattern. To see this consider three-consonant onset clusters with /s/ as the first element. All such three-consonant onset clusters, like the two-consonant cluster in (6.15), violate the sonority sequencing principle, as is shown in the representation of *straw*:

(6.16)

sonority

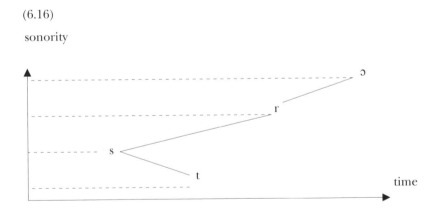

time

But by considering the structure of such three-consonant onsets, a pattern for onsets with /s/ in begins to appear more clearly. Observe that three-consonant onsets are well-formed only if the two consonants following /s/ constitute a permissible onset cluster. For example, /pw/ is not a permissible onset cluster, hence /spw/ is an ill-formed onset, but /pj/ is a permissible onset cluster, hence

/spj/ is a well-formed onset. This fact clearly suggests that /s/ simply does not count in the syllable structure of NAERD, but stands outside the syllable; it is, so to speak, an extra-syllabic segment. By interpreting /s/ in this way, all two-consonant and three-consonant onsets which begin with /s/ conform to the sonority sequencing principle. Thus if /s/ is viewed in this way, it is still possible to maintain that the sonority sequencing principle is the overall governing principle in the construction of NAERD syllable onsets.

6.5.2 Codas

In § 6.3 it was pointed out that the coda and the peak together make up a third unit, the rhyme. § 6.3 also established that the rhyme of a stressed syllable minimally must contain two segments to be well-formed: either it must have two segments branching from the peak (as in *see* and *sigh*) or it must have a one segment peak followed by a one segment coda (as in *hit*). But it is also common practice to state what the maximum structure of the rhyme is. This is an issue which is still being debated by phonologists. Here the view will be adopted that the rhyme in NAERD can maximally contain three segments. This view is supported by such examples as the following:

(6.17)

a	hill	b	helm	c	heal	d	*/heɪlm/
	fit		film		file		*/faɪlm/

These data suggest that in NAERD a rhyme can have the structure VC, VCC or VVC (C = consonant, V = vowel), but if extended to VVCC it becomes ill-formed as attested by (6.17d). That is, once the rhyme exceeds three segments, a constraint steps in and rules it out. Clearly, it is easy to think of well-formed structures which exceed this three segment limit on rhymes. Consider e.g. *mind, bounce, glimpse, text* to mention just a few. But such examples are not real counter-examples, just as onsets with initial /s/ were not real counter-examples. They are part of a regular pattern, as will become clear presently.

But what principle governs the composition of the coda? Consider first the permissible two-consonant codas listed in (6.18a) with an example of each permissible combination represented in (6.18b):

(6.18)

a.

	p	t	tʃ	k	b	d	dʒ	f	θ	s	ʃ	v	z	m	n
p	-	+	-	-	-	-	-	-	+	+	-	-	-	-	-
t	-	-	-	-	-	-	-	-	+	+	-	-	-	-	-
tʃ	-	+	-	-	-	-	-	-	-	-	-	-	-	-	-
k	-	+	-	-	-	-	-	-	-	+	-	-	-	-	-
b	-	-	-	-	-	+	-	-	-	-	-	-	+	-	-
d	-	-	-	-	-	-	-	-	+	-	-	-	+	-	-
dʒ	-	-	-	-	-	+	-	-	-	-	-	-	-	-	-
g	-	-	-	-	-	+	-	-	-	-	-	-	+	-	-
f	-	+	-	-	-	-	-	-	+	+	-	-	-	-	-
θ	-	+	-	-	-	-	-	-	-	+	-	-	-	-	-
s	+	+	-	+	-	-	-	-	-	-	-	-	-	-	-
ʃ	-	+	-	-	-	-	-	-	-	-	-	-	-	-	-
v	-	-	-	-	-	+	-	-	-	-	-	-	+	-	-
ð	-	-	-	-	-	+	-	-	-	-	-	-	+	-	-
z	-	-	-	-	-	+	-	-	-	-	-	-	-	-	-
ʒ	-	-	-	-	-	+	-	-	-	-	-	-	-	-	-
m	+	+	-	-	-	+	-	+	-	-	-	-	+	-	-
n	-	+	+	-	-	+	+	-	+	+ -	-	-	+	-	-
ŋ	-	-	-	+	-	+	-	-	+	-	-	-	+	-	-
l	+	+	+	+	+	+	+	+	+	+	+	+	+	+	+
r	+	+	+	+	+	+	+	+	+	+	+	+	+	+	+

b.

								depth	lapse					
								eighth	hats					
		hatched												
	act									six				
					mobbed							mobs		
								width				adze		
					judged									
					begged							begs		
	shaft							fifth	chefs					
	bathed							smiths						
lisp	list	cask												
	mashed													
					lived							lives		
					sheathed							paths		
					buzzed									
					rouged									
limp	dreamt				skimmed	nymph						m's		
rant	bench				land	hinge	tenth	glance						fans
			sink		hanged		length	sings						
yelp	filt	belch	silk	bulb	filled	bulge	alf	health	false	Welsh	delve	fills	film	kiln
harp	heart	arch	park	herb	hard	urge	turf	birth	purse	harsh	serve	parse	firm	fern

A closer examination reveals that of these 76 well-formed two-consonant codas, 55, or 75 %, conform to the sonority sequencing principle. This principle is then the major organising principle of two-consonant codas, as it is in onsets. The remaining 21 attested combinations all violate the sonority sequencing principle. In these the final consonant is the more sonorous of the two consonants found in the coda. This is illustrated in (6.19) showing the sonority structure of the 'offending' word *six*:

(6.19)

sonority

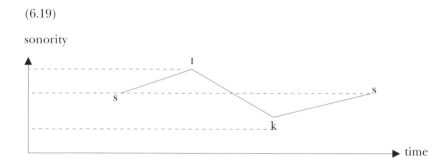

But in all the clusters which violate the sonority sequencing principle, the place of articulation of this final consonant is either dental or alveolar. That is, just as only /s/ violated the general onset structure, it is possible to limit the number of consonants which are allowed to violate sonority sequencing in the coda to those which are dental or alveolar. Some regularity involving again extra-syllabic consonants seems then to be at work in the coda, a regularity which will explain why the 21 'offending' combinations are in fact not ruled out.

But before any final conclusion is drawn, consider first codas consisting of more than two consonants. Codas of more than two consonants involve the following combinations:

(6.20)

a.

	t	s	θ
ds	+	-	-
ks	+	-	+
mp	+	+	-
ns	+	-	-
ŋk	+	+	-
lp	+	-	-
lk	+	+	-
lf	-	-	+
ls	+	-	-
rk	+	-	-
rm	-	-	+
rp	+	+	-

b.

midst		
next		sixth
tempt	glimpse	
against		
succinct	sphinx	
sculpt		
mulct		
		twelfth
whilst		
infarct		
		warmth
excerpt	corpse	

and further combinations appear when the two-consonant combinations listed in (6.18) have one of the suffixes /t, d, s, z/ added to them, as in e.g. *hilts, depths, widths, lists, casks, bulbs*.

What do the combinations in (6.20) then tell us? (6.20) confirms the pattern found in two-consonant combinations, namely that three-consonant combinations in the coda (whether they are morphologically simple or morphologically complex) conform to the sonority sequencing principle, and that if this is violated, but the cluster remains well-formed, the segment or segments which appear after the last segment conforming to the sonority sequencing principle is one or more of /t, d, s, z, θ/, i.e. an obstruent drawn from the places of articulation dental or alveolar. In other words, the provisional conclusion drawn on the basis of two-consonant combinations in the coda is borne out by three consonant combinations. The conclusion is then that the predominant organising principle of the coda, and then also of the rhyme, is the sonority sequencing principle. If this principle or the constraint that the rhyme maximally can contain three segments is violated, the segments which violate are all drawn from the following set: /t, d, s, z, θ/. To this set should be added /dʒ/ because of such well-formed strings like *lounge, range*. Like in onsets, there are then segments in the coda, and hence the rhyme, which do not count as real members of the syllable. Such **extra-syllabic** segments are all drawn from the same small subset of dental-alveolar and in one case alveopalatal consonants. Sometimes such consonants are known as coronal consonants. In many phonological contexts the behaviour of coronal consonants is unmarked. Their status as extra-syllabic here is then not exceptional but ascribable to this property.

Observe finally that four-consonant combinations in the coda, which arise when one of the three-consonant combinations listed in (6.20) has a suffix added, as the examples in (6.21) show:

(6.21)

excerpts   tempts   texts

which confirm the pattern of coda structure established on the basis of three-consonant combinations or combinations with fewer consonants.

6.5.3 The main points about the structure of onsets and codas

The rules which govern the structure of onsets and codas in NAERD may be summarised as follows:

- The sonority sequencing principle is the predominant principle governing onset and coda structure
- In the onset, two segments which otherwise obey the sonority sequencing principle cannot constitute a well-formed onset, if they are drawn from the same place of articulation, or if they constitute two successive oral constrictions
- In onset-initial position, /s/ may form two-consonant onsets with /p, t, k/ and three-consonant onsets with combinations of /p, t, k/ plus whatever other sonorant these stops form a well-formed two-consonant onset with
- /s/ in two- or three-consonant onset clusters is regarded as not being part of the syllable structure proper
- The structure of the coda is closely tied up with the structural restrictions associated with the rhyme, in particular that the rhyme minimally must contain two segments and maximally three segments
- If the maximal structure of rhymes is exceeded, the violating segments occurring in the coda must be one or more of the following /t, d, s, z, dʒ, θ/.

6.6 The syllabification of polysyllabic words

So far this chapter has only considered the structure of monosyllabic words. But words regularly consist of more than one syllable. Such **polysyllabic** words pose the problem of deciding where the boundaries between the syllables should be placed. This section outlines the rules for the placement of syllable boundaries in polysyllabic words.

Given that the structure of syllables is such that they have indispensable peaks, the boundaries between syllables must be near the optional elements. This corresponds well with the intuition of many native speakers who, when asked, would syllabify words like *dependent, monogamy* as shown in (6.22):

(6.22)

de.pen.dent   mo.no.ga.my

where dots indicate syllable boundaries. How do we know for sure that this is the correct syllabification? One way of finding out is to ask native speakers to pronounce words like *dependent* and *monogamy* in such a way that they duplicate each syllable. The result of such a test will be *de-de.pen-pen.dent-dent, mo-mo.no-no. ga-ga.my-my*. Let us assume then that the syllabification shown in (6.22) is correct. This means that the following syllabifications are also accurate:

(6.23)

a.	glo.ri.fy	b.	im.port	c.	a.pron
	le.ga.li.ty		mo.nu.men.tum		at.las
	pho.ne.tics		nigh.tin.gale		pen.tath.lon
	se.cond		al.ter.nate		a.cri.mo.ny

What are the rules for these syllabifications then? Starting with (6.22) and (6.23a), the general rule clearly is that a single consonant between vowels syllabifies with the following vowel, i.e. is an onset rather than a coda. This regularity results in a CV.CV. CV structure rather than in a VC.VC.VC structure. This structure is not only characteristic of English and NAERD, but held to be a general pattern universally.

When English prefers to place consonants in the onset, as reflected in the CV-structure, should the string VCCV then also follow this pattern and be syllabified such that CC become the onset of the following vowel? This can be answered by considering (6.23b) and (6.23c). From these two sets it is clear that CC become the onset if the two constitute a permissible onset. In (6.23b) no CC constitute a permissible onset. They all violate the sonority sequencing principle. As a consequence, the syllable boundary falls between the two consonants as shown in (6.24a). In (6.23c) CC in two instances syllabify with the following vowel. In these two instances, CC constitute a permissible onset. In the remaining instances CC are not permissible onsets, because the place of articulation of the two consonants coincide (see. § 6.3 above). The syllable boundary therefore falls between the two consonants in these instances, as shown in (6.24b)

(6.24)

a.				b.		
	im.port	*/mp-/			a.pron	/pr-/
	mo.nu.men.tum	*/nt-/			at.las	*/tl-/
	nigh.tin.gale	*/ŋg-/			pen.tath.lon	*/θl-/
	al.ter.nate	*/lt-/, */rn-/			a.cri.mo.ny	/kr-/

On the basis of the polysyllabic words considered thus far, the rule that accounts for syllable boundary placement can then be formulated as follows:

(6.25)

within polysyllabic words, consonants are syllabified in such a way that as many as possible are placed in syllable onsets but without violating the rules for permissible onset clusters

Observe that this rule not only accounts for the syllabification of two successive consonants within words. It also accounts for strings of more than two consonants. For example, the strings *astray* (VCCCV-), *imprison* (VCCCV-) and *instrument* (VCCCCV-) will be syllabified as *a.stray*, *im.pri.son* and *in.stru.ment* in accordance with the rule given in (6.25).

The observant reader will have noticed that the syllabification resulting from the application of the rule in (6.25) sometimes conflicts with the claim that checked vowels cannot occur in an open stressed syllable. As a result of the rule given in (6.25), words like *matrimony, petrol, bulletin, rusty, nippy* will be divided into the following syllables:

(6.26)

/ˈmæ.trɪ.moʊ.nɪ/   /ˈpe.trəl/   /ˈbʊ.lə.tɪn/   /ˈrʌ.stɪ/   /ˈnɪ.pɪ/

but this clearly places /æ/, /e/, /ʊ/, /ʌ/ and /ɪ/ in open stressed syllables, contrary to their status as checked vowels, because the following consonants syllabify with the succeeding vowel.

This fact presents a problem, but not one which cannot be solved. In fact, it is commonly assumed that the consonant which immediately follows a stressed checked vowel belongs to both the preceding syllable and the following syllable. That is, the assumption is that such consonants are **ambisyllabic**. If curly brackets for a moment represent syllable boundaries, in particular '{' denotes 'begin-

ning of syllable' and '}' denotes 'end of syllable', a syllabification assuming ambisyllabic segments will look as shown in (6.27):

(6.27)

/{ˈmæ{t}rɪ}{moʊ}{nɪ}/   /{ˈpe{t}rəl}/   /{ˈbʊ{l}ə}{tɪn}/

/{ˈrʌ{st}ɪ}/   /{ˈnɪ{p}ɪ}/

Such a syllabification prevents the checked vowels /æ/, /e/, /ʊ/, /ɪ/ and /ʌ/
from occurring in an open stressed syllable, because at least one consonant now
closes the syllable of which they are the peak. The rule that results in the syllabifications shown in (6.27) may be formulated as follows:

(6.28)

> *consonants which follow a stressed checked vowel belong to both the syllable of which the checked*
> *vowel is the peak and the following syllable, provided such ambisyllabicity results in permissible*
> *onsets and codas*

Observe that the rule in (6.28) has the effect that the clusters /tr/ in *matrimony*
and *petrol* get syllabified such that both consonants belong to the onset of the
second syllable, because /tr/ is a permissible onset, but such that only /t/ and
not /tr/ belongs to the coda of the stressed syllable, because /tr/ is not a permissible coda. In the word *rusty*, on the other hand, the cluster /st/ belongs in
toto to both the coda of the first syllable and the onset of the second syllable,
because /st/ is both a permissible coda and a permissible onset.

Ambisyllabic segments are then found only when the structure requires a
checked vowel to occur in a closed syllable. Observe, finally, that ambisyllabicity
commonly surfaces if native speakers are asked to pronounce each syllable of
such words as *bulletin* and *petrol* twice. This will result in bul-bul. le-le. tin-tin and
pet-pet. trol-trol, i.e. the ambisyllabic consonants will by such a test appear in
two successive syllables. The ambisyllabicity of, for example, /t/ in *petrol* also appears from the fact that it exhibits both syllable-final features and syllable-initial
features, whereas the /t/ of, for example, *matron* (*ma.tron*) exhibits only syllable-
initial features in accordance with the fact that /t/ in this word belongs to the
second syllable only, since the first open syllable contains a free vowel.

6.7 Summary of syllable structure

Let us conclude this chapter with a summary of the main points about syllable structure in NAERD:

- The syllable consists of an indispensable peak (the vowel) and two further optional units: the onset referring to what comes before the peak and the rhyme referring to what follows the peak
- The rhyme is further divided into peak and coda. The rhyme must minimally contain two segments and maximally three segments
- The generally organising principle of the syllable is the sonority sequencing principle, according to which the peak of the syllable is flanked by segments which gradually decrease in sonority
- Permissible onsets obey the sonority sequencing principle. Onset segments violating the sonority sequencing principle do not belong to the core structure of the syllable
- Permissible codas obey the sonority sequencing principle. Segments violating the restriction on the number of segments allowed in the rhyme do not belong to the core structure of the syllable. Such segments are one or more of /t, d, s, z, θ, dʒ/
- The syllabification of polysyllabic words maximises the CV-structure, i.e. places as many segments in the onset as possible without violating the rules for permissible onsets
- To prevent checked vowels from occurring in an open syllable, consonants are interpreted as constituting the coda of one syllable and the onset of the following syllable, i.e. to be ambisyllabic.

Further reading
Very good introductions to English syllable structure can be found in Lass 1984, Giegerich 1992. See also Gimson 1962, Bauer et al 1980, the latter dealing with American English. A comprehensive but also quite technical account based on the principles of generative phonology is found in Kenstowicz 1994.

CHAPTER 7

Word stress in American English

7.1 Introduction to word stress

It is a characteristic feature of English polysyllabic words that one syllable is more prominent than the other(s) when these words are uttered in isolation. For example, in the words *waiter, England, primary* the first syllable is the strongest syllable, just as in *ahead, regret, immediate* the second syllable is the most prominent. Following common practice, this prominence will be referred to as **stress**, although strictly speaking stress is only one among several features which makes stressed syllables stand out as more distinct.

More specifically, the features which contribute to making syllables stressed are the following:

- greater muscular effort, i.e. more stress
- longer duration
- distinct as opposed to blurred vowel quality, i.e. absence of /ə/ in stressed syllables
- pitch variation, either shift of pitch level or variation due to tone movement on the prominent syllable itself or due to a step up or step down in the immediate vicinity of the prominent syllable

Not all stressed syllables display all four features. All features are found in those syllables which have what will be referred to as **primary stress**. But polysyllabic words may have more than one stressed syllable. For example, in words like *blameworthy* or *perpendicular* there is not only one syllable which carries primary stress, but the penultimate (last but one) syllable in *blameworthy* and the first syllable in *perpendicular* are also stressed. Because these syllables are less prominent, however, they will be said to have **secondary stress**. Syllables with secondary stress only display the first three features listed above. They lack pitch variation.

The description given below outlines the rules for stress – both primary and secondary – in **non-compound** words and **compound** words when these are uttered in isolation. It is a basic assumption of this account that the stress of derived words is predictable from their underived counterparts. For example, the stress pattern of *universal* is determinable on the basis of the underived form *universe.* In formulating the main stress rules, the following concepts will be used: **root** which refers to an **underived form** (for example *sing*), **suffix** which refers to an inflectional or derivational ending (as in *singing* and *singer* respectively), **prefix** which refers to a word or a syllable placed before a root (as in *replay, foreplay, counterattack, unhappy*), **syllable** which refers to the structural unit that polysyllabic words can be divided into and whose obligatory element is a vowel or a syllabic sonorant consonant. Finally, **penult** and **antepenult** will be used to refer to the last syllable but one and the last syllable but two respectively.

As just stated, the following sections will deal with stress in both compound and non-compound words. § 7.2 deals with stress in non-compounds and § 7.3 with stress in compound words. It is important to emphasise that the following stress rules are the main rules for these two types of word stress in NAERD. Given the limited space available here, it is evident that not all rules and constraints regarding word stress assignment can be included. So when the reader encounters stress patterns which contravene the rules specified here, then this is due to the admittedly incomplete and only very general rules which will be proposed in the following sections.

7.2 Stress rules in non-compounds

To account for stress in non-compound words, the following four main stress rules will be needed: **the root stress rule**, **the antepenult rule**, **the prefix rule** and **the word-class rule**. These rules all concern the assignment of primary word stress. But words of three or more syllables as a rule also receive a secondary stress. The general pattern is for secondary stress to fall two syllables to the right or two syllables to the left of the syllable carrying primary stress. In the following account of stress rules, only primary stress rules will be given. Secondary word stress will be dealt with in § 7.2.5 below.

7.2.1 The root stress rule
The root stress rule applies to roots of two or three syllables. The root stress rules assign stress to the first syllable in such roots, as exemplified by the stress pattern in the following words:

(7.1)

2 syllables	3 syllables
ˈfaggot	ˈhandicap
ˈlisten	ˈnursery
ˈdolphin	ˈCanada
ˈheaven	ˈvitamin
ˈstudent	ˈhospital
ˈbrother	ˈveteran

It should be noted that these words can all be said to be underived. They do not consist of a root and a prefix or a suffix.

However, some disyllabic and trisyllabic words fail to comply with this pattern. They fall into two groups. These are listed in (7.2)

(7.2)
a. *Ber'lin, Ju'ly, ca'reer, kanga'roo, Tenne'ssee, pio'neer*
b. *A'laska, No'vember, ana'conda*

The words in (7.2a) have stress on the second or the last syllable and those in (7.2b) have stress on the penultimate (last but one) syllable. The words in (7.2a) belong to a very large class of foreign words which behave in the same way. Their irregular stress pattern may then be explained as being due to the fact that they are either foreign loan words of particularly French origin or place names.

The exception to the root stress rule exemplified by (7.2b), on the other hand, is explicable in terms of the structure of the words. As appears from the words given in (7.2b), the penultimate vowel in these is followed by a cluster of two or more consonants. This structure is a heavy cluster and attracts stress to the syllable of which the vowel immediately before the cluster is the peak. This condition is called the **consonant cluster condition**. Although it is able to explain the non-initial stress assignment in the words in (7.2b) plus a host of other words such as *ve'randa, To'ronto, as'bestos*, the consonant cluster condition does not help to account for the stress pattern in, say, *ca'sino, Ha'vana, co'lossal, ba'nana* with stress on the penultimate and not on the first syllable as the root stress rule predicts. These have to be considered as exceptions to the root stress rule.

7.2.2 The antepenult rule

Words of four or more syllables – be they root or roots plus suffixes (unless the latter are the so-called strong suffixes or the so-called weak suffixes) – have stress on the last syllable but two (antepenult syllable). Consider the following list of words which exemplify the application of this rule:

(7.3)

di'ameter	*bi'ology*	*me'lodious*
de'mocracy	*accessi'bility*	*spec'tacular*
sim'plicity	*car'bonium*	*or'thography*

However, words which contain one of the **strong suffixes** fail to comply with the antepenult rule. (7.4) lists some typical strong suffixes and words in which they occur, from which it is clear that these strong suffixes attract primary stress:

(7.4)

-ade	*lemo'nade*
-aire	*questio'naire*
-ation	*manifest'ation*
-cation	*signifi'cation*
-ee	*tu'tee*
-esque	*pictu'resque*
-ese	*Japa'nese*

Another type of strong suffix whose attractive power is less strong but which still exerts influence on the stress pattern in the word in which it occurs is the suffix *-ic*, including *-ical(ly)*, *-icism*, *-ics*. Words with this suffix have stress on the syllable immediately before the suffix:

(7.5)

characte'ristic	*dra'matic*
pho'netic	*ro'manticism*
dra'matically	*sta'tistics*

Finally, a set of suffixes fails to exert any influence on the stress pattern at all, even though their addition may result in words which strictly speaking should receive antepenultimate stress. These **weak suffixes** include all inflectional endings and a number of derivational suffixes. Here are some examples:

(7.6)

-(e)d	*'culminated, 'circulated*
-(e)s	*oe'sophaguses, 'Beatrice's, 'pulverises*
-(ing)	*'culminating, 'circulating*

Again, there exist words whose stress pattern cannot be predicted on the basis of the antepenult rule, nor the two associated suffix rules, the strong suffix condition and the weak suffix condition. These are words like the following:

(7.7)

| *anec'dotal* | *homi'cidal* | *sui'cidal* |
| *advan'tageous* | *cou'rageous* | *fa'llacious* |

Words of this type simply have to be considered as exceptions to the general pattern.

7.2.3 The prefix rule

Prefixes are somewhat more difficult to describe than suffixes. This is because prefixes are often bound to the root, so the root cannot stand alone. For example, the words *perceive* (*per + ceive*), *transmit* (*trans + mit*) and *pronounce* (*pro +*

nounce) all consist of roots which do not constitute independent words. None-theless, such words plus many more will be assumed to contain a prefix, because it is possible to replace the prefixes with other prefixes as the following words illustrate: *receive, submit, announce, conceive, admit, renounce.*

As can be seen from the list of words which concluded the preceding paragraph, primary stress does not fall on a prefix. Instead the root receives the primary stress. This pattern is further confirmed by the following list:

(7.8)

ac'cept	*inter'rupt*	*con'sole*
re'ply	*un'kind*	*pro'hibit*
pre'cede	*con'stituent*	*ex'ception*

The rule which accounts for the stress assignments in these words is then simply the root stress rule discussed above in §7.2.1. But the absence of stress on the prefix in the words in (7.8) does not entail that the prefix never receives stress. Not only does it sometimes receive secondary stress (marked with a lowered stress mark) when it is polysyllabic, followed by another prefix or belongs to the category of strong prefixes, as shown in (7.9):

(7.9)

polysyllabic	two prefixes	strong prefix
inter'fere	*decom'pose*	*anti'Catholic*
contra'dict	*disim'bark*	*hyper'tension*

but the prefix may also receive primary stress under certain conditions. These are described below and concern the stress rule termed the word-class rule.

7.2.4 The word-class rule

The basic group of words with primary stress on the prefix involves nouns which have identical verb counterparts, except that the primary stress in these verbs falls on the root and not on the prefix. Consider the following list:

(7.10)

noun	verb
'address	*a'ddress*
'ally	*a'lly*
'conflict	*con'flict*
'import	*im'port*
'increase	*in'crease*
'insult	*in'sult*
'object	*ob'ject*
'permit	*per'mit*

But the existence of a verbal counterpart is not a prerequisite for a noun to conform to this pattern. The word class-rule is a rule which describes the norm for prefixed nouns and this is for the prefix to have primary stress. Some more examples of nouns are listed in (7.11), all of which lack verbal counterparts:

(7.11)

'absence	'expert	'comfort
'diagram	'intercourse	'omnibus
'radiogram	'stereotype	'heterochrome

Given that prefix stress is the norm in nouns which have a prefix, the stress pattern in nouns like co'mmand, ex'change, ad'vice have to be regarded as exceptions. It should be noted that there are also verbs (and adjectives as well as adverbs) which take primary stress on the prefix: 'profit, 'surface, 'prosecute, 'analyse, 'indicate. Such words are then further exceptions to the general rule.

7.2.5 Secondary word stress

The assignment of stress to polysyllabic words often involves more than identifying one syllable as stressed. Depending on the number and nature of the syllables, a polysyllabic word may also have one or more secondary stressed syllables. Assigning secondary stress is chiefly rhythmically conditioned, so that a syllable with secondary stress is found two syllables to the left and two syllables to the right of the syllable with primary stress. This is called **the secondary word stress rule**. It is important to note that this rule describes the general pattern. The presence of special prefixes with a specific informative function may change this pattern. The secondary stress following the primary accent is also not found as consistently as the secondary stress preceding the primary stress. (7.12) lists some examples:

(7.12)

ˌadvan'tageous	imˌpressio'nistic
ˌperpen'dicular	ˌperpenˌdicu'larity
'tempoˌrary	'cemeˌtery
ˌine'xactiˌtude	ˌunˌsyste'matic

Observe that secondary stress often falls on a syllable which in another form of the same word carries primary stress. For example, the second secondary stress in ˌperpenˌdicu'larity falls on the syllable which in the form ˌperpen'dicular has primary stress. In other words, the primary stress leaves a trace in the form of a secondary stress if it is shifted two syllables to the right. If a primary stress is shifted only one syllable to the right, the trace it leaves appears on the syllable which precedes the one with former primary stress, provided there is one. This may be illustrated with advan'tageous which is derived from ad'vantage. When the stress is shifted one syllable to the right the former primary stress appears as secondary stress on the first syllable. The rule which accounts for the appearance of traces in the form of a secondary stress, a trace which has been left by a former primary stress, is known as the **trace rule.**

7.2.6 Summary of word stress in non-compound words

The following rules with associated sub-rules account for primary and secondary stress in NAERD non-compound words:

- **ROOT STRESS RULE (RSR) – consonant cluster condition (ccc)**

- **ANTEPENULT RULE (APR) – strong suffix condition (ssc) weak suffix condition (wsc)**

- **PREFIX RULE (PR)**

- **WORD CLASS RULE (WCR)**

- **SECONDARY WORD STRESS RULE (SWSR)**

As an illustration of how the stress rules work, consider the stress patterns in the following words: *semiacceptability, antidocumentarism, unpolitical, nonmedicinality*

(7.13)

semiacceptability	*acˈcept*		RSR, PR
		acˈceptable	RSR, PR, wsc
		acˌceptaˈbility	APR, SWSR
		ˌsemiacˌceptaˈbility	APR, SWSR
antidocumentarism	*ˈdocument*		RSR
		ˌdocuˈmentary	ssc, SWSR
		ˌdocuˈmentarism	ssc, wsc, SWSR
		ˌantiˌdocuˈmentarism	ssc, wsc, SWSR
unpolitical	*ˈpolitic*		RSR
		poˈlitical	ssc
		ˌunpoˈlitical	ssc, SWSR
nonmedicinality	*ˈmedicine*		RSR
		meˈdicinal	APR
		meˌdiciˈnality	APR, SWSR
		ˌnonmeˌdiciˈnality	APR, SWSR

7.3 Stress in compounds and compound-like combinations

The attention is now directed towards stress in combinations of words. Two types of combinations of words will be considered: compounds and compound-like combinations. By a compound is meant a unit which consists of two or more roots, each of which may constitute a word on its own. A compound-like combination is a collocation whose constituent roots also form a unit but not as close-knit a unit as that of a compound. Like the constituent roots of compounds, the constituent roots of compound-like combinations may also individually constitute a word. Here are some examples:

(7.14)

compounds	compound-like combinations
wall-paper	*cottage cheese*
overdose	*town hall*
White House	*home-made*
moreover	*runner-up*
blood-thirsty	*world-wide*

The difference with respect to stress pattern between the two types is that compounds have only one primary stress (on the first or the second element), whereas compound-like combinations have two primary stresses (one on each element). In addition to compounds and compound-like combinations, this section will also briefly deal with **complex compounds** and **complex compound-like combinations**. (7.15) lists two examples of each type:

(7.15)

complex compounds	complex compound-like combinations
wall paper factory	*town hall servitor*
White House representative	*State of the Union speech*

which are characterised by consisting of more than two elements, where the first two constitute a compound or a compound-like combination. The stress pattern of complex compounds and complex compound-like combinations follow that of the corresponding simple ones: one primary stress in complex compounds and two primary stresses in complex compound-like combinations.

7.3.1 Stress in simple compounds

As stated already, compounds are characterised by having only one primary stress (the following discussion of stress in compounds and compound-like combinations disregards the occurrences of secondary stress), and the normal case is for a compound to have stress on the first element. (7.16) lists some examples:

(7.16)

nominal as second element	participle as second element	adverb/adjective as second element
ˈbuilding block	ˈheart-broken	ˈcomeback
ˈstopwatch	ˈsnow-covered	ˈhangover
ˈWhite House	ˈhand-written	ˈseasick

second element as a variation of the first

ˈmish-mash
ˈding-dong
ˈzig-zag

The other possibility that the primary stress falls on the second element of the compound is also found, but this pattern is much less frequent and, unlike in English English RP, it is usually not found when the second element is a participle or an adjective:

(7.17)

nominal as second element	adverb/adjective as second element
Great ˈBritain	thereˈafter
New ˈYork	moreˈover
prime ˈminister	
week-ˈend	

Foreign learners should pay particular attention to the compounds with stress on the second element, as these compounds often represent an unexpected stress pattern.

7.3.2 Stress in simple compound-like combinations

Simple compound-like combinations are characterised by having primary stress on both elements. This pattern may be illustrated with the following examples:

(7.18)

nominal as second element	participle as second element	adverb/adjective as second element
ˈlogˈcabin	ˈdog-ˈtired	ˈrunner-ˈup
ˈstoneˈwall	ˈhome-ˈmade	ˈknee-ˈdeep
ˈcottageˈcheese	ˈunder-ˈdeveloped	AˈttorneyˈGeneral

**second element as
a variation of the first**

ˈhelter-ˈskelter
ˈhanky-ˈpanky
ˈhocus-ˈpocus

As a special characteristic, the compound-like combinations may change the stress pattern in connected speech from two primary stresses to one primary on the first element when the compound-like combination functions as premodification:

(7.19)

functions as subject complement	functions as premodification
The snow is ˈknee-ˈdeep	They walked in ˈknee-deepˈsnow
The patient is ˈdog-ˈtired	A ˈdog-tiredˈpatient

This variation is due to considerations of rhythm. By dropping a primary stress when functioning as premodification, a pattern of alternating stresses is created.

7.3.3 The stress of complex compounds

The most common type of complex compound involves a compound plus another noun. Stress in compounds involves one primary stress, usually on the first element. This pattern is repeated in complex compounds. Thus in the following examples, the primary stress falls on the first element:

(7.20)

ˈWhite House representative   ˈseasick tablet
ˈpickup truck
ˈping-pong tournament   ˈice cream cone

A complex compound of the kind listed in (7.20) can itself be part of a more complex compound as shown in (7.21):

(7.21)

ˈWhite House representative dispute
ˈping-pong tournament results

In principle, this process of creating gradually more complex compounds may continue indefinitely. The limit is only drawn when a complex compound cannot be successfully decoded. For example, the reader may try and decipher the following (unlikely) compound: *lawn-tennis tournament referee license test committee member.*

7.3.4 The stress of complex compound-like combinations

As in the case of complex compounds, the most common type of complex compound-like combinations is one which consists of a compound-like combination plus another noun. The stress pattern of compound-like combinations, one primary stress on each element, is repeated in complex compound-like combinations. Thus in the following complex compound-like combinations, the first two elements receive primary stress:

(7.22)

'State of the 'Union speech	'House of 'Commons debate
'cottage 'cheese factory worker	'foot and 'mouth disease alert

and, as in the case of complex compounds, the possibility of constructing yet more complex compound-like combinations is only halted when decoding is no longer successful.

7.3.5 Summary of stress in compounds and compound-like combinations

The stress pattern found in NAERD simple or complex compounds and compound-like combinations may be summarised as follows:

- Simple compounds have only one primary stress. This primary stress may fall on the first or the second element of the compound. Primary stress on the first element is the more common pattern. Examples: '*fresh-water*, *Lake* '*Placid*
- Simple compound-like combinations have two primary stresses. These primary stresses fall on the two elements of the combination. Example: '*down* '*payment*
- Complex compounds have only one primary stress. This primary stress falls on the first element of the complex compound. Example: '*fresh-water reservoir*
- Complex compound-like combinations have two primary stresses. These fall on the first two elements of the complex compound-like combination. Example: '*town* '*hall servitor*.

7.4 Rhythm

7.4.1 Types of rhythm

It is a characteristic feature of speech, be it English or some other language, that it is organised in units of timing each marked by some prominent element. This heartbeat, as it were, of the pronunciation is what is referred to as the rhythm of the pronunciation. In general, such markers of rhythm fall at regular intervals, so regular that the stretches of speech, or the rhythmic groups, between such prominent elements are conceived to be of the same length. For this reason, the prominent elements of rhythm are often said to be **isochronous**.

Conceivably, any element extending in time may constitute a rhythmic group. Thus segments, syllables or stretches of syllables are all potential groups of rhythm. In practice only the latter two have been shown to serve this function. Segments vary too much in length and recur too quickly to be perceived as rhythmic units. The duration of several syllables is long enough and the duration of one syllable is also of sufficient length to constitute such a unit. Even parts of syllables may serve as rhythmic groups.

Languages in which syllables constitute the units of rhythm, i.e. where the syllables are of equal duration without notable variation in prominence, are termed **syllable-timed**. French is one such language. Spanish, Italian, Greek are also syllable-timed languages. That is, in such languages the syllable governs the rhythmic beat of the language. However, since the syllables fail to be completely homogenous, but vary in structure and prominence, the more general term **syllable-based** is probably a better description of the rhythm of such languages.

Languages in which the units of rhythm are made up of strings of syllables where each string or group is initiated by a stressed syllable and where the material of each group has notable variation in duration, prominence and vowel quality are termed **stress-timed** languages. English is such a language. German, Danish and Swedish are also stress-timed language. That is, in such languages stressed syllables govern the rhythmic beat of the language. However, the beats of stress-timed languages do not fall at completely regular intervals. The beats are not completely isochronous. For this reason, the more general term **stress-based** is a better description of such languages. The stress-based rhythm of English may be illustrated with the following sentence:

(7.23)

ˈBolinger had been reˈvisiting the ˈbar ˈlonger than she ˈknew

If one taps a finger on a table each time a stressed syllable in (7.23) is pronounced, the tapping will fall at intervals which are roughly equal in time. This means that when the pronunciation material between two such stressed syllables includes several syllables (as between the first two stressed syllables in

(7.23)), the speech tempo will accelerate and vowel reduction, for example, will be evident. Conversely, with few or no syllables between such stressed syllables (as between the fourth and fifth stressed syllables in (7.23)), the tempo will decelerate and lengthening may take place. Such compensation, in one or the other direction, results in a rhythmic pattern in which groups of syllables have roughly the same length. Each such rhythmic group of syllables is called a **foot**.

By comparison, a syllable-timed pronunciation of (7.23) would result in the first foot ('*Bolinger.....re-*) having 6 times, the second foot ('*visiting the*) having 4 times the duration of the third foot ('*bar*) which contains just one syllable (the other two feet contain 5 and 4 syllables respectively). A pronunciation of (7.23) showing these length differences would be typical of an Indian's rendition of this sentence. A typical feature of English spoken by Indians (in India or outside) is that the syllable-based rhythm of the native language is transferred to the English pronunciation. The effect is a 'ratatat' rhythm quite distinct from the English stress-based rhythm, but it illustrates well how the two types of rhythm differ in deliverance.

7.4.2 The foot

The foot, as stated in the preceding section, is a unit of rhythm which organises syllables into groups. The first syllable of each foot is stressed. This syllable marks the beginning of the foot. A diagram of the foot structure of (7.23) looks as follows:

(7.24)

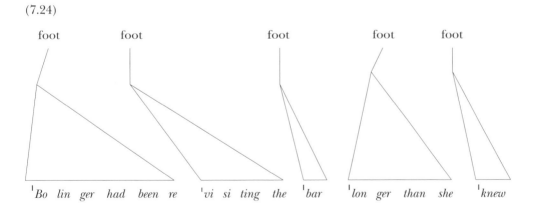

From this it is quite clear that foot structure does not follow grammatical structure. For example, not all the syllables of the Verb Phrase *had been revisiting* belong to the same foot. The first three syllables belong to the first foot and the remaining syllables to the second foot. A consequence of aligning unstressed syllables to the preceding foot is that if a sentence begins with one or more unstressed syllables, such unstressed syllables belong to the preceding foot or, if no such foot exists, become unfooted.

But the foot can be motivated in another way than as a unit which governs rhythm. Allophonic rules depend on the foot. For example, a foot-initial position is where /p, t, k/ are strongly aspirated. Devoicing of /r/ and /l/ after /p, t, k/ is also bound to foot-initial position. Segmental evidence supporting the foot is then plentiful.

Having recourse to the foot also helps explain variations in stress patterns. Compare the following stress patterns:

(7.25)

a.   ˌthirˈteen   b.   ˈthirˌteen ˈgirls
      ˌHeathˈrow   ˈHeathˌrow ˈAirport
      ˌthirty-ˈone   ˈthirty-ˌone ˈstudents
      ˌPicaˈdilly   ˈPicaˌdilly ˈCircus

The stress pattern of the word which is repeated in (7.25) is the reverse in (b.) of what it is in (a.). The pattern changes from secondary-primary to primary-secondary. Stating the mechanism of this rule requires access to the notion of foot, as the reversing of the stress patterns may involve more than one syllable at the time.

One important aspect of the foot deserves special mention. The foot is also used to refer to a unit in versification consisting of stressed and unstressed syllables. But the phonological foot should not be confused with the **foot of versification**. As observed and shown in (7.24), the phonological foot is a unit of one or more syllables in which the first syllable is always stressed. The foot of versification, on the other hand, does not always begin with a stressed syllable, but it can also be unstressed. The foot in versification structures the lines of a composition, typically a poem, into a recurrence of regular patterns of stressed and unstressed syllables. The regular rhythm of a poetic line created by such a regular pattern is called **metre**. Depending on the foot structure, the metre may be iambic, anapaestic, trochaic, dactylian, the most common types of metrical feet. Iambs and trochees are disyllabic and anapaests and dactyls are trisyllabic units. Iambs have the structure *w*(eak) followed by *s*(trong) syllable, trochee has the structure *s* followed by *w*, whilst the structure of anapaests is *w w s* and that of dactyls *s w w*. Depending on the number of feet, i.e. iambs, trochees etc., in each line, a metrical line of verse is named e.g. dimeter if it contains two feet, tetrameter if it contains four feet, pentameter if it contains five feet, hexameter if it contains six feet. Below follow examples of metrical feet in which the feet of versification are marked by vertical bars.

(7.26)

iambic pentameter: (Gray, *Elegy*)

w | s w | s w | s w | s w | s
The ploughman homeward plods his weary way

trochaic pentameter: (Browning, *One Word More*)

s w | s w | s w | s w | s w
There they are my fifty men and women

dactylian dimeter: (Ralph Hodgson, *Eve*)

s   w   w | s w w
Eve, with her basket was
s   w   w | s   w   w
Deep in the bells and grass

The foot of versification not only differs from the phonological foot by not always beginning with a stressed syllable. Unlike the phonological foot, the foot of versification also has a regular recurrent pattern which creates the characteristic purified rhythm of much poetic language. Such a purified rhythm is very different from the 'prose rhythm' of ordinary speech. The foot of versification and its organisation of metrical lines then contribute in an important way to the characteristics of poetic language. At the same time as they mark poetic language as different from ordinary 'prose' language, feet and metre create a norm or expected standard for poets to follow or deliberately deviate from. Although it thus leads a different life in poetic language, the foot of ordinary prose language shares with the foot of versification the structural unity that they both span or encompass a string of stressed and unstressed syllables. Verse is then a good example of how the phonological structure of rhythm, in particular how the phonological structure of what could be called a purified or perfect rhythm, is put to use, however restricted this use may be.

7.4.3 Main points about rhythm
The main points about rhythm may be summarised as follows:

- Rhythm is the regular recurrence of some prominent element which produces the perceptual heartbeat of speech
- Each stressed syllable governs the rhythm of NAERD. Therefore the rhythm of NAERD is stress-based
- Each unit of rhythm which in NAERD begins with a stressed syllable is called a foot. Each foot is approximately of the same length
- The foot is not only an important structural unit in the description of rhythm, but it also constitutes the domain of a number of phonological rules

- The foot is also an important unit in the description of the metrical structure of verse. The foot of versification has a less restricted structure than the foot of 'prose' language.

Further reading
A very good introduction to English word stress can be found in Giegerich 1992. See also Laver 1994, and Bauer et al 1980, the latter dealing with American English. A comprehensive account is Halle & Keyser 1971 or Chomsky and Halle 1968. On the use of rhythm in verse, see Wales 2001, Leech 1969.

CHAPTER 8

Intonation in American English

8.1 The nature and function of intonation

The previous chapter explored the stress of individual words (compounds as well as non-compounds) and adduced rules which account for the assignment of stress to words of two or more syllables or to compound words. It was established that the prominence of a stressed syllable is produced by long duration, greater muscular effort, usually distinct vowel quality and not least by the presence of pitch. As a rule, the tone of lexical stress has a falling pitch in NAERD. But not only do monosyllabic words also receive stress when they occur in a string of continuous speech. The pitch used in a given utterance to mark a stressed syllable is also not always a falling one. It may be rising, falling-rising or level and it may involve a wide or a narrow pitch range. This and the following sections deal with the stress and pitch pattern of continuous NAERD speech and explore how such phenomena can be described in a systematic way. Following common practice, such patterns will be referred to as the **intonation** of NAERD.

Before we look at the pitch patterns of NAERD, it is appropriate to specify in more detail what the term intonation implies and how it differs from the also widely used term tone. The two terms, intonation and tone, refer to two distinct ways in which pitch is used in languages. In **tone languages** pitch serves the phonological function of distinguishing individual words or individual syllables. As an example of a word-based tone language, Swedish or Norwegian may be mentioned. Take for example the two Swedish words *anden* 'the spirit' and *anden* 'the duck' whose pitch contours are represented in (8.1a). The first word is characterised by a single fall in pitch, whereas the second is characterised by a fall-rise-fall pitch, and these tone features alone distinguish the two words. As another example, consider the Etsako words shown in (8.1b) (Etsako is a language spoken in Nigeria) in which different tones are associated with different syllables. Again, in this language the syllable-bound tones alone keep the words apart. (For the implications of transcribing tone between two horizontal lines, see the discussion in the following paragraph).

(8.1)

a. Swedish   *anden* 'the duck'   *anden* 'the spirit'

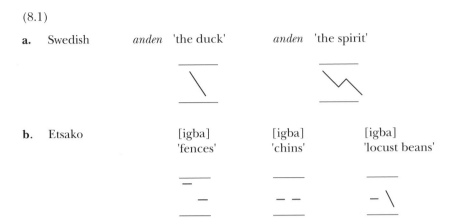

b. Etsako   [igba]   [igba]   [igba]
                  'fences'   'chins'   'locust beans'

NAERD, like other English accents, does not employ tone as exemplified by Swedish or Etsako. Instead NAERD is an **intonation language**. This means that pitch is not associated with single syllables and single words, but is distributed over a larger unit than the word such as the phrase or the sentence. This unit is referred to as the **tone group**.

As a way of determining what exactly it means that a language is intonation-based, consider the utterance *Is there another organ in the church?* The pitch or intonation of this utterance may be represented as shown in (8.2):

(8.2)

Is there another organ in the church?

The two horizontal lines represent the width of the pitch span and the strokes in between syllables. The top line represents the potentially highest pitch limit of a given speaker and the bottom line the potentially lowest pitch limit of a given speaker. It is important to stress that these lines represent relative and not absolute values. What this representation shows is that an intonation-based language like English (and in fact many other European languages) has a systematic melody and that this melody varies depending on which part of the utterance we look at. Clearly, (8.2) contains two different melodic chunks: one which encompasses *church* and only this syllable and another which encompasses all the syllables preceding *church*. The former is the most prominent syllable of the utterance. This syllable is called the **nucleus**. What is characteristic of this syllable in (8.2) is that it is associated with stress and a dynamic tone, in particular a rising tonal glide. On the other hand, the chunk preceding the nucleus, which is called the **head** and which consists of less prominent stressed syllables (marked as long strokes) and unstressed syllables (marked as short strokes), is intoned at the same pitch level, in particular at a level which is a little below medium pitch level. If the nucleus is followed by one or more syllables, as in an utterance like (8.3):

(8.3)

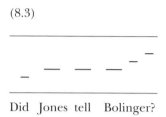

Did Jones tell   Bolinger?

these syllables mark the rising quality of the nucleus by stepping up in pitch. They can also mark a step down in pitch, depending on the type of nucleus used in the utterance in question. Such post-nuclear syllables are known as the **tail**.

§ 8.2 below explores the finer details of the structure of the tone group, i.e. head, nucleus and tail. What is important to observe at this juncture is the systematic and recurrent pattern which is characteristic of an intonation-based language like English. It is important to observe that continuous speech is organised in tone groups and that these, as a rule, consist of head, nucleus and tail. The reservation 'as a rule' refers to the fact that only the nucleus is an obligatory element of the tone group. Head and tail are optional elements but they are very often present.

Tone in tone languages, like Swedish, serves the function of identifying lexical meanings as was illustrated in (8.1). Tone has a contrastive function just like phonemes in these languages. The function of intonation in an intonation-based language like English is also to express meaning, but not lexical meaning. If the tone group as a whole is considered, then the function of intonation is to specify the **information structure** of utterances. It signals what is **new information**, i.e. information not shared by hearer and speaker, and what is **given information**, i.e. presupposed information, that is, information shared by speaker and hearer. New information is associated with the nucleus, the most prominent part of the tone group. Given information is associated with the head of the tone group. If we narrow the scope to a consideration of the nucleus only (plus the tail if present), then the function of intonation can still be said to contribute to the meaning of utterances. In particular, the intonational variation found in this part of the tone group signifies i) **attitudes** of the speaker, ii) **utterance types** and iii) **grammatical** distinctions. As an example of the first function, consider the two nucleus types shown in (8.4a) and (8.4b), which are both possible pronunciations of the utterance *would you mind closing the door*:

(8.4)

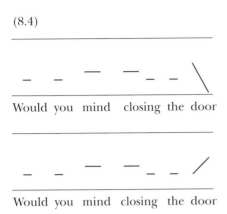

Would you mind   closing the door

Would you mind   closing the door

The first possibility (a), with a falling nucleus, would be used if the speaker is
annoyed/irritated or simply wants to issue a command, whereas the second one
(b), with a rising nucleus, would not be used in a context of irritation but signals
the speaker's polite request. That variation in the nucleus (and tail if present)
can lead to a different utterance type, the second function mentioned above,
may be illustrated with a statement like (8.5a), which is normally pronounced
with a falling nucleus. However, if it is pronounced with a rising pitch as in
(8.5b), it will be interpreted as a (yes/no)-question:

(8.5)

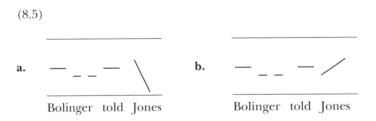

a.   b.

Bolinger told Jones   Bolinger told Jones

So that the pronunciation in (8.5b) corresponds to the meaning conveyed by
the *yes/no*-utterance type, '*did Bolinger tell Jones?*'. Finally, as an example of the
third category that intonation may express grammatical distinctions, consider
the two different nucleus assignments in (8.6). In (8.6a), the first syllable in
naturally constitutes the nucleus, while in (8.6b) the second syllable in *behave*
carries the main prominence.

(8.6)

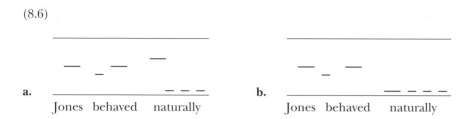

a.   Jones   behaved   naturally   b.   Jones   behaved   naturally

These two different nucleus assignments can be said to have grammatical function because in (8.6a) the intonation signals that *naturally* is an integrated adverbial (adjunct) and in (8.6b) that it is a non-integrated adverbial (disjunct).
In (8.6a), *naturally* means 'in a natural way' and in (8.6b) *naturally* means 'as
might be expected' or 'of course'.

To summarise: in an intonation-based language like NAERD, pitch is linguistic behaviour which is associated with and distributed over strings of speech.
This behaviour is **systematic**, displaying recurrent structural pitch chunks (head,
nucleus and tail) which may be replaced by other pitch chunks resulting in different communicative and particularly attitudinal meanings. Intonation is also
conventional in that there is tacit agreement between speakers employing this
pitch pattern that specific pitch patterns signal specific meanings without this
following from the physiological property of the pitch. Finally, it should be
stressed that intonation is **language specific**. The intonation is not the same in
all intonation-based languages, but each language has its own system. Intonation may even be accent-specific. For example, the intonation of NAERD is not
completely the same as the intonation of English English RP.

8.2 What is represented between the two horizontal lines?

In the previous section intonational patterns of NAERD (as well as the tones of
tone-based languages) were represented between two horizontal lines, but very
little was said about this system of representation. This section explains in more
detail the implications of this very common way of representing linguistic pitch.

Consider for this purpose the following tonetic transcription:

(8.7)

Did   he   have   to   tell   Bolinger   as   soon   as   they   had   received   the   prize?

In this transcription system, the upper horizontal line represents the highest pitch limit of a given speaker and the bottom horizontal line the lowest pitch level of a given speaker. In other words, the interval between the two horizontal lines constitutes the **pitch span** of a given speaker. Between the horizontal lines, long strokes represent stressed syllables and short strokes unstressed syllables. The relative position of a stroke or a dot between the two lines represents the relative pitch level of the syllable in question. It is important to emphasise that this pitch level is **relative** and not absolute. Placing one syllable at a given pitch level within the two horizontal lines simply reflects this syllable's pitch level as compared with the pitch level of its neighbouring syllables. The placement reflects that it is judged higher, lower or as being at the same level as its neighbouring syllables. The transcription system is also relative in another sense in that what is represented between the two lines is as much a representation of the pitch in the speech of a large man as a representation of the pitch in the speech of a small child.

The last stressed syllable in (8.7) is different from the other stressed syllables in this utterance. Not only is it the most prominent of all the syllables (the nucleus). It is also pronounced with a **dynamic** pitch contour. By this is meant that the pitch level changes during the articulation of this syllable. In particular, it starts off with a pitch value whose level is a little below medium level and rises to a level which is a little above medium level. This is represented by the slanting stroke. Other dynamic contours than a **rise** are also possible. The dynamic change may also involve a **fall**, a **fall-rise** or a **rise-fall**. The extension of the dynamic change may also vary. The extension of the rise associated with *prize* in (8.7) does not involve the entire pitch span. But in NAERD it is possible to pronounce a syllable with a fall which extends over almost the entire pitch span. Such a fall would be represented (if it is associated with an utterance final monosyllabic nucleus as in (8.7)) with a stroke which starts near the top line and falls to the bottom line.

As observed already, strokes represent stressed syllables and dots unstressed syllables. This implies that the overall melody of the utterance is represented in terms of syllables, not in terms of individual consonants and vowels. The reason for this is that every syllable in NAERD obligatorily contains a voiced segment (a vowel or a sonorant consonant, cf. Ch. 4, 5) and different pitch levels are produced by different rates of voicing. Pitch is then naturally linked to syllables. But it is important to stress that this **interlinear** transcription in terms of syllables represents a simplification of the actual pitch variation found in real utterances. It does not show all the pitch variations but only the pitch of the dominant vowel frequencies, i.e. those of the stressed syllables. This is because the human ear does not perceive the pitch variation in unstressed syllables. Nor does the interlinear transcription express pitch differences of brief duration and within a narrow pitch span. For this reason, many prominent syllables are shown in the system as level and without micro-variations.

Below in § 8.7 this interlinear transcription is replaced by a simpler and less explicit transcription system, which specifies only stressed syllables and marks the pitch of the nucleus with a stress mark which is different from that used to specify other stressed syllables. But some knowledge of the NAERD pitch pattern is required before this simpler system can be introduced and understood. This knowledge is best acquired by using the more explicit interlinear transcription system. Therefore the new simpler transcription system will not be introduced before the reader has become familiar with NAERD intonation by reading and using the interlinear transcription system.

8.3 The tone group – structure and demarcation

8.3.1 Structure

In an intonation-based language like NAERD, a stretch of continuous speech is organised into what in § 8.1 was called tone groups. This section explores in detail the internal structure of the tone group of NAERD.

A tone group is an information unit to which a recurrent intonation contour applies. § 8.1 established that the tone group may contain up to three elements: firstly, an obligatory syllable which is more prominent than any other syllable in the tone group. This syllable is called the **nucleus**. The obligatory status of the nucleus means that if a tone group consists of only one syllable, then this syllable necessarily constitutes the nucleus. Secondly, the tone group may contain two optional elements. These two optional elements are called the **head** and the **tail**. The head comprises all the pre-nucleus syllables and the tail comprises all the post-nucleus syllables. Head and tail may be present or absent independently of one another.

Because it is the most prominent syllable of the tone group, the nucleus has what will be called **primary accent**. A syllable with primary accent is characterised by: i) strong prominence and ii) either a dynamic tone, if the nucleus is tone group-final, or a static tone followed by a downward/upward shift of tone (or sometimes no shift of tone) if the nucleus is tone group non-final, i.e. if the tone group has a tail. In addition, the nucleus contains such properties as longer duration and distinct rather than blurred vowel quality, but these two properties are found in all NAERD stressed syllables and not just in syllables with primary accent.

In the unmarked or neutral pronunciation of an utterance in NAERD, the nucleus falls on the last potentially prominent (stressed) syllable. Thus in the following utterances, the typical pattern is for the nucleus to fall on -*ceived* in (8.8a) and *Bo-* in (8.8b):

(8.8)

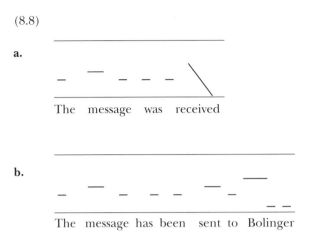

a.

The   message   was   received

b.

The   message   has been   sent   to   Bolinger

This nucleus placement signals that the new information occurs at the end of the utterance, i.e. what is focused on is the reception in (8.8a) and that Bolinger got the message in (8.8b). At the same time, this pattern also signals that 'the message' is presupposed knowledge and that this knowledge probably appears from the context.

The system of options for selecting the primary stress or nucleus is referred to as the **tonicity** of the tone group. If the primary accent falls on the last potentially prominent syllable, the tonicity is said to be **unmarked**. **Marked** tonicity, on the other hand, is when the primary stress falls on a different syllable than the last potentially prominent syllable. For example, if the primary stress is promoted to the first syllable of *message* in (8.8a), the special effect is to focus on the fact that the message reached it destination but that, by contrast, something else did not. This marked tonicity is shown in (8.9) (which has a rising tail because it is a statement question):

(8.9)

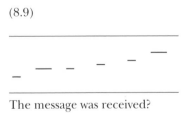

The message was received?

The nucleus is divided into subtypes. In particular, the present account will operate with the following five types: **fall, rise, fall-rise, rise-fall and level**. The first three of these nucleus types involve a shift in pitch level either in the form of a glide or in the form of a step-wise shift. Moreover, the first two may vary as to where within the pitch span they start and as to where within the pitch span they end. The last is static and does not involve any variation in pitch level. The exact details of these nucleus types as well as their communicative functions will be dealt with in § 8.4.

The tone group in (8.8b) contains not only a nucleus, as it should, but also a head and a tail. The **head** extends from the beginning of the tone group and to the nucleus, i.e. in (8.8b) the head comprises the syllables *the message has been sent to.* The tail comprises any syllable which follows the nucleus. Thus in (8.8b) the tail is the component part which consists of the two last syllables of *Bolinger.* (8.10) gives two more examples of utterances with all three components present, with indications of which is which:

(8.10)

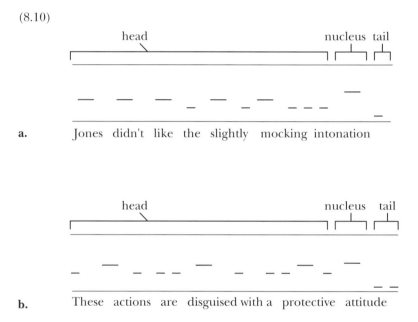

It is apparent from the examples in (8.8) – (8.10) that the pitch level of the stressed syllables of the head is a little below medium level and that the pitch level of the unstressed syllables of the head is a little below the level of the stressed syllables. This head structure is referred to as **medium head**. Medium head is the neutral and unmarked pitch level for NAERD heads. But heads can also be high or low. **High heads,** which are characteristic of a lively, enthusiastic delivery, have a pitch level which is above medium pitch level:

(8.11)

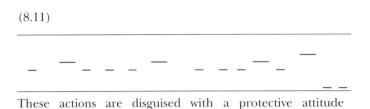

These actions are disguised with a protective attitude

Low heads, which are characteristic of parenthetic sequences, have a pitch level which is lowered to a level corresponding to that held by the unstressed syllables of medium heads, cf. (8.10).

Both (8.10a) and (8.10b) contain a **tail**. The tail is the component part of the tone group which comprises any post-nucleus material. In (8.10a) the last syllable of *intonation* constitutes the tail. In (8.10b) the two last syllables of *attitude* constitute the tail. Whilst the pitch level of the head is independent of the nucleus, the pitch level of the **tail** is bound to the nucleus and serves the function of accentuating the nature of the nucleus. For example, in both (8.10a) and (8.10b), the tail signals that the preceding nucleus is a low fall by being pronounced at a very low pitch level. Conversely, if the nucleus is a rising one, the tail contributes to this pattern by being pronounced at a higher pitch level than the nucleus, in particular, if the tail contains two or more syllables, by describing a stepwise rising contour as shown in the yes/no question in (8.12):

(8.12)

These actions disguised with a protective attitude

Are these actions disguised with a protective attitude?

Thus although it is optional, the tail when it is present in the tone group enters into a close and predictable relation with the nucleus.

It is a characteristic structure of the tone group that it contains one and only one nucleus. This syllable carries primary stress by virtue of being the most prominent syllable of the tone group. But by examining the tone group in (8.10a), for example, it is clear that the syllables *Jones, didn't, like, slight-* and *mock-* also receive stress. They differ from the syllable with primary stress (*-na-* of *intonation*) in two ways. Firstly, they are not pronounced with a dynamic pitch contour; secondly they do not involve a pitch level which differs from the level of the preceding syllables; and thirdly they are not pronounced with as much prominence as the syllable with primary stress. Such syllables carry what will be termed **secondary stress**. Finally, the remaining syllables of the tone group, all of which lack the features of those syllables which carry either primary or secondary stress, are **unstressed** syllables.

It is important to note that the syllables which receive stress (primary or secondary) in continuous speech are not just those syllables of polysyllabic words or compounds which receive lexical stress. Monosyllabic words which occur in a string also receive stress (primary or secondary) (cf. *Jones*, and *like* in (8.10a)) if they belong to the category of **content words**. The stress which is assigned to syllables in continuous speech is called **sentence stress.** Typically content words, i.e. nouns, lexical verbs, adjectives and adverbs, receive sentence stress, and, in the case of polysyllabic words and compounds, sentence stress coincides with lexical stress. But every polysyllabic word does not necessarily receive sentence stress. If a polysyllabic word belongs to the group of form words, i.e. is a preposition, conjunction, pronoun, determiner, auxiliary verb or article, then it does not in an unmarked pronunciation receive sentence stress.

The main points about the structure of the tone group are summarised below:

- The stress assigned to syllables in tone groups is called sentence stress. In polysyllabic words, sentence stress coincides with lexical stress
- The tone group can be divided into three component parts: head, nucleus and tail
- The nucleus is the only obligatory part of the tone group. The nucleus is the most prominent syllable of the tone group. It carries primary stress
- The system of options for selecting the nucleus within the tone group is called tonicity
- It is unmarked for the nucleus to fall on the last potentially prominent syllable of the tone group
- In addition to being the most prominent, the syllable with primary stress is also characterised by either a dynamic pitch or a static pitch followed by a shift in pitch level (except when the primary accent is level)
- The prominent syllables which occur in the head and the tail carry secondary stress. They do not involve as strong prominence as the syllable with primary stress; nor do they display the pitch features of the syllable with primary accent.

8.3.2 Demarcation

§ 8.2.1 established that continuous speech is made up of strings of information units, the so-called tone groups, each of which is constructed around a nucleus, the obligatory syllable with primary stress. § 8.2.1 also looked at the structure of the tone group and established the terminology used to describe its component parts. This section will explore how the boundaries between the tone groups are drawn and what principles govern such a demarcation.

Corresponding to the term tonicity, which was used in the previous section to refer to the system of options for selecting the nucleus of the tone group, this section will use the term **tonality** to refer to the system of options for placing boundaries between tone groups. To illustrate how the system of tonality works consider the following passage:

(8.13)

> Judge Charles Richey| would not talk with us directly| but when a third party asked Judge Richey about these matters| he asserted| that he had never met or spoken to John Dean| at any time about any subject ||

In this passage, vertical terminal bars have been inserted to mark tone group boundaries. A tone group terminated by double bars (||) is **final**, whereas a tone group terminated by a single bar (|) is **non-final**.

The placement of boundaries in (8.13) is **unmarked**. This means that the tonality as shown in (8.13) is what one would expect in a neutral pronunciation of this passage. But if the number of boundaries is increased, as shown in (8.14), by inserting two extra single bars (after *party* and after *met*), the tonality of the passage would still remain unmarked:

(8.14)

> Judge Charles Richey| would not talk with us directly| but when a third party| asked Judge Richey about these matters| he asserted| that he had never met| or spoken to John Dean| at any time about any subject ||

Similarly, a tonality with fewer boundaries than those used in (8.13) as displayed in (8.15), which lacks a boundary after *Richey* and *asserted*:

(8.15)

> Judge Charles Richey would not talk with us directly| but when a third party asked Judge Richey about these matters| he asserted that he had never met or spoken to John Dean| at any time about any subject ||

is also not marked. However, if the number of boundaries is reduced even further to the point where there is only one after *matters*, the result is **marked** tonality, because the effect would be that of reeling off the utterance by heart without thinking about the meaning. Analogously, inserting yet more boundaries than those already present in (8.14) as shown in (8.16):

(8.16)

> Judge Charles Richey| would not talk| with us| directly| but when a third party| asked| Judge Richey| about these matters| he asserted| that he had never met| or spoken| to John Dean| at any time| about any subject ||

would also make the tonality of the passage marked. Such a pronunciation would resemble the delivery characteristic of dictation which in its extreme form has a boundary after each word.

It should be clear from these examples that the distinction between marked and unmarked tonality is not a clear-cut one. It has to be accepted that a grey-zone exists between not only how few boundaries count as marked and how few count as unmarked, but also between how many boundaries count as unmarked and how many count as marked. The impossibility of drawing a clear limit between marked and unmarked tonality reflects the fact that tonality varies according to the speech situation in question (register). As a rule, informal conversation language will have fewer boundaries, formal conversation will, usually, have more boundaries, whereas the language of, say, lecture rooms or church rooms will contain many boundaries. An important factor determining the number of boundaries is then how much effort the speaker puts into getting his message across to the listener.

Whilst the number of boundaries may vary within a certain limit, there is less leeway with respect to the location of the boundaries. It is unmarked for tone group boundaries to coincide with the boundaries between **major syntactic categories**. The boundaries between major syntactic categories are the boundaries which fall between **sentence elements** (subject, verb, complement, adverbial), **phrase elements** (premodification, head, postmodification), **co-ordinated structures** and those between **subclause and matrix clause**. As an example of how this pattern of coincidence is observed, consider the following syntactic representation of the passage in (8.14) with the tone group boundaries inserted:

(8.17)

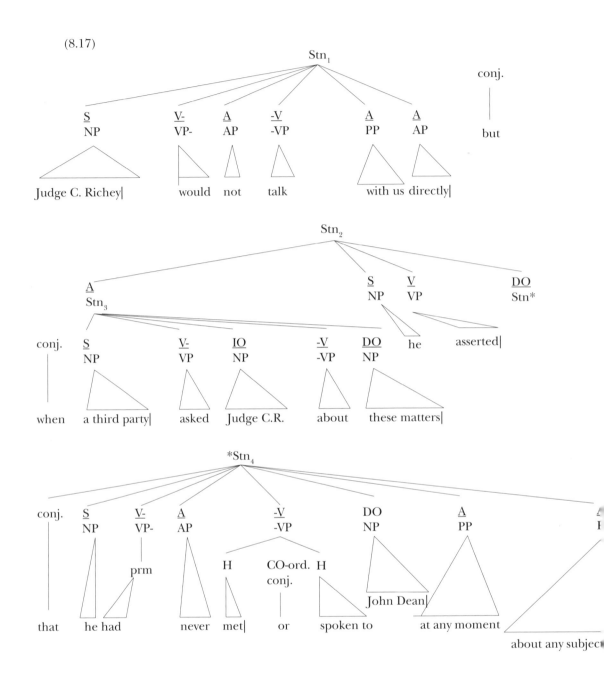

As can be seen from (8.17), tone group boundaries coincide with major syntactic boundaries. In particular, the first single bar coincides with the boundary between subject and predicate, the second single bar coincides with the boundary between two co-ordinated sentences, the third single bar coincides again with the boundary between subject and predicate, the fourth single bar coincides with the boundary between (part of) adverbial and subject (of the matrix clause), the fifth single bar coincides with the boundary between verb and direct object, the sixth single bar coincides with the boundary between two co-or-dinated verbs and the seventh single bar coincides with the boundary between direct object and adverbial.

As further illustration that this hypothesis of co-incidence between tone group boundary and major syntactic boundary is a valid one, consider the option that a tone group boundary is inserted between a preposition and the prepositional complement (for example between *with* and *us* in sentence 1) or between a de-terminer and the nominal element of a noun phrase (for example between *these* and *matters* in the sentence 2) or between an auxiliary verb and the head of the verb phrase (for example, between *had* and (*never) met* in sentence 4). Clearly, such boundary placements would be very odd and highly marked, exactly be-cause they do not coincide with major syntactic boundaries. This does not mean that such options are completely ruled out. It merely means that they are not the obvious choice in a neutral pronunciation in e.g. running conversation, but would be in dictation.

It is not just grammatical cues which may serve to identify tone group bound-aries. Phonetic cues such as **length** and **pitch variation** also help identify the de-marcations. In particular, the material which precedes a boundary has longer duration and /or involves a shift in pitch, so that it stands out, to a greater or lesser extent, as different from the material which follows the boundary, unless, of course, the tone group is final. As illustration of how these cues help identify tone group boundaries, consider the following transcription of (8.14):

(8.18)

Judge Charles Richey| would not talk with us directly| but when a third party|

asked Judge Richey about these matters| he asserted| that he had never met| or

spoken to John Dean| at any time about any subject ||

Observe first that before '|' (single bar) the nucleus may have any of the following realisations: LR(= low rise), MF (= mid fall), L (= level) and FR (= fall-rise). FR is particularly found in tone groups with marked tonicity, whereas LR, MF and L are used in tone groups with unmarked tonicity. Before '||' (double bar) , LF (= low fall) and MR (= mid rise) are the most common nucleus types, the first type being used in statements and *wh*-questions, the latter in *yes/no*-questions and statement questions with unmarked tonicity. The following section looks at these nucleus types and their use in greater detail.

The phonetic cues which signal tone group boundaries in (8.18) may be summarised as follows:

The **first** boundary (after *Richey*) has before it a relatively long (and prominent) syllable followed by an unstressed syllable which is at a higher pitch level than the long (and prominent) syllable. On the other side of the boundary the pitch level has fallen to a level which is a little above the lowest level.

The **second** boundary (after *directly*) has before it a relatively long (and prominent) syllable whose pitch level is a little higher than the pitch level of the prominent syllables preceding it. This syllable is then followed by an unstressed syllable which has stepped down to a lower pitch. On the other side of the boundary, the successive unstressed syllables are pronounced at a lower pitch level.

The **third** boundary (after *party*) is marked primarily by the longer (and more prominent) syllable preceding the boundary. Pitch level plays a minor part in signalling the division between the two tone groups, this being by and large the same on either side of this boundary.

The **fourth** boundary (after *matters*) has before it a long (and prominent) syllable followed by an unstressed syllable at the same pitch level. On the other side of the boundary, the pitch level of the two successive unstressed syllables has fallen to a low level.

The **fifth** boundary (after *asserted*) has before it a long (and prominent) syllable at a low pitch level which is then followed by an unstressed syllable which has stepped up to a pitch level a little below medium level, i.e. to a higher pitch level. On the other side of the boundary, the pitch level of the three successive unstressed syllables has fallen to a low level.

The **sixth** boundary (after *met*) has immediately before it a relatively long (and prominent) syllable whose pitch level starts close to the lowest pitch level and glides to a pitch level which is a little below medium level. On the other side of the boundary, the pitch has fallen to a low level.

The **seventh** boundary (after *Dean*) has immediately before it a long (and prominent) syllable which starts at a medium pitch level and glides to a level a little above the bottom level. On the other side of the boundary, the immediately following unstressed syllable is pronounced at a low pitch level.

The **last** boundary (after *subject*) has before it a long (and prominent) syllable at medium pitch level followed by an unstressed syllable which has stepped down to a level close to the lowest pitch level. This kind of fall in pitch is the unmarked signal of a final declarative utterance.

It should be apparent from this summary that the most important factors which contribute to the phonetic signalling of tone group boundaries are variation in pitch level on either side of the boundaries, length and prominence of the nucleus and sometimes the presence of syllables with dynamic tones.

Given the information summarised in specifically (8.17) and (8.18), the main points about the demarcation of tone groups can be stated as follows:

- The system of options for placing tone group boundaries is referred to as tonality
- Tonality is unmarked if tone group boundaries coincide with major syntactic boundaries
- It is impossible to predict exactly how many tone group boundaries a given string of utterances will contain. There is a grey zone between what counts as an appropriate number of boundaries and what counts as too few and what counts as too many boundaries
- Tone group boundaries are signalled by duration and prominence, change in pitch level and occasionally dynamic pitch contours.

8.4 The classification of nucleus types

8.4.1 Simplex and complex nuclei

As the component part of the tone group which signals new information, the nucleus is the most prominent part of the tone group. The previous section established that this prominence is achieved through strong stress, long duration and not least pitch. It was also established that by pitch is meant **variation in pitch** level either such that the nucleus changes in pitch during its articulation or such that the pitch level of the nucleus differs from the pitch level of the following syllable(s). The first possibility is found when the nucleus is the last syllable of the tone group, i.e. when the tone group is tailless. The second possibility is found when the nucleus is followed by one or more syllables, i.e. when the tone group has a tail.

A second property of the nucleus, which has not been mentioned so far, is that it can be **simplex** or that it can be **complex**. The pitch of a simplex nucleus moves in one direction only. If it moves towards a lower pitch level the nucleus is a **fall**, if it moves towards a higher pitch level it is a **rise**, and if it involves neither a rise nor a fall, the nucleus is **level**. The pitch of a complex nucleus, on the other hand, moves in two directions and this can be done in two ways. Either it involves first a rise and then subsequently a fall. This is called a **rise-fall**. The second possibility is that it first falls and then rises. This kind of nucleus is called a **fall-rise**.

In principle, the simplex nuclei may begin and end anywhere within the pitch span. But following common practice, the present account will reduce this infinite variation to the following distinctive patterns:

(8.19)

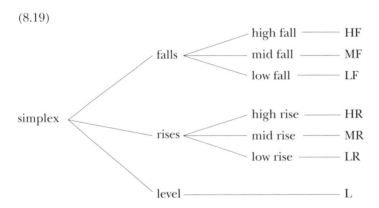

The complex nuclei will be classified as either **fall-rise** or **rise-fall**. This reduction is possible because the only kind of fall-rise that is common is low and the only rise-fall that is common is high. Thus the system of complex nuclei may be shown as follows:

(8.20)

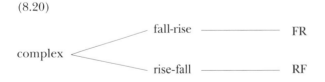

Since the use of **RF** is very restricted and only used to signal strong emphasis, it will receive no further attention in this chapter, except for the brief description in § 8.4.2 below.

8.4.2 The interpretation and transcription of simplex and complex nuclei

It is not enough to list the distinctive nucleus patterns as shown in (8.19) and (8.20). It is also necessary to describe how each subtype is realised and specify how each subtype is transcribed.

The realisation of each nucleus type depends on the exact structure of the tone group. If the nucleus is **tone group final**, the pitch variation will be realised as a glide up or down on the nucleus only. On the other hand, if the tone group contains a tail, i.e. the nucleus is **tone group non-final**, the pitch variation will be realised as a step up or step down. The exact pitch movement of these nine nucleus types appears from (8.21) in which the two utterances *Jones phoned the police* and *Jones phoned the officer* are transcribed with all the nine nucleus types given in (8.19) and (8.20) and in which each nucleus type is given a detailed description:

high fall   without a tail   with a tail

Jones phoned the police   Jones phoned the officer

The **high fall** is realised by a pitch movement which involves almost the entire pitch span. A high-fall starts at a level which is close to the highest pitch within the pitch span and then falls to the lowest level within the pitch span. If the nucleus is tone group final, the high-fall is realised as a glide; if the nucleus is tone group non-final, i.e. the tone group has a tail, the pitch movement involves a step down from the nucleus to the tail.

mid fall   without a tail   with a tail

Jones phoned the police   Jones phoned the officer

The **mid fall** is realised by a pitch movement which involves a relatively narrow part of the pitch span. A mid fall starts at medium level and falls to a level which is a little higher than the lowest level. If the nucleus is tone group final, the mid fall is realised as a glide; if the nucleus is tone group non-final, i.e. the tone group has a tail, the pitch movement involves a step down from the nucleus to the tail.

low fall   without a tail   with a tail

Jones phoned the police   Jones phoned the officer

The **low fall** is realised by a pitch movement which involves the lower part of the pitch span. A low fall starts at medium level and falls to the lowest level within the pitch span. If the nucleus is tone group final, the low fall is realised as a glide; if the nucleus is tone group non-final, i.e. the tone group has a tail, the pitch movement involves a step down from the nucleus to the tail.

high rise   without a tail   with a tail

Jones phoned the police   Jones phoned the officer

The **high rise** is realised by a pitch movement which involves the higher part of the pitch span. A high rise starts at medium level and rises to the highest level within the pitch span. If the nucleus is tone group final, the high rise is realised as a glide; if the nucleus is tone group non-final, i.e. the tone group has a tail, the pitch movement is realised as a step up from the nucleus.

mid rise   without a tail   with a tail

Jones phoned the police   Jones phoned the officer

The **mid rise** is realised by a pitch movement which involves a relatively narrow part of the pitch span. A mid rise starts at medium level and rises to a level which is a little lower than the highest level. If the nucleus is tone group final, the mid rise is realised as a glide; if the nucleus is tone group non-final, i.e. the tone group has a tail, the pitch movement is realised as a step up from the nucleus.

low rise   without a tail   with a tail

Jones phoned the police   Jones phoned the officer

The **low rise** is realised by a pitch movement which involves the low part of the pitch span. A low rise starts at the lowest level and rises to a level which is a little below medium level. If the nucleus is tone group final, the low rise is realised as a glide; if the nucleus is tone group non-final, i.e. the tone group has a tail, the pitch movement is realised as a step up from the nucleus.

level   without a tail   with a tail

Jones phoned the police   Jones phoned the officer

The **level** is realised by no pitch movement. The pitch of a level nucleus is the same as the pitch of the prominent syllables of the head. This applies to both final and non-final nuclei.

rise-fall   without a tail   with a tail

Jones phoned the police   Jones phoned the officer

The **rise-fall** is realised by a complex pitch movement which involves the entire pitch span. A rise-fall starts at medium level and always glides to the highest pitch level. If the nucleus is tone group final, the glide is continued down to the lowest pitch level. If the nucleus is tone group non-final, i.e. the tone group has a tail, the second pitch movement involves a step down.

fall-rise   without a tail   with a tail

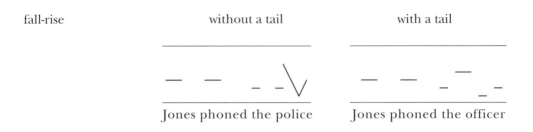

Jones phoned the police   Jones phoned the officer

The **fall-rise** is realised by a complex pitch movement which involves a low fall followed by a low rise. If the nucleus is tone group final, both pitch movements are associated with the nucleus. If the nucleus is tone group non-final, i.e. the tone group has a tail, the down glide is associated with the nucleus and the following low rise is realised either as a glide up or as steps up.

8.5 The use of the NAERD nuclei

To get an overview of the use of the NAERD nucleus types, it is useful to return to the two binary oppositions marked/unmarked and final/non-final tone groups. In NAERD, specific nuclei are unmarked in final – or to be more accurate – potentially final tone groups, i.e. those tone groups which are followed by ||. Similarly, specific nuclei are unmarked in non-final tone groups, i.e. those tone groups followed by |. § 3.5.1 explores first the patterns found in final tone groups. Since these patterns are largely predictable on the basis of utterance types, such as statement, imperative, question. § 3.5.1 lists the unmarked choice of nuclei in some very common utterance types when these are final.

8.5.1 The unmarked nuclei in final tone groups
The following common utterance types will be examined with respect to unmarked nucleus behaviour:

(8.21)
statements
yes/no questions
wh-questions
statement questions
imperatives
exclamations
echo-questions

The examination of each utterance type will follow the same pattern. Firstly, it will specify the grammatical characteristics of each utterance type; secondly, it will list the illocutionary meaning typically associated with each utterance type; thirdly, the examination specifies the most typical nucleus type associated with the utterance type in question, and, finally, the examination lists two examples of each utterance type with associated tonetic transcriptions, one with a tone group final nucleus and one with a tone group non-final nucleus.

Statements:
i) finite verb and subject verb word order.
ii) unit which provides information
iii) unmarked nucleus type: **low fall**
iv) examples:

The train was well on its way to Dundee

The train was pulling in at the platform

yes/no questions:
i) subject verb inversion
ii) unit which seeks information about a yes/no matter
iii) unmarked nucleus type: **mid rise**
iv) examples:

Has something been done?

Is something the matter?

wh-questions:
i) introduced by one of the interrogative pronouns *who, whom, whose, which, what, why, where, when, how*
ii) unit which seeks information about a specific matter with respect to identity, reason, place, time, manner
iii) unmarked nucleus type: **low fall**
iv) examples:

What is well on its way to Dundee?

When is the train pulling in at the platform?

statement questions:
i) no overt grammatical properties indicate that these are questions; presence of finite verb, normal subject verb word order
ii) unit which seeks information about a yes/no matter
iii) unmarked nucleus type: **mid rise**
iv) examples:

The staff has phoned the police?

The train is pulling in at the platform?

imperatives:
i) verb in base form; usually no surface subject present
ii) unit which instructs the listener to perform some action
iii) unmarked nucleus: **low fall**
iv) examples:

Smile your sweetest smile!

Smile and be happier!

exclamations:
i) usually no sentence structure; often introduced by *what* and *how*
ii) unit which expresses an emotional reaction such e.g. surprise, disappointment, disapproval, encouragement
iii) unmarked nucleus type: **high fall**
iv) examples:

What a sweet smile!

How delightful a president!

echo-questions:
i) no specific grammatical structure
ii) unit which expresses (feigned) disbelief in what another speaker said or (feigned) failure to hear what another speaker said
iii) unmarked nucleus type: **high rise**
iv) examples:

(8.22)

Am I a fool?   She refused to receive the letter?

From this overview, it is clear that only four nucleus types are unmarked in final tone groups: **low fall**, **mid rise**, **high rise**, and **high fall.** The way they are used in NAERD is summarised (8.23):

(8.23)

nucleus types in final tone groups:

statements
wh-questions
imperatives   LF
greetings

yes-no-questions
statement questions   MR

exclamations   }   HF

echo-questions   }   HR

It is important to note that the pattern summarised in (8.23) is not always followed. In § 8.8 below, it will be shown that specific grammatical constructions sometimes quite regularly do not comply with these general rules, even in cases which can be considered unmarked. Thus it is important to note that the overview in (8.23) represents the general and typical pattern in final tone groups, but just this.

8.5.2 The unmarked nucleus types in non-final tone groups

A non-final tone group is a tone group which in the notation used here is terminated by a single bar (|). The single bar indicates that the speaker has not finished his string of speech, that the tone group is followed by one or more tone groups. The nucleus types found in such **connected** non-final tone groups may be one of the following types:

(8.24)

nucleus types in non-final tone groups:

MF, LR, L, and FR

MF, LR, and L are particularly common and may be chosen freely. FR is less common in non-final tone groups and most often found when tonicity is marked and the nucleus does not fall on the last prominent syllable of the tone group.

The transcription of the following passage illustrates the use of the non-final nuclei:

(8.25)

Well, I can only suggest that you pursue your complaint with a member of the staff;

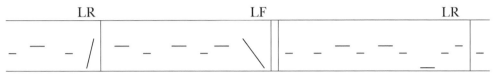

my friend and I took these seats in good faith. Can we then be held responsible for

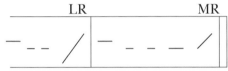

any mistakes made by the rail staff?

To understand the way intonation works in non-final tone groups, it is necessary to keep in mind that the connection between utterance type and choice of nucleus type, as summarised in (8.23), applies only to final tone groups, i.e. those followed by ||. Non-final tone groups, i.e. those followed by |, are not encompassed by these rules. Consequently, in the transcribed passage in (8.25) the two final tone groups, the first of which ends in *faith* and the second of which ends in *staff*, have the two final nucleus types, LF and MR respectively. The first has a LF because it functions as a statement, the second has a MR because it functions as a *yes/no*-question. But all the other tone groups are not encompassed by the rules that apply to final tone groups. As non-final tone groups, they are encompassed by the rules summarised in (8.24). That is, their nucleus types can be any one of the types MF, LR, L or FR. This implies that although all the tone groups before the first || can be said to constitute a statement collectively, it is only the last one which actually signals statement by having a LF. All the non-final ones do not. Similarly, although all the tone groups from the first || to the last || can be said to constitute a *yes/no*-question collectively, it is only the last one which actually signals *yes/no*-question by having a MR. All the non-final ones do not.

The main points about the nucleus types in final and non-final tone groups may be summarised as follows:

- Final tone groups are followed by || in the notation used here
- The choice of nucleus types in final tone groups is linked to the grammatical structure of the utterance which the tone group terminates
- Depending on the grammatical structure, the nucleus type of a final tone group may be a LF, MR, HF, HR
- Non-final tone groups are followed by | in the notation used here
- The nucleus types in non-final group may be a MF, LR, L or FR
- The choice of nucleus types in non-final tone groups is not linked to grammatical structure

8.6 Some communicative implications of the nucleus types

As just established in § 8.5, the unmarked nucleus patterns found in final and non-final tone groups are those shown in (8.26):

(8.26)
final: LF, MR, HF, HR
non-final: MF, LR, L, FR

This distribution of nucleus types implies that the communicative meaning of LF, MR, HF, HR must be **completeness** by virtue of the fact they occur in final tone groups, and that the communicative meaning of MF, LR, L, FR must be **incompleteness** by virtue of the fact they occur in non-final tone groups.

In the present account, it will be assumed that the main function of non-final MF, LR, L is to signal incompleteness (FR will be assumed to have a more complex function). However, it appears from the overview in (8.23) that LF, MR, HF, HR not only signal completeness. This overview also states that LF, MR, HF, and HR have additional meanings. In particular, LF signals provision of information or request for information, MR signals request for information, HF signals exclamation and HR signals amazement. But as was stressed in § 8.4.1, these meanings apply in specific grammatical structures when the situation is unmarked. But sometimes the final nucleus types appear in other utterance types than those in which their occurrence is considered unmarked. For example, an imperative has LF as the unmarked nucleus type. But sometimes an imperative may instead be associated with a MR. In this case the effect is that the imperative gets interpreted as a polite request, i.e. MR signals kindness. MR and LF as well as the non-final FR can all be said to signal special meanings when they occur in other final utterance types than those they typically appear in. In addition to the already mentioned pair **completeness/incompleteness**, these special meanings concern **certainty/uncertainty** and **kindness/unkindness**.

As illustration of how the choice of a different nucleus type affects the meaning certainty/uncertainty, consider the following statement:

(8.27)

— — ‾ — — ＼

Jones is always polite

which, if final, would be pronounced with a LF signalling not only completeness but also certainty. However, it is also possible to pronounce this utterance with a FR, as shown in (8.28). This would give it the distinctive meaning 'not quite certain' or 'reservation':

(8.28)

— — ‾ — — ＼／

Jones is always polite

i.e. the meaning uncertainty becomes dominant (it would moreover make the utterance non-final). Consider also an often cited example like the following which, if pronounced with a LF, expresses that the speaker never lends his car at all:

(8.29)

— — — — — — —

I'm not lending my car to anybody

but if pronounced with a FR expresses that he is particular about whom he lends his car to:

(8.30)

— — — — — — — —

I'm not lending my car to anybody

These examples concern the meaning certainty/uncertainty. An example illustrating how the choice of a different nucleus type affects the meaning kindness/unkindness, an imperative such as the following may be used. When pronounced with a LF, which is the norm in (final) imperatives, the meaning is neutral with respect to kindness/unkindness:

(8.31)

Please shut the door

But if it is pronounced with a MR, the utterance signals polite request, i.e. a more kind attitude. Similarly a *wh*-question, whose unmarked nucleus type is a LF, may have a MR associated with it, as shown in (8.32):

(8.32)

Who did he lend his car to?

Again the effect is to signal a kinder attitude on the part of the speaker, i.e. the enquiry is more polite.

It is also possible to use a LF in an utterance whose unmarked nucleus type is a MR with a kindness/unkindness effect. A *yes/no*-question has in an unmarked pronunciation a MR, but if it is associated with a LF as in (8.33):

(8.33)

Will you put your boots on now?

the signal it sends is unkind attitude, impatience or the meaning conveyed by an imperative.

Lastly, as an example of how completeness/incompleteness may be affected by an alternative choice of nucleus type, consider the following **enumeration**. Observe first, as will be described below in § 8.8.2, that in an enumeration each listed item constitutes a tone group on its own and that it is unmarked for each of these tone groups, except the last one, to have a non-final nucleus. The last item listed, on the other hand, has unmarked LF. This characteristic pattern of enumerations is shown in (8.34):

(8.34)

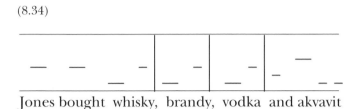

Jones bought whisky, brandy, vodka and akvavit

If, then, this pattern is violated by assigning the last tone group the same nucleus type as in the non-final tone groups, as shown in (8.35):

(8.35)

Jones bought whisky, brandy, vodka and akvavit

the effect is marked, and it signals that the list of enumerated items is not complete but could have more items added to it. That is, the meaning of completeness typically associated with the pattern in (8.34) has changed to one of incompleteness.

The interaction between communicative meaning and the occurrence of marked and unmarked nucleus types in different utterance types is summarised below

- In final statements, LF is unmarked and signals among other things certainty. If associated with a FR, this meaning is changed to uncertainty or reservation
- In final imperatives, LF is unmarked signalling, among other things, neutral attitude with respect to kindness/unkindness. If associated with a MR this meaning is changed to one of kindness
- In final *wh*-questions, LF is unmarked and the signal it sends is, among other things, neutral with respect to kindness/unkindness. If associated with a MR, this meaning is changed to one of kindness
- In final *yes/no* questions, a MR is unmarked and the signal it sends is neutral with respect to kindness/unkindness. If associated with a LF, the meaning is changed to one of unkindness or irritation

8.7 Simplified transcription

As anticipated above, it is possible to replace the interlinear transcription system with a simpler transcription system in which stress and intonation are represented jointly in terms of a total of 6 **tonetic stress marks**. This section outlines the principles of such a system.

As a start, recall the following facts about the stress system in NAERD: i) 3 degrees of stress occur in NAERD, viz. primary stress (associated with the nucleus), secondary stress (associated with all the stressed syllables except the nucleus) and no stress (associated with unstressed syllables); ii) the nucleus has associated with it either a tonal glide or a subsequent stepwise shift in pitch level, and this variation in pitch – whether it is manifested as a glide or a stepwise shift – can be one of the following types: HF, MF, LF, HR, MR, LR, FR and L.

The new simplified transcription system marks these three degrees of stress in the following way. Unstressed syllables are never marked; only stressed syllables have stress marks assigned to them. A syllable with secondary stress is marked with the traditional single apostrophe, i.e. " ' " , before the syllable which has this degree of stress. The syllable with primary stress, on the other hand, may be marked with any one of the following four stress marks, depending on the pitch pattern associated with it:

(8.36)

↘	marks HF, MF, LF
↗	marks HR, MR, LR
∨	marks FR
→	marks L

Again these marks are placed immediately before the syllable which carries primary stress. As an example of how this simplified transcription system is used to represent tone and stress, consider again the passage transcribed in (8.25), which is repeated in (8.38) and transcribed not only in terms of the interlinear transcription system but also in terms of the tonetic stress mark system:

(8.37)

→ Well, I can ˈonly sug ⌝gest that you purˈsue your comↃplaint with a ˈmember of the

Ↄstaff; my ˈfriend and⌝I ˈtook these ˈseats in ˈgood Ↄfaith. Can we ˈthen be ˈheld

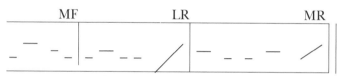

reↃsponsible for ˈany mi⌝stakes ˈmade by the ˈrail ⌝staff?

But since the point about introducing the tonetic stress mark system is to abolish the interlinear system all together, a transcription of the passage in (8.37) using only tonetic stress marks will take the form of (8.38), in which, moreover, all consonants and vowels are transcribed phonetically:

(8.38)

→ wel | aɪ kən ˈoʊnli sə⌝dʒest | ðət jʊ pərˈsu jər kəmↃpleɪnt | wɪð ə ˈmembər əv ðə

Ↄstæf | maɪ ˈfrend ənd ⌝aɪ | ˈtʊk ðiz ˈsits ɪn ˈgʊd Ↄfeɪθ || kæn wɪ ˈðen bɪ ˈheld

rɪↃspɑnsəbl | fər enɪ mɪ⌝steɪks | ˈmeɪd baɪ ðə ˈreɪl ⌝stæf ||

By comparing the two transcription systems, it is clear that the system based on tonetic stress marks is less explicit than the interlinear system. It is clearly less explicit because: i) it contains no exact clues as to the pitch level of the syllables constituting the nucleus or the nucleus and the tail if the latter is present, ii) it contains no information about the pitch span involved in the nucleus or the nucleus and the tail if the latter is present, but only indicates the direction of the pitch movement, and iii) it does not specify the pitch level of the syllables constituting the head of the tone group. In sum, the tonetic stress marks system is not as detailed and specific as the interlinear notation. Consequently, encoding and decoding tonetic stress marks require quite a detailed knowledge of the structure of intonation in NAERD. This is the reason that this chapter has started by using the interlinear system.

Obviously, more detail can be added if each tone group in the transcription given in (8.38) is specified with respect to the kind of fall and rise it contains. This may be achieved simply by attaching the already introduced abbreviations HF, MF, LF and HR, MR, LR, L to each tone group. This is shown in (8.39):

(8.39)

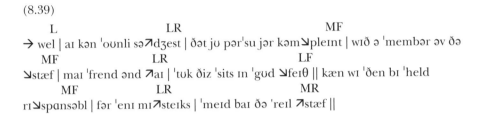

Choosing between (8.38) and (8.39) is a question of how much detail is required in a given representation. In the present context, the amount of detail specified in (8.38) will suffice, provided that such a transcription is supplied with a detailed account of the intonational patterns of NAERD. The five nucleus types of the tonetic stress marks system are then simply a further reduction of the system outlined above in section § 8.4.1, as shown in the following overview:

(8.40)

simple system   complex interlinear system
tonetic stress marks

simple system tonetic stress marks	complex interlinear system
F	HF
	MF
	LF
R	HR
	MR
	LR
FR	FR
L	L

The main characteristics of the tonetic stress marks system are summarised below:

- Tonetic stress marks indicate both stress and pitch
- Unstressed syllables are not marked in this system
- Syllables with secondary stress are marked by ' in front of them
- Syllables with primary stress are marked by one of the following stress marks: ↘, ↗, ∨, →. which indicate that the direction of pitch movement is falling, rising, falling-rising, and level respectively
- The tonetic stress marks represent an implicit system by leaving out details about the exact pitch level, pitch movement and pitch span

8.8 The intonation of some characteristic syntactic constructions

(8.41) below lists a set of seven characteristic and often occurring syntactic constructions all of which can be said to be associated with a fairly predictable intonation pattern:

(8.41)
tag questions
alternative questions/constructions
enumerations
relative clauses
adverbials
dialogue mechanism
vocatives
comment clauses

This section examines the intonation of each of these constructions. A closer examination shows that the intonation patterns of adverbials, dialogue mechanisms, vocatives and comment clauses are very similar. The same applies to alternative questions and enumerations. For these reasons, each of these two sets of constructions will be examined under one heading below. Tag questions fall outside these two groups of construction. § 8.8.1 is therefore devoted solely to this construction type.

8.8.1 Tag questions
Tag questions may be described in the following way:

Tag questions:

grammatical characteristics: kind of *yes/no*-question appended (tagged onto) a clause (matrix clause) which can be a declarative, an imperative clause or an exclamation. It contains an inverted pronoun subject (or *there*) and a primary or modal auxiliary. The finite auxiliary verb form of the matrix clause is repeated in the tag; if no auxiliary is found, a form of *do* is inserted. If the matrix clause is declarative and positive, the tag is usually negative, and if the matrix clause is declarative and negative, the tag is usually positive

communicative function: a tag question is characteristic of spoken English and functions as a marker of linguistic interaction, often with question force; it corresponds to German *nicht wahr*, French *n'est-ce-pas*

examples   You enjoyed the steak, didn't you?
Finish you meal, will you?
How well she has behaved, hasn't she?

Two questions have to be addressed when determining the intonation of tags. Firstly: does the tag constitute an independent tone group or is it intoned together with the matrix clause? And secondly: should the nucleus associated with such tag-constructions be falling, rising or falling-rising? The answer to the first question is that it is unmarked for the tag question to make up the tail partly or fully, that is, unmarked for it not to form an independent tone group. The answer to the second question depends on a set of factors, in particular the following: the grammatical properties of the matrix clause and the question force contained in the tag, and for declaratives whether both matrix and tag are positive or whether both are negative or whether they have the most common structure, matrix positive and tag negative or matrix negative and tag positive, i.e. opposite values. (8.42) sums up the correlation between type of matrix clause and choice of nucleus type in both marked and unmarked cases:

(8.42)

matrix clause	*unmarked nucleus type*	*marked nucleus type*
declarative (opposite values)	FR	LF
declarative (same values)	FR	
exclamation	LF	
imperative	LF	FR

(8.43) lists examples of all eight types of pattern with tonetic stress marks added:

(8.43)

	FR	LF
declarative (opposite values)	he has 'killed the ⌄cat, 'hasn't he	it is 'very ⌄cold, 'isn't it
	FR	
declarative (same values)	you'd ⌄like that 'would you	
	LF	
exclamation	how 'well she ⌄sings, 'doesn't she	
	LF	FR
imperative	'shut the ⌄door, 'will you	'keep your 'mouth ⌄shut, 'will you

That the otherwise relatively uncommon nucleus type, FR, is the norm in tags following declaratives is to do with two facts: i) that tonicity is marked in that the tag constitutes the tail and the primary accent does not fall on the last potentially prominent syllable, and ii) that the second part of this complex nucleus type is a rise and, all other things being equal, a rising intonation is characteristic of a *yes/no*-question. This implies that the use of FR in connection with tags after declaratives mostly functions like a question, or at least has the effect of leaving it open to the listener to agree or disagree with the speaker. When the nucleus type is not FR but LF, the implication is that the listener is expected to agree with the speaker. Thus the example *it is 'very ⌄cold, 'isn't it* pronounced with a LF would be a natural pronunciation when it is twenty below zero.

Whilst tags after exclamations do not allow the same variation as after declaratives (because there is very little admixture of a question in an exclamation), tags after imperatives can be both LF and FR. LF is the unmarked possibility and signals simply that the whole utterance is a directive. But the other possibility that the nucleus type is a FR signals that the utterance as a whole is now a mixture of a directive and a question. This pronunciation would be natural in a context where the speaker wishes to soften the directive and express a kind attitude.

In general, the intonation of tags is a complex matter. It is also possible that the tag constitutes a separate tone group. This and other possibilities have not been discussed here. In a basic introduction like the present one, the general patterns shown in (8.42) and (8.43) will suffice.

8.8.2 Alternative questions/constructions and enumerations

The intonation of alternative constructions shares many features with the intonation of enumerations. For this reason, these two types of construction will be treated together here.

alternative questions/constructions

grammatical characteristics	an alternative construction is a question or a statement that consists of two parts between which the speaker can choose
communicative function	unit which seeks or provides information about a choice between two possibilities
examples	She may go shopping or she may go camping Is he from Edinburgh or Glasgow?

enumerations

grammatical characteristics	construction which names items on a list one by one
communicative function	unit which provides information about the items on a list one by one
examples	The box contained beer, juice, milk and mineral water We have dealt with questions, statements, imperatives and exclamations

For both these two types of construction, the following patterns are unmarked:

i)   to let each of the items listed individually constitute a tone group (it is also unmarked for short alternative constructions to constitute one tone group)

ii) for all tone groups except the last one to have non-final nucleus types

iii) for the last tone group to have a LF, if the alternative construction or enumeration is finished and leaves no more possibilities open

iv) for the last tone group to have a MR or FR, if the alternative construction or enumeration is unfinished or open-ended

(8.44) below lists two examples of alternative constructions, the first of which is not open-ended and the second of which is open-ended:

(8.44)

                           LR   LF

a.   He may 'go to ↗Melbourne | or he may 'go to ↘Sidney

                           LR   MR

b.   Would you 'like ↗red 'wine | or ↗white 'wine

Accordingly, because it is not open-ended, (8.44a) has a LF in the last tone group, whereas (8.44b) has one of the non-final nucleus types in the last tone group, as the enumeration is open-ended. Recall that the nucleus type in the first tone group in both examples may be any of the non-final ones.

Similar examples illustrating the intonation pattern found in enumerations are given in (8.45). Again (8.45a) is not open-ended whilst (8.45b) is open-ended:

(8.45)

                        LR   LR   LR

a.   We have 'dealt with ↗questions | ↗statements | im↗peratives | and

                 LF

    excla↘mations

b.   LR   LR   LR   MR

    There were ↗carrots | ↗leeks | ↗radishes |and ↗peas

and again the pattern is that the non-open-ended list of items in (8.45a) has the final nucleus type LF associated with the last tone group, whilst the open-ended list of items in (8.45b) has a non-final nucleus type associated with the last tone group, signalling that more items could be added to the list. In both instances, the nuclei in the non-final tone groups are the non-final type LR, but they could be any one of the non-final nucleus types.

8.8.3 Relative clauses

Relative clauses may be **restrictive** and **non-restrictive**. (8.46) lists examples of each type:

(8.46)

a.
restrictive: The man she is going to marry is the richest person in Norway
                     The person who did that is an idiot
                     He was definitely one of the nicest persons that I have ever met

b.
non-restrictive: Peter, who lives in Norway, is a very rich man
                      The rich Dane, to whom I addressed the letter, now lives in Norway

The tonality varies according to which of the two types of relative clause a given sequence contains. Non-restrictive relative clauses are preceded and followed by terminal boundaries. The first boundary is a |, the second also a | if the relative clause is non-final and a || if it is final. Thus the tonality of the examples in (8.46b) is as shown below:

(8.47)
                    Peter | who lives in Norway | is a very rich man
                    The Norwegian | to whom I addressed the letter | now lives in Denmark

In addition, non-restrictive relative clauses are often pronounced at a lower pitch level and delivered more rapidly than what precedes and follows them.

The tonality of restrictive relative clauses is not quite so simple as that of the non-restrictive ones. As a rule, they are followed by a terminal boundary, either | or ||. Whether they are also preceded by a boundary, in particular a |, depends on the length of the sequence which precedes the restrictive relative clause. If this sequence is very short, as in the first example in (8.46a), there is no boundary at the beginning of the relative clause. The distribution of boundaries in this example would then be as shown in (8.48):

(8.48)
                    The man she is going to marry | is the richest person in Norway

On the other hand, if the sequence preceding the restrictive relative clause is long, as in the third example in (8.46a), there is usually a boundary before the relative clause:

(8.49)

He was definitely one of the nicest persons | that I have ever met

Finally, if both restrictive relative clause and the sequence which precedes it are very short, no boundaries are inserted at all. This may be illustrated by the second example in (8.46a) which would have a boundary after *idiot* only.

The nucleus types found in relative clauses do not differ from those found in other final and non-final utterance types. This is the reason that this brief discussion of relative clauses has focused on tonality only.

8.8.4 Sentence adverbials, dialogue mechanisms, comment clauses and vocatives

As stated above sentence adverbials, dialogue mechanisms, comment clauses and vocatives are intoned in roughly the same way. For this reason, they will be treated together in this section. Consider first a description of the four construction types:

sentence adverbials

grammatical characteristics	adverbial consisting of one or more words which does not modify one utterance element alone, but the utterance as a whole and, thus has a peripheral status to utterance structure. Sentence adverbials occur initially (I-position), medially (M-position) and in terminal position (T-position)
communicative function	to comment on the information of the utterance or the style in which it is pronounced; a third possibility is that they have conjunction-like function
examples	Fortunately, the Norwegian acted naturally He had to leave, however Strictly speaking, it was a stupid thing to do She evidently didn't like the Norwegian The Norwegian couldn't see the point, as a matter of fact The Norwegian of course had to leave early On the other hand, there was no point trying again

dialogue mechanisms

grammatical characteristics   usually short sentences which occur before, in the middle of or after direct speech. Dialogue mechanisms occur in I-position, M-position and T-position

communicative function   to specify who the speaker of the direct speech is

examples   She said, "I don't want to marry the Norwegian."
"The Norwegian," she remarked, "is not very rich."
"I'm not going to marry him," she told everybody else

comment clauses

grammatical characteristics   incomplete sentences consisting of either a first person personal pronoun or a second person personal pronoun plus a finite verb but without a complement, or a subjectless non-finite clause. Comment clauses occur in I-position, M-position and T-position and are loosely attached to the matrix clause

communicative function   to establish contact between speaker and listener. When *I* is subject, the function is to express speaker's attitude or degree of certainty; when *you* is subject, the function is to catch and maintain the listener's attention

examples   You see, she is going to marry that Norwegian
I do, I have to admit, rather like the Norwegian
It is difficult to tell, you know
I don't know whether she will do it, to be honest,
Crudely speaking, there were about 100 guests

vocatives

grammatical characteristics   a noun phrase whose head may be a proper noun, a common noun or a pronoun which is a term of address. Vocatives appear in I-position, M-position and T-position.

communicative function	may have several functions: to serve as an opener of conversations, to ensure that the listener knows he is being addressed, to describe the addressee in a positive or negative way or as a means of showing respect for the addressee
examples	Monica, could you do that again? There is, your lordship, no reason to worry How do you like that, honey? Mr President, is this sufficient? Can't you see, you idiot, that this is the whole idea Answer the door, somebody

The intonational patterns of these four construction types may be summarised as follows. In **I-position**, the general pattern for all four construction types is that they all constitute independent tone groups and their nuclei may be any one of the non-final ones (and sometimes also MR). In **M-position**, the pattern is also very often the same in all construction types. In M-position they normally constitute (a part of) the tail, the only exception being one-word sentence adverbials which form part of the head of the tone group. In **T-position**, all four construction types again follow the same pattern. In this position, they constitute (part of) the tail. These observations are summarised in the following overview:

(8.50)

	sentence adverbials	dialogue mechanisms	comment clauses	vocatives
I-position	independent tone group non-final nucleus including MR	independent tone group non-final nucleus including MR	independent tone group non-final nucleus including MR	independent tone group non-final nucleus including M
M-position	constitute (part of the) the tail	constitute (part of the) the tail	constitute (part of the) the tail	constitute (part of the) the tail
T-position	constitute (part of the) the tail	constitute (part of the) the tail	constitute (part of the) the tail	constitute (part of the) the tail

8.9 Summary of the main points

Intonation as the term has been used in this chapter refers to the distribution of pitch and stress over a stretch of utterances of typically more than one word's length. In NAERD, and in English in general, intonation is systematic, conventional and specific. That intonation is systematic is manifested by the recurrent division of speech into tone units, the so-called tone groups, and the repeated division of each tone group into an obligatory nucleus (typically the last potentially stressed syllable of each tone group) and optional heads and tails, where the former always carries primary stress, frequently expressed by variation in pitch, and the latter two contain syllables with secondary stress and unstressed syllables. Intonation is also conventional because specific meanings by unspoken agreement are attached to the pitch variation. Firstly, the intonation determines what information is shared between speaker and hearer and what is new information and hence not shared by speaker and hearer. The nucleus is associated with new information and what precedes the nucleus, i.e. the head, refers to known material. Secondly, less general and more specific meanings are associated with the pitch variation found in the nucleus and often the subsequent tail. Depending on whether the nuclear variation is falling, rising or a combination and what utterance type these nuclear variations occur in, the specific meanings expressed have to do with completeness/incompleteness, kindness/unkindness, certainty/uncertainty. These meanings concern what may be described, using a general term, the speaker's way of looking at things, and the meaning of intonation in NAERD is then not lexical as in tone languages proper but a property of speech that expresses the speaker's attitude. Lastly, intonation is described as specific. This refers to the fact that intonation is language-specific. The intonation of English is not the same as the intonation of, say, German, French or Danish. In fact, intonation is accent-specific. The intonation of NAERD is not the same as the intonation of English English RP, although they are similar, but the intonation of other varieties of American English is probably very similar to the system described in this chapter as characteristic of NAERD, so similar that what has been said above applies by and large to other forms of American English pronunciation as well. As a conclusion to this chapter, the main points about intonation in NAERD are repeated in the following bulleted list:

- Intonation in NAERD is the melody, created by a combination of pitch and stress, which is distributed over a stretch of utterances to convey meaning
- Intonation in NAERD is systematic, dividing speech into a recurrent system of tone groups each with the typical structure: obligatory nucleus, optional head and optional tail

- The meaning conveyed by intonation is either general specifying what is new and what is known information, or more specific indicating the speaker's attitudes
- As a variable structural unit which can have a falling, a rising or a falling-rising pitch, the nucleus is specifically associated with different attitudinal meanings
- The nucleus is typically the last potentially stressed syllable of the tone group. This pattern is known as unmarked tonicity. Tonicity is then the system of options for selecting the nucleus
- Boundaries between tone groups coincide with major syntactic boundaries. Having tone group boundaries at regular intervals is known as unmarked tonality. Tonality is then the system of options for selecting tone group boundaries
- Tone groups before a pause are classified as final. The pitch variation of the nucleus of final tone groups varies, depending on the grammatical structure of the utterance
- Final tone groups which are statements, *wh*-questions, imperatives and exclamations have a falling nucleus. Final tone groups which are *yes/no*-questions and statement questions have a rising nucleus
- Tone groups that are followed by other tone groups are non-final. The nuclei of non-final tone groups can be falling, rising and level
- Intonation is often represented between two horizontal lines. In this interlinear transcription, the top line represents the highest pitch level and the bottom line the lowest pitch level. Each syllable is marked by a short stroke if it is unstressed and a long stroke if it is stressed. The pitch variation is indicated by the relative placement of each syllable/stroke in between the two horizontal lines
- The interlinear transcription system may be replaced with a simpler system with tonetic stress marks and no horizontal lines. In this system, the tonetic stress marks indicate stress and nucleus as well as the direction of the pitch variation.

Further reading

A comprehensive introduction to intonation is Cruttenden 1986. The works of Bolinger 1972, 1986, 1989 are also very comprehensive, as is Halliday 1970. See also Laver 1994, Gussenhoven 2004 and Bauer et al 1980, the latter dealing specifically with American English. Ladd 1996, for example, represents a more abstract and less phonetic approach to pitch phenomena.

PART III

CHAPTER 9

Variation and change

9.1 Types of inter-segment influence

This chapter is an introduction to how phonemes or what also above was referred to as phonological segments (see Ch. 2.) influence one another. The chapter is called 'variation and change' because this inter-segment influence will be looked at from two different viewpoints. The first viewpoint is represented by the word 'variation'. In this chapter variation stands for the fluctuation found in the present-day pronunciation of segments which is caused by contiguous sounds. This variation occurs typically in contexts of fast conversational speech and it serves the purpose of minimising the speaker's articulatory effort. The string *of course* may serve as an example. The pronunciation of the final /v/ of *of* is typically not [v] in this string, unless the speech tempo is slow and deliberate, but instead it is [f], i.e. strong, because /v/ is followed by the strong obstruent /k/. That is, the contiguous strong /k/ influences /v/ so /v/ is pronounced strong like /k/, since it involves less effort to pronounce two consecutive strong segments than to pronounce one weak followed by one strong segment. Variation as it is used in this chapter is then not quite the same as variation when it refers to the free and bound variation of phonemes as described in chapter 2. Free and bound allophones or variants do not depend on tempo and style. Bound allophones always occur and free allophones crop up in both slow and fast speech. Nor does variation in this chapter refer to the variation in accent and dialect contingent upon such factors as the regional origin of the speaker of North American English. Such variation will be considered in greater detail in chapter 10.

Variation in the sense used here is frequently called **assimilation** which then, to return to the string *of course,* is a process in which one segment becomes more like (sometimes identical to) another contiguous segment as a result of inter-segment influence. Assimilation is observable variation, variation which is found among speakers of NAERD (and other varieties of English). This is the reason that it was described as characteristic of present-day English in the previous paragraph. Variation such as assimilation where input and output of the process are not temporally ordered is also called **synchronic** variation. By contrast, processes in which input and output are temporally ordered so that there are, say, 50 years, a century or perhaps several centuries between input and output are called **diachronic**. Thus a process such as that which changed some varieties of American English from rhotic to non-rhotic and then often back to rhotic (see the discussion in Ch. 4 above), a process which spanned several hundred years, can be used as an example of a diachronic process. Exactly how many years a synchronic period spans and when it ceases to be synchronic and enters a diachronic development is not of direct concern here (and not easy to establish) nor important in order to understand the distinction between synchronic and diachronic. What is more important is that it requires two or more synchronic stages for a process to be regarded as diachronic.

Diachronic process is what has motivated the other important word that enters the heading of this chapter, viz. 'change'. Whilst 'variation' stands for synchronic variation, specifically present-day assimilations, 'change' stands for the situation where one segment has changed, either as a result of neighbouring sounds or as a result of rotations in the phonological subsystem it enters into, but where input and output to the change or process are temporally ordered. The change affecting rhoticity in some varieties of American English has already been mentioned. But as this is not segment induced (phonetically motivated), a better (and classic) example is the influence that a /j/ or /i/ exerted some time before the seventh century, that is, some time before the first attested forms of English appeared. This influence is known as *i*-umlaut (see further below), a sound change which, as a result of the presence of /j/ or /i/, fronted back vowels and raised front vowels. In the seventh century when English was first written down (the English of the seventh to the eleventh centuries is known as Old English) the effects of this fronting and raising could be seen, but the /i/ and /j/ causing the change had disappeared. So when the Old English forms of the words *full, fill, man, men* are compared with the reconstructed pre-Old English forms of the same words (marked with an asterisk. i.e. *), those Old English words whose reconstructed forms have /i/ or /j/ in them turn up with fronted/ raised root vowels:

(9.1)

pre-Old English	Old English
*ful	ful
*fuljan	fyllan (→ fill)
*man	man
*manni	men

Since the loss of sounds like /i/ and /j/ does not happen overnight, it is reasonable to assume a lapse of a considerable amount of time between the use of the forms in the left-hand column and the use of the forms in the right-hand column – between input and output of this sound change. Support for such a time lapse can be found in the close affinity between the pre-Old English forms and the related but older East Germanic language, Gothic. The Gothic forms of the words in (9.1) are very similar to the pre-Old English ones. As Gothic had almost ceased to exist by the fifth century AD, the input to *i*-umlaut, i.e. the pre-Old English forms in (9.1), probably dates back to the fourth or the fifth century, whilst the output to *i*-umlaut, i.e. the Old English forms in (9.1), does not appear until the seventh century. Input and output to *i*-umlaut are then clearly temporally ordered, and *i*-umlaut thus serves as a nice (and frequently used) example of what is covered by the word 'change' in this chapter and of what is often (in other contexts) referred to as a diachronic or historical change.

Variation is the first inter-segment influence to be considered in this chapter. To recapitulate, variation here refers to the present-day transformation that segments undergo so they become like or sometimes identical to contiguous segments. This transformation typically happens in fast informal speech, and the speaker's unconscious desire to pronounce what involves least articulatory effort is instrumental in this process. The technical term used for such transformations is assimilation. The loss of segments as when *hands* is pronounced [hænz] and not [hændz] is also a segment-induced transformation. Such a transformation to zero so that a segment is completely lost is known as **elision**. As it is conditioned by fast speech and by a desire to minimise the articulatory effort, this kind of loss will also be regarded as an instance of assimilation and treated together with those types of inter-segment transformations which do not lead to deletions. Clearly, elision also shares with assimilation the property that input and output are not temporally ordered. Another process which is not conditioned by fast speech but which, like elision, affects whole segments and inserts rather than deletes is **epenthesis**. As a whole-segment process, epenthesis will be discussed together with elision, although it is not induced by fast speech.

9.2 Types of assimilation

The standard way of classifying assimilations which do not lead to deletions involves a description of the **direction** of the influence and a description of the **phonetic parameter** which is the target of the assimilation. The direction of the influence involved in the assimilation can be either one way (**uni-directional**) or two ways (**bi-directional**), and in principle any phonetic parameter can be the target of assimilation, but typically the target is one of strength, place or manner of articulation. Assimilations may be further categorised as **allophonic** or as **phonemic** and as **word-internal** or as **word-external**. The former distinction refers to whether the output of the assimilation is identified with another phoneme than the input, and the latter is to do with the stretch of phonological material to which the assimilation applies. The sections below will describe these characteristic distinctions of assimilation in more detail, using the following strings as examples: *open, of course, miss you, all those cars, in the closet, hate you* and *anthem.*

9.2.1 Phonetic parameter and direction

open and *of course* illustrate well how assimilations may vary both with respect to phonetic parameter and with respect to direction. Besides the common pronunciations of *open* and *of course* given in (9.2a), the alternative pronunciations given in (9.1b) are also frequent, particularly in high tempo speech:

(9.2)

	a.	**b.**
open	[ˈoʊpən]	[ˈoʊpm̩]
of course	[əv ˈkɔrs]	[əf ˈkɔrs]

In the case of *open*, the two pronunciations differ in that in (9.2b) after the loss of [ə] in an unstressed syllable the alveolar nasal [n] has changed to (syllabic) bilabial [m]. The loss of [ə] occurs first whereby [p] and [n] become contiguous. Once they are contiguous, mutual influence is possible, and the bilabial [p] influences the following [n] so it acquires the bilabial place of articulation of [p] and becomes [m]. Since the direction of influence is one way, viz. from [p] to [n], and the direction of influence is from a sound to a following sound, this kind of inter-segment influence is termed a **unidirectional** and **progressive** assimilation. Moreover, as it turns an alveolar into a bilabial, the phonetic target of this influence is place of articulation. In sum, the assimilation represented by the pronunciation [oʊpm̩] for *open* may then be described as a unidirectional, progressive **place** assimilation.

Consider now the string, *of course*. As regards this string, (9.2a) differs from (9.2b) with respect to the pronunciation of *of*. In (9.2a) it is pronounced [əv], in (9.2b) the pronunciation is [əf], that is, a weak labiodental fricative (in **a.**) has become a strong labiodental fricative (in **b.**). The cause of the change [v] →[f] is the following strong (velar) [k], whose strength is anticipated in the preceding labiodental [v], so this acquires the same strength as [k] and becomes [f]. The direction of this influence is backward and not forward as in *open*. For this reason, the type of assimilation exemplified by *of course* is **regressive**, rather than progressive, but it is like *open* in being **unidirectional** as the direction of the influence is from [k] to [v] only. The phonetic target of this assimilation is energy (strength), changing weak [v] to strong [f]. In sum, the assimilation represented by the pronunciation [əf ˈkɔrs] for *of course* may then be described as a unidirectional, regressive **energy** assimilation.

The target of an assimilation is not always energy and place. Manner of articulation is also a frequent parameter affected by assimilation. The strings *in the closet* and *all those cars* illustrate how manner can be changed as a result of assimilation. Compare the two pronunciations of these strings listed below:

(9.3)

	a.	**b.**
in the closet	[ɪn ðə ˈklɑzət]	[ɪn nə ˈklɑzət]
all those cars	[ˈɔl ðoʊz ˈkɑrz]	[ˈɔl loʊz ˈkɑrz]

The **b.**-versions are typical of fast speech and differ from the **a.**-versions in the way the initial consonants of *the* and *those* are pronounced. In fast speech these consonants frequently change so they become identical to the previous consonant, as it involves less articulatory effort to pronounce the same consonant twice than two different consonants consecutively. The inter-segment influence leading to [ð] → [n] and [ð] → [l] is forward and one way only, and since the difference between [n]/[l] and [ð] is one of sonorant versus obstruent, the variations in (9.3b) are examples of manner assimilations. In addition to manner, the place parameter is also affected: [ð] is dental, whilst [n]/[l] are alveolar. In sum the transformations given in (9.3b) may then be described as **unidirectional, progressive manner and place** assimilations.

The assimilations considered so far have all been uni-directional. But assimilations can also result from the mutual influence of segments. Such bi-directional assimilations are shown in the **b.**-versions in (9.4) which are characteristic of a higher speech tempo:

(9.4)

	a.	**b.**
miss you	[ˈmɪs ju]	[ˈmɪʃʃu]
hate you	[ˈheɪt ju]	[ˈheɪtʃu]

miss you exemplifies assimilation of [sj] → [ʃʃ] which is further reduced to [ʃ]. This assimilation involves two processes. Firstly, [sj] → [ʃʃ] involves the transference of sibilance and strength from [s] to [j] so that [j] becomes [ʃ], and secondly, the transference of the place property palatality ([j] is a palatal in NAERD) from [j] to [s], which changes [s] into a more retracted sibilant which in NAERD is [ʃ]. Subsequently [ʃʃ] is reduced to [ʃ]. The change [j] → [ʃ] is a progressive assimilation affecting place and manner of articulations as well as strength, and the change of [s] → [ʃ] is a regressive assimilation which affects place of articulation. Because it is a complex process working both forwards and backwards and involving mutual influence, this kind of assimilation is **bi-directional**.

The string *hate you* is also an example of a bi-directional assimilation, although a less obvious instance of this. The change of [tj] → [tʃ] in the fast speech version of this string also involves two processes. Firstly, [j] → [ʃ], and secondly [t] + [ʃ] → [tʃ]. The first part of the process is a progressive assimilation whereby the preceding [t] strengthens, fronts as well as changes the manner of articulation of [j] so it becomes [ʃ]. The second part of the process is a fusion of two separate segments. As a result of a regressive assimilation, [t] is retracted and articulated with a bunched tongue because of the bunched tongue of the following palato-alveolar [ʃ]. The natural output of this fusion is [tʃ]. Because it is a complex process which involves mutual influence working both regressively and progressively, the assimilation process exemplified by *hate you* is also bi-directional.

9.2.2 Allophonic or phonemic assimilations

Assimilation may also be categorised as either phonemic or allophonic depending on which phoneme the output of the assimilation is identified with. If the output of the assimilation is an allophone of a different phoneme than the input phoneme, then the assimilation is **phonemic**. The assimilations considered so far have all been phonemic. For example, the output of the assimilation illustrated by *of course* is [f] (*of* becomes pronounced [əf] and not [əv] as a result of the following strong [k]). [f] is an allophone of the phoneme /f/ and not of the phoneme /v/. The output of this assimilation is then identified with another phoneme than it was as input and *of course* is an example of a phonemic assimilation. As another example, consider the string *in the closet*. The output of this assimilation is that *the* is pronounced [nə] and not [ðə] as a result of the preceding nasal sonorant [n]. [n] is an allophone of the phoneme /n/ and not of the phoneme /ð/. The output of the assimilation is then identified with another phoneme than it was as input. The change of [ð] → [n] in *in the closet* is thus also an instance of a phonemic assimilation.

A nonphonemic or **allophonic** assimilation, on the other hand, is characterised by the output being identified with the same phoneme as the input. The string *anthem* may serve as an example. Frequently *anthem* is pronounced with a dental rather than alveolar *n* as a result of the following dental fricative [θ]. The output of this regressive place assimilation, albeit different from the input, does not deviate enough from the input to be identified with another phoneme than /n/. It is therefore an allophonic assimilation because the bound dental variant is an allophone of the phoneme /n/ in NAERD. If dental and alveolar had been contrastive places of articulation in NAERD (as they are in some languages), this assimilation would have been phonemic.

Other variant pronunciations often mentioned as examples of allophonic assimilations are the devoiced sonorant allophones occurring not always obligatorily after strong obstruents. Thus in *try* and *clay*, for example, /r/ and /l/ become devoiced after strong (and hence voiceless) /t/ and /k/ as a result of a progressive strength assimilation. Such devoiced output pronunciations will be identified with the same phonemes as they were as inputs because voiced and devoiced sonorants are not phonologically contrastive in NAERD. Instead the difference between voiced and devoiced sonorant is allophonic, i.e. a difference found among variants of one phoneme, and the assimilations occurring in, for example, *clay* and *try* are therefore allophonic.

9.2.3 Word-internal and word-external assimilations

Only one aspect of assimilations remains to be described now, viz. the stretch of phonological material to which assimilations apply. In NAERD this stretch of phonological material, or **domain** as it is usually called, can be either one word or two consecutive words. When the domain is one word, the target sound and the inducing sound occur within the same word. This is known as **word-internal** assimilation and characteristic of the assimilations found in *open* and *anthem*. In these, both target sounds, [n] in both words, and inducing sounds, [p] and [θ] respectively, occur within the boundaries of one word. By contrast, when the domain is two consecutive words the target sound and the inducing sound belong to different words. Such assimilations are termed **word-external**. Word-external assimilations are exemplified by *have to* and *miss you*. In the first example, the target sound [v] in *have* belongs to the first word, while the inducing sound is the initial [t] of the second word. In *miss you*, which represents a bi-directional assimilation changing [s] + [j] to [ʃ] + [ʃ], both target and inducing sounds belong to either word. Thus in word-external assimilations, the mutual influence of sounds takes place across a word boundary.

It is not possible to say that particular kinds of assimilation favour particular domains, except that bi-directional assimilations typically occur across word boundaries. Both word-internal as well as word-external assimilations can be unidirectional and word-internal assimilations do not affect the place parameter exclusively, just like word-external assimilations affect strength, place and manner alike.

Assimilations are very common in informal fast speech. They are frequently treated with contempt and thought to be the result of bad, incorrect or sloppy language. People who deplore the use of assimilation often do not realise that they will themselves be among those speakers who assimilate both uni-directionally and bi-directionally as shown in the following list of examples.

(9.5)

fat boy	['fæp 'bɔɪ]	[t] → [p]
that cup	['ðæk 'kʌp]	[t] → [k]
good bye	['gʊb baɪ]	[d] → [b]
good girl	['gʊg 'gɜɫ]	[d] → [g]
ten minutes	['tem 'mɪnɪts]	[n] → [m]
this ship	[ðɪʃ 'ʃɪp]	[s] → [ʃ]
I'm going to come	[aɪŋ gənə 'kʌm]	[m] → [ŋ]

give me it	[ˈgɪm mi ɪt]	[v] → [m]
have to	[ˈhæf tə]	[v] → [f]
his sons	[hɪs ˈsʌnz]	[z] → [s]
has your father	[hæʒʒər ˈfɑðə]	[z]+[j] → [ʒʒ]
what did you say	[ˈwʌt dɪdʒə ˈseɪ]	[d]+[j] → [dʒ]

9.3 Elision and epenthesis

Assimilation, as it has been understood so far, is present-day variation in the pronunciation of individual sounds following from inter-segment influence. As
pointed out above, a similar inter-segment influence can be observed to occur
under the same conditions which deletes rather than changes a sound. This complete loss of sounds is known as **elision**, and since it, like assimilation, occurs
typically in high tempo speech and is an option chosen by the speaker (uncon-
sciously) to minimise the articulatory effort, a discussion of elision belongs naturally in the present context. Both assimilations and deletions are whole-segment
processes. For this reason, a third phenomenon which applies to whole segments
too, is also dealt with in this chapter. **Epenthesis**, as this whole-segment process is
called, inserts rather than deletes a segment, but unlike assimilation and elision,
epenthesis is not conditioned by speech tempo or articulatory ease.

9.3.1 Elision

As established above, the term **elision** is employed to describe a situation where
a sound is lost completely. The following types of elision are particularly frequent in NAERD: i) the loss of a consonant where this consonant would otherwise lead to clusters of three or more consonants. This rule affects specifically
the alveolar stops /t/ and /d/ and applies to word-internal as well as word-external domains as shown in (9.6):

(9.6)

text number	[ˈtekst ˈnʌmbər] → [ˈteks ˈnʌmbər]
cold night	[ˈkoʊld ˈnaɪt] → [ˈkoʊl ˈnaɪt]
facts	[fækts] → [fæks]
twelfths	[twelfθs] → [twelfs]
drink good wine	[ˈdrɪŋk ˈgʊd ˈwaɪn] → [ˈdrɪŋ ˈgʊd ˈwaɪn]
shields	[ʃildz] → [ʃilz]

ii) the loss of [ə] where this vowel is followed by [r] and another vowel. Examples:

(9.7)

shivering	[ˈʃɪvərɪŋ] → [ˈʃɪvrɪŋ]
miserable	[ˈmɪsərəbl] → [ˈmɪsrəbl]
summary	[ˈsʌməri] → [ˈsʌmri]
satisfactory	[sæDɪsˈfæktəri] → [sæDɪsˈfæktri]

iii) the loss of [r] where the following syllable contains an [r]. In this case, elision is not induced by an immediately contiguous sound. Examples (note that [ər] is used instead of [ɚ]):

(9.8)

southerner	[ˈsʌðərnər] → [ˈsʌðənər]
surcharge	[sɜrˈtʃɑrdʒ] → [sɜˈtʃɑrdʒ]
secretary	[ˈsekrəteri] → [ˈsekəteri]

iv) the loss of [ɪ], [ʊ] and specifically [ə] in unstressed syllables. As described in Ch. 5, vowels in unstressed syllables typically lose distinctness. Distinct peripheral vowels become less distinct and centralised, so in syllables which lack stress [ə] may replace most vowels. Very often this process is taken one step further and the vowel of the unstressed syllable is lost completely. This process applies to the unstressed syllables of content words as well as to the weak forms of form words. Examples:

(9.9)

He would have liked to come and open an exhibition
[hɪ wʊd həv ˈlaɪkt tə ˈkʌm ən ˈoʊpən ən eksəˈbɪʃən] →
[hɪd əv ˈlaɪk tə ˈkʌm n̩ ˈoʊpm̩ ən eksəˈbɪʃn̩]

v) the loss of consonants in unstressed syllables either before identical consonants, as when [ˈlaɪkt tə] → [ˈlaɪk tə] in (9.9), or in form words as when also in (9.9) [hɪ wʊd həv] → [hɪd əv]. In iv) and v), it is possible to speak of a 'conspiracy' of two rules. Deletion occurring in high tempo speech (like assimilation) interacts with the rule that vowels and consonants tend to weaken or disappear in contexts of no stress, and the result of this conspiracy is the possibility of quite extensive reductions and elisions.

9.3.2 Epenthesis

The opposite process of elision is insertion or **epenthesis**. Epenthesis either occurs in word-marginal positions or between two previously contiguous segments, and the epenthesised sound may be a consonant or a vowel, but, as pointed out above, it is not restricted to specific speech forms such as high tempo speech like the two other whole-segment processes, assimilation and elision. The following types of epenthesis between two contiguous segments are the most common ones: i) insertion of a vowel between two consonants, the latter of which is a potentially syllabic sonorant:

(9.10)

film	[fɪlm] → [fɪləm]
athlete	[ˈæθlit] → [ˈæθəlit]

ii) insertion of [ɪ], particularly in Southern American English after non-close vowels before palatals and velars:

(9.11)

bag	[bæg] → [bæɪg]
bush	[bʊʃ] → [bʊɪʃ]
much	[mʌtʃ] → [mʌɪtʃ]

iii) insertion of an oral stop between a nasal and an oral stop or fricative. The inserted oral stop has the same place of articulation as the nasal. This insertion is the result of the velum closing before the oral closure of the following stop or fricative is formed:

(9.12)

something	[ˈsʌmθɪŋ] → [ˈsʌmpθɪŋ]
length	[leŋθ] → [leŋkθ]
prince	[prɪns] → [prɪnts]

9.3.3 Summarising whole-segment processes

Assimilation, elision and epenthesis apply to whole segments and are the result of inter-segment influence in present-day pronunciation of NAERD. Assimilation and elision occur in the context of fast informal speech and minimise the speaker's articulatory effort. Epenthesis occurs independently of speech tempo and, albeit articulatorily motivated, does not facilitate the articulatory gesture. The following points should be noted about assimilation:

- The effect of assimilation is that one sound becomes more like or identical with another sound
- Virtually any phonetic parameter may be the target of assimilation, but typically they are place, manner or strength or combinations of these
- The domain of an assimilation can be a word or across a word-boundary
- The direction of influence can be from one sound to another or it can be mutual between two sounds
- If the output of an assimilation is identified with another phoneme than the input phoneme, the assimilation is phonemic; if the output is identified with the input phoneme, the assimilation is allophonic

and in a diagram these points appear as follows:

(9.13)

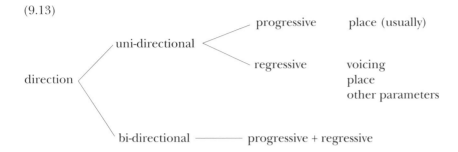

direction

uni-directional
- progressive — place (usually)
- regressive — voicing
  place
  other parameters

bi-directional ———— progressive + regressive

The following list summarises the main points about elision:

- The effect of elision is sound loss
- Elision typically reduces three or four consonant clusters by one; very often the elided consonant is an alveolar stop; the domain can be a word or across a word boundary
- /r/ is lost not as a result of an immediately contiguous sound, but because of another /r/ occurring within the same word
- Non-distinct vowels and specifically schwa are lost as a result of fast speech or lack of stress or both
- The consonants of form words are lost as a result of fast speech or lack of stress or both

It has been mentioned several times in the preceding that assimilation and elision are motivated by the speakers' unconscious wish to minimise the articulatory effort. But putting assimilation and elision down to this strategy does not explain why these transformations follow the course they do or why they do not always happen. Whilst the latter perhaps is explicable in terms of speech tempo – and even this is not unproblematic – the former is difficult to handle when examined in more detail. To see this, consider, for example the strings *I'm going to come* [aɪŋ gənə ˈkʌm] and *give me it* [ˈgɪm mi ɪt] listed in (9.5). The first string represents a change of [mg] → [ŋg], the second a change of [vm] → [mm], that is, the former a place assimilation of bilabial to velar and the latter place and manner assimilations of labiodental obstruent to bilabial nasal. But if the motivation is minimising the articulatory effort, *I'm going to come* could as well involve homorganisation of [mg] → [gg] and *give me it* of [vm] → [vv], none of which are more complex process-wise than what is found in attested assimilations. It simply is not easy to say why the one and not the other possibility occurs and underlines with how much caution a term like motivation of change should be used.

9.4 Diachronic change

This part of chapter 9 deals with the issues covered by the word change, the other important word occurring in the heading of this chapter. Change refers in this chapter to diachronic change, the kind of change where the input and the output to a sound change are temporally ordered. As in § 9.2, only changes induced by other segments will be considered. Traditionally, a sound change induced by other segments involves the transference and subsequent predominance of some phonetic property, as when in *i*-umlaut the high, front property of /i/ or /j/ transforms a preceding non-front and non-high vowel to a front and non-low vowel. But in this chapter 'induced by other segments' refers also to the situation where the change of a vowel or a consonant occurs as a result of a sometimes quite extensive and massive restructuring of the subsystem of phonemes of which the vowel or the consonant is a member. The vowel rotations, in so far as they can be said to be diachronic, like The Northern Cities Shift and The Southern Vowel Shift, illustrate this type of change (see Ch. 5.). The inducing property of such rotations is not contiguous sounds in a string of speech as in assimilations and *i*-umlaut, but the inducing property is the restructuring of sounds that are contiguous in the sense that they fill specific slots in the phoneme system. Phonetically induced changes like *i*-umlaut are sometimes referred to as **combinatorial** changes whereas changes which are triggered by restructurings in the phonological system will be referred to as **system-dependent** (the latter sometimes appear under the somewhat misleading name **isolative**). The former also frequently involve **phonologicalisation**, the process whereby allophones become phonemes, the latter do not as they fail to produce allophones. This section on diachronic change starts with combinatorial change and discusses how phonologicalisation is manifest in combinatorial changes. Subsequently, the mechanism of system-dependent changes will be looked into and a possible extension of the 'domain' of phonologicalisation will be considered in connection with this type of change.

9.4.1 Combinatorial i-umlaut

As outlined above in § 9.1, *i*-umlaut occurred before the first attested forms of English appeared in the 7th century AD. It is the result of the presence of a /i/ or /j/ turning a preceding back vowel into a front vowel or, if it is already front, raising a front vowel to one with a closer quality. If we take the present-day words *full, fill, foot, feet* as examples, then the effect of *i*-umlaut on root vowels can be illustrated as follows, in which unattested forms are marked with * (in the following *o* represents long *o*):

(9.14)

stage 1		stage 2		stage 3	
pre-Old English		pre-Old English		Old English	PDE
*ful	→	*ful	→	ful	full
*fuljan	→	*fylljan	→	fyllan	fill
*fot	→	*fot	→	fot	foot
*foti	→	*føti	→	føt/fet	feet

What (9.14) shows is that at some point before the 7th century, in the pre-Old English period, root vowels begin to appear as front vowels if followed by a /i/ or /j/, but remain back vowels when no /i/ or /j/ follow. This variation is apparent from stage 2 and the appearance of *fyl- and *fø- is a result of assimilation, a regressive place and/or height assimilation. At stage 2 the vowel phonemes /u/ and /o/ thus have two bound allophones: /u/ has the allophone [y] when followed by /j/ or /i/ and the allophone [u] elsewhere, and /o/ has the allophone [ø] when followed by /j/ or /i/ and the allophone[o] elsewhere. In principle, this allophonic variation predicted by a following /j/ or /i/ could have continued well into present-day English, if it had not been for a series of changes occurring so that the Old English forms of these words appear quite a lot different today. To simplify somewhat, what happened was that post-root /j/ was lost just like vowels after roots were lost or weakened, but the exact details are not important here. The effect of these changes is quite dramatic because, as is apparent from stage 3 above, it is now no longer possible to predict when the root vowel is front, i.e. /y/ or /ø/, and when it is back, i.e. /u/ or /o/, because the conditioning environments have disappeared. Instead /y/ now occurs in exactly the same context as /u/ and /ø/ in exactly the same context as /o/, and when /y/ is found the meaning is 'verb', and when /u/ occurs the meaning is 'adjective' (this is apparent from the present-day English forms), just like /ø/ results in the meaning 'plural' and /o/ in the meaning 'singular'. Sounds that occur in the same environment and whose presence results in different meanings or distinguish meaning are phonemes (as described in Ch. 2). The development described by *i*-umlaut is then that sounds which arose in the pre-Old English period as a result of assimilation and which for some time led a life as bound allophones become phonemes once the conditioning environment of the bound allophones disappears. *i*-umlaut is then a diachronic process, diachronic because there is a time span of several hundred years between input and output, which creates new phonemes. In particular, as shown below, both /o/ and /u/ are split into two phonemes (recall that more vowels than /o/ and /u/ are affected by *i*-umlaut, but not included here):

(9.15)

The creation of new sound contrasts as a result of the loss of the environment of bound allophones is a classic instance of what is referred to in the literature as **phonologicalisation**. Thus the term phonologicalisation in its core use presupposes allophonic variation and that the number of phoneme contrasts increases as a result of phoneme **splits**.

i-umlaut is a classic instance of a combinatorial diachronic change involving phonologicalisation. It is combinatorial because a phonetic context creates new allophones of root sounds and it is diachronic and involves phonologicalisation because the loss of endings, and hence the inducing context, in the course of several centuries places former allophones in contrastive and unconditioned contexts. It remains to be seen if similar processes exist in American English. Given that the overall structure of the lexicon was largely determined as English developed its American branch, clear-cut instances like *i*-umlaut are not likely to abound in American English.

9.4.2 Combinatorial changes in American English

A closer examination confirms the prediction of the last paragraph that few instances of conditioned changes exist in American English which result in phonologicalisations. Two splits are fairly well-known and hence potential candidates. The first is the characteristic insertion of [j] followed by an inglide after /æ/ in the context of an alveolar nasal or strong alveopalatal fricative in Southern American English:

(9.16)

can't [kænt]	→	[kæjənt]
ash [æʃ]	→	[æjəʃ]

This change contributes to what is often referred to as the 'Southern drawl' and involves a combinatorial change triggered by the following consonant whose front characteristic is copied and leaves the duplicate [j] followed by a transition sound [ə]. The effect of southern **breaking**, as this process is sometimes referred to, is that /æ/ is sometimes realised [æ] and sometimes [æjə]. The inducing environment of the [æjə]-realisation is not likely to disappear as the inducing environment in *i*-umlaut. Southern breaking will therefore not result in phonologicalisation of allophones. But not only will the inducing context not disappear, the effect of the change is also such that even if the inducing context disappears the possibility of new contrasts in identical environments, as in *i*-umlaut, does not arise. Southern breaking creates a new syllable, in particular the output string of the process has one syllable more than the input string. So long as the output is interpreted as involving the addition of a syllable, southern breaking involves the creation of an extra potential environment of contrast, not a new contrast. Southern breaking thus creates material which is present simultaneously. The relation between material occurring simultaneously is syntagmatic, whereas the relation between phonological contrasts which can occur in the same context and which do not occur simultaneously is paradigmatic. The phonologicalisation represented by southern breaking, in so far as this can now be said to be an established feature of the phonological system of Southern American English, is then syntagmatic. But if reduction steps in and deletes material in the output of southern breaking, turning [æjə] into a diphthong, which is a likely development, the possibility of paradigmatic contrast, like in *i*-umlaut, becomes real.

The other split constituting a potential example of phonologicalisation in American English is the division of /æ/ in the Mid-Atlantic states and New York City into /æ/ and /æ:/, the latter frequently realised as the vowel of *yeah* or *idea*, i.e. [ɪə]. This /æ/-splitting, as it will be referred to below, has the following effect when it occurs:

(9.17)

ham [hæm]	→	[hæ:m]	*hælf* [hæf]	→	[hæ:f]
man [mæn]	→	[mæ:n]	*pass* [pæs]	→	[pæ:s]
			path [pæθ]	→	[pæ:θ]

The lengthening, and frequent subsequent diphthongisation of [æ:] → [ɪə], occurs at least before the nasals /m, n/ and the fricatives /f, v, s, z, θ/, but the context in which this lengthening is found varies somewhat from area to area, but as a rule does not take place before strong stops, /ŋ/ and /l/. Thus *cap, mat, sang, pal* have [æ].

But since /æ/-splitting does not always occur in the expected environment, minimal pairs crop up in some varieties of American English which exhibit this split. Thus in some varieties, *can* (auxiliary verb) unexpectedly has short [æ] whereas *can* ('tin') has [æ:]. Similarly, *have* unexpectedly has short [æ], whereas *halve* has [æ:]. Clearly, the emergence of such minimal pairs makes /æ/-splitting a potential phonologicalisation process. But again the phonological difference does not follow from the loss of conditioning environment as in classic *i*-umlaut. The difference is a result of the failure of an allophonic splitting process occurring in specific words. Arguably, /æ/-splitting is then the result of an interaction of lexical features and phonetic environment and not the result of the latter only. Depending on how rigid our phonological analysis is, in particular how much we stick to the principle of 'once a phoneme always a phoneme', /æ/-splitting can then be seen as leading to two separate phonemes, /æ/ and /æ:/, or as allophonic variation from which specific lexical items are exempted. This is not the place to argue for one or the other position. It is sufficient to say that from one point of view, /æ/-splitting can be said to represent phonologicalisation in which combinatorial change plays a part as it involves an increase in the phoneme inventory.

9.4.3 System-dependent change: consonant shift and vowel shift

Combinatorial changes, as discussed in the preceding sections, involve context-induced and phonetically motivated inter-segment transformations. When these changes lead to new phonological contrasts, they exemplify phonologicalisation as in the classic case of *i*-umlaut. However, a change is not always the result of the phonetic influence of a contiguous segment. That a sound is contiguous to other sounds with which it interacts in a phonological system can also bring about a change. Contiguity in this sense refers not to sequential and syntagmatic vicinity, but to the inter-segment dependencies that exist because segments which occupy specific slots in a system of paradigmatically related phonemes (a syntagmatic relation holds between elements that occur simultaneously, a paradigmatic relation holds between elements that occupy the same position and enter a relation of contrast in this position). A change triggered by this second kind of contiguity is found either i) when one or a series of phonemes vacates the slot it or the series occupies and a contiguous segment or series in the phonological system moves into the vacated slot, or ii) when a phoneme or a series of phonemes is put under pressure to leave the slot it or the series occupies as a result of the movement of a contiguous phoneme or series of phonemes in the system. As it does not create allophones nor is phonetically induced but instead follows from system-internal restructurings, such a change is termed system-dependent (sometimes isolative) and also not thought to exemplify phonologicalisation. This section looks at two such system-dependent changes: the first from the pre-Old English period which affected consonants, and the second from Middle English (the 450 years in the history of English from 1066 to 1500) which affected vowels. Both accounts will reveal that the term system-dependent is appropriate for the type of change represented by these two shifts. Neither is separate, unique and without connection to other phonological segments, but the interaction with other sounds is of a different kind than in combinatorial changes. Both accounts will also deal with the obviously problematic contention that only combinatorial changes instantiate phonologicalisation.

The change from the pre-Old English period is the restructuring of the consonant system known as **the First Germanic Consonant Shift** which affected all the languages belonging to the family of Germanic languages (basically English, Dutch, German and the Scandinavian languages). There is general agreement that the source language from which the Germanic languages, among many others, have derived had a consonant system consisting of the following series of stop consonants, where -*h* stops represent voiced aspirates and -^{w} stops represent labiovelars (*bh, dh, gh* were probably 'breathy voiced' consonants, produced with a 'sighing' voice quality, and not voiced aspirates, but this is not relevant here). This source language is known as Indo-European and is in the neighbourhood of six thousand years old:

(9.18)

Indo-European	bh	dh	gh	g^wh
	b	d	g	g^w
	p	t	k	k^w

There is also general agreement that in early Germanic, approximately 3 thousand years later, this system underwent the following changes (the labiovelars are ignored henceforth as they by and large merged with the velars):

(9.19)

i)	bh	dh	gh	→	β	ð	ɣ
ii)	b	d	g	→	p	t	k
iii)	p	t	k	→	f	θ	x

That is, the voiced aspirates *bh, dh, gh* changed to voiced fricatives (β = voiced bilabial fricative, ɣ = voiced velar fricative), the voiced stops became voiceless stops and the voiceless stops became voiceless fricatives (x = voiceless velar fricative as in present-day Scottish English *loch*). Although they occurred around three millennia ago, these changes have left traces which can still be seen today when words in Germanic languages are compared with the corresponding words in, say, non-Germanic Latin (L), Greek (G) or Sanskrit (Skr), none of which were affected by the First Germanic consonant shift.

(9.20)

Non-Germanic		Germanic
bhratar (Skr),		
thugater (G) (th<*dh*)	→	*brother, daughter, goose*
hamsa (Skr) (h<*gh*)		
kannabis, dent-, genus	→	*hamp, tooth, kin*
piscis, tres, cord-	→	*fish, three, heart*

This quite massive change in the consonant system in the parent language of the Germanic languages is an example of phonological restructuring triggered by a segment or a series of segments – in this case a series – vacating the slots the series occupies. More specifically, what probably started this change was a strategy to get

rid of *bh, dh, gh* which, except in the Indo-European sub-family of Indic languages, had become 'illegitimate'. But more factors are involved than illegitimacy
making *bh, dh, gh* vacate their slots and become voiced fricatives. A particular preferred type of obstruent system also played a role in the development. What is
meant by a preferred type of obstruent system becomes apparent if the effect of
the First Germanic Consonant Shift is regarded as consisting of three steps where
the first step is i) in (9.19), the shift of *bh, dh, gh* → β, ð, ɣ. After this first step, but
before steps ii) and iii) have occurred, the obstruent system looks as follows:

(9.21)

β	ð	ɣ
b	d	g
p	t	k

However, there is a problem with this system in that it violates a constraint hold-
ing for most languages: that a weak obstruent series requires the presence of the
corresponding strong series. The system in (9.21) violates this constraint because it has the weak fricatives β, ð, ɣ but lacks the corresponding strong *f, θ, x-*
series. Consequently, step ii) shifting *p, t, k* to the missing *f, θ, x* applied. This
fricativisation or weakening resulted in the following system:

(9.22)

β	ð	ɣ
b	d	g
f	θ	x

But again the system in (9.22) does not comply with the general constraint hold-
ing for most languages that a weak obstruent series requires the presence of the
corresponding strong series: weak *b, d, g* are not matched by strong *p, t, k* in
(9.22). Therefore the third step of (9.19), the change of *b, d, g* to strong *p, t, k*
took place, so the obstruent system in Early Germanic had the following form:

(9.23)

β	ð	ɣ
p	t	k
f	θ	x

which is the output of the First Germanic Consonant shift as is apparent from
(9.19). In English β, ð, ɣ later strengthen to voiced stops so that when the first
attested form of English appears in the 7th century, *b, d, g* rather than β, ð, ɣ are
phonemes.

These later developments need not concern us here. What is sufficient for the present purpose is that the First Germanic Consonant Shift is an example of a diachronic sound change with a considerable time span between input and output (probably several millennia) which is best described as a chain process in which one transformation entails the next and so on. The triggering factor setting about this change is not one or more phonetic properties of neighbouring sounds. Probably, the shift is triggered by the fact that the so-called voiced aspirates, *bh, dh, gh*, became 'illegal' or 'not wanted' and shifted to voiced fricatives. The appearance of voiced fricatives set about a whole-sale restructuring of the obstruent system of early Germanic, making other stop series vacate their places in the system to occupy new places: strong stops becoming strong fricatives and weak stops becoming strong stops. Thus it is best explained if consonants are interpreted as members of a space in which they are not only phonetically defined, but also occupy specific slots allowing them to be organised in series which depend on each other. In such a space, the movement of contiguous series inevitably will set parallel series in motion. To call it a chain process presupposes such a view of consonant systems. As a chain process, the First Germanic Consonant Shift is a system-dependent sound change induced by a reorganisation of the phonological obstruent system of early Germanic, not a change motivated by a phonetic context (like combinatorial *i*-umlaut). As such, the First Germanic Consonant Shift also does not create allophones. Instead when phonemes vacate slots in a phonological system, either new sounds fill the vacated slots or other phonemes are forced to vacate the slots they fill. But in neither case do allophones arise as a result of these reorganisations, and the number of phoneme contrasts does not increase, that is, phoneme splits do not occur. Instead the result is that particular phonemes become associated with a different set of words than they were before the change, and the phonetic sounds which had phonemic status before the change are not the same as those that have phonemic status after the change. The absence of allophones in the First Germanic Consonant Shift entails that it is not thought to instantiate phonologicalisation, as this term normally presupposes the promotion of allophones to phonemes as in the case of *i*-umlaut. But it is not obvious that a shift like the First Germanic Consonant Shift should not involve phonologicalisation, even though it fails to create more phoneme contrasts. Since it creates other contrasts by reshuffling the contrastive consonants of sets of words, the shift clearly affects the phonological system. As such, the term phonologicalisation is as appropriate for this kind of process as it is for a process involving allophonic promotion. As a consequence, phonologicalisation will here be assumed to cover not only sound systematisation involving allophonic promotion, but also such restructurings in the system of phonemes which either reshuffle the distribution of particular phonemes in particular sets of words or assign phoneme status to sounds with no prior phonemic or allophonic status.

The second instance of a sound change not induced by a phonetic context to be considered here is the change that took place in the Middle English vowel system, a change which is commonly referred to as **the Middle English Great Vowel Shift**. As the name suggests, the Great Vowel Shift affected only vowels, raising all non-open long vowels one step up unless they were close, i.e. at the top of the system (recall figure (5.1) in Ch.5), in which case they diphthongised as they could raise no further. This process started in the 15th century and can be visualised as shown below (length is marked by ':'):

(9.24)

```
              i:            u:
      ↙       ↑             ↑      ↘
ei            e:            o:              ou
              ↑             ↑
              ɛ:            ɔ:
```

(9.24) shows the effect of the Great Vowel Shift in the 16th century. That is, at this point /i:/ and /u:/ had diphthongised, /e:/ and /o:/ had raised to /i:/ and /u:/ and so on. Later, at least in the kind of English which forms the basis of NAERD, further changes took place so that in present-day NAERD the effect of the Great Vowel Shift and subsequent changes may be illustrated as follows:

(9.25)

input to vowel shift		output to vowel shift		present-day NAERD	
i:	→	ei	→	aɪ	*fight*
e:	→	i:	→	i	*feet*
ɛ:	→	e:	↗		*feast*
a:	→	a:	→	eɪ	*fate*
u:	→	ou	→	aʊ	*foul*
o:	→	u:	→	u	*fool*
ɔ:	→	o:	→	oʊ	*foal*

Like the First Germanic Consonant Shift, the Great Vowel Shift is a **chain process** in which the change of one series of vowels triggers the movement of another series which again entails the shift of a third series and so on. By series is meant two vowels which share one of the height features close, half-close or half-open (see Ch. 5). It is debated whether this chain process started by the diphthongisation of the close vowels /i:/ and /u:/, leaving empty slots for more open vowels to move up into (this mechanism is known as a **drag chain** because, metaphorically speaking, more open vowels are dragged up into vacated positions), or whether it started by the most open series pushing the vowels above out of position entailing that further vowels above were pushed out of their positions, eventually diphthongising the close vowels (this mechanism is known as a **push**

chain). Probably, the Great Vowel Shift was a combined push/drag process. Evidence from Northern English dialects supports this view. In northern dialects, the input system to the Great Vowel Shift lacked /o:/ which had been fronted to /ø:/, that is, the input system looked as follows:

(9.26)

i: u:
e:, ø:
ɛ: ɔ:
a:

After the application of the Great Vowel Shift, a northern system like that in (9.26) shows no diphthongisation of /u:/. Because of the empty slot between /u:/ and /ɔ:/, /u:/ did not diphthongise because there was no /o:/ to push /u:/ out of place (but /ɔ:/ moved up to fill the empty slot left by the fronted /o:/ by a drag process). On the other hand, among the front vowels close /i:/ diphthongised, suggesting that a push chain was involved among these vowels. The absence of a diphthongisation of /u:/ suggests two things: first that the Great Vowel Shift probably started with the raising of /e:/ and /o:/, and second that both a push and drag mechanism was involved. If it started with the rising of the half-close /e:/, /o:/, then this explains why diphthongisation in the North of England occurs among the front but not among the back vowels, and if neither the lowest nor the highest of the input vowels move first, both push and drag mechanisms inevitably must be involved.

It is not so important in this context whether the Great Vowel Shift involved a push or drag mechanism nor where in the system it started. The overall implications of the process are more important. The overall implications are that, like the First Germanic Consonant Shift, the Great Vowel Shift is a change that affected the sound system as a whole shifting series of sounds, in this case long vowels, such that the shift of one series triggers the shift of other series. Thus the Great Vowel Shift is best understood if vowels are interpreted as members of a space in which they are not only phonetically defined but also described as occupying specific slots in this space, allowing them to be organised in series. As in the First Germanic Consonant Shift, contiguity in such a system of slots can affect sounds that share phonological features such that the shift of one series, sharing certain phonological features, sets parallel series in motion. In this respect, the First Germanic Consonant Shift and the Great Vowel Shift are similar. Because it is not induced by phonetic context but the change is to do with sounds occupying specific slots in a system of phonological contrasts, the Great Vowel Shift is also a system-dependent change like the first Germanic Consonant Shift. They probably differ in that the overall driving force of the First Germanic Consonant Shift was to fulfil the general requirement that a weak obstruent series should be matched by the corresponding strong series as well as to get rid of a systemically isolated series, whilst the driving force of the Great Vowel Shift, once the process had started, was to preserve phonological distinctions.

As regards phonologicalisation, the Great Vowel Shift is parallel to the First Germanic Consonant Shift. Like the latter, the Great Vowel Shift does not increase the number of phoneme contrasts. In other words, no splits occur as no allophones arise as a result of the shift. But despite the lack of allophonic promotion, the vowel shift nonetheless affects the phonological system. Not only does it make sounds which before the change lacked the ability to contrast meaning phonemes, but it also reshuffles the lexical incidence of long vowels. The set of words associated with, say, /i:/ or /e:/ before the change is not the same set of words that has these vowels after the change. As discussed in connection with the First Germanic Consonant Shift, this kind of restructuring is difficult to regard as anything else than instances of phonologicalisation, albeit not the classic instance involving allophonic promotion.

9.4.4 System-dependent changes in North American English

Moving into slots occupied by other phonemes and vacating phoneme slots which are subsequently filled by new phonemes characterise instances of system-dependent changes that are found in present-day North American English. Two instances of such system-dependent changes will be considered here. Both instances have been discussed briefly in Ch. 5 under the two headings, the Northern Cities Shift (NCS) and the Southern Vowel Shift (SVS) (see also Ch. 10 below). In so far as there are some advanced speakers who exhibit full implementation of these shifts, it is justifiable to regard NCS and SVS as diachronic changes.

NCS involves the following shifts of monophthongs repeated from Ch. 5:

(9.27)

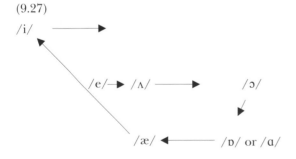

The first stage of NCS is the raising of /æ/, a raising which is common everywhere in North America before the nasals /m/ and /n/. The second stage fronts /ɒ///ɑ/, which moves forward to fill the slot vacated by /æ/. /ɔ/ subsequently moves into the space formerly occupied by /ɒ///ɑ/. /e/ is then retracted, pushing /ʌ/ backwards to fill the slot that /ɔ/ occupied before it moved downward and forward. Finally, /i/ shifts to the back as a reaction to the movement of /e/. These shifts are all interrelated and, except for the initial movement of /æ/, caused by the movement of other monophthongs. The shift of /æ/, the initial stage of NCS, pulls /ɒ///ɑ/ into front position just like the movement of /ɒ///ɑ/ pulls /ɔ/ down and forward. These shifts are clear instances of drag chain processes. The movement of /ʌ/ and /e/ involves a push chain mechanism. The raising of /æ/ makes both /e/ and /i/ leave their slots. /e/ is retracted colliding with /ʌ/, which in response moves backward, just like /i/ also responds to /æ/- raising by abandoning its place in the pre-shift system. Like the Great Vowel Shift, NCS then exemplifies both drag and push chains and like the Great Vowel Shift it is a system-dependent change. If vowels are not seen as members of a system whose members fill slots, it is difficult to explain why the shifts involved in NCS actually occur. Interestingly, NCS affects both subsystem A and subsystem B vowels. This suggests a general applicability of the phonological vowel space description at the same time as it supports the phonetic class of monophthongs. The implications of NCS are principally the same as the implications of the Great Vowel Shift. Phonologically, vowels are organised in a system of slots. These slots maintain differences of meaning. When these slots are invaded by occupants of other slots or occupants vacate slots and approach other slots, the vowel system responds with general restructuring so meaning differences can be upheld.

SVS, the other major North American vowel shift, is also not explicable without recourse to the phonological system that vowels enter into. SVS involves the following shifts repeated from Ch. 5:

(9.28)

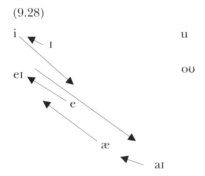

As described in Ch. 5 briefly, SVS is a chain process involving mutual influence of both monophthongs and diphthongs. In fact, SVS like NCS probably comprises both drag and push mechanisms (see also Ch. 10 below). The first stage of SVS is the monophthongisation of /aɪ/ and fronting of the nucleus (first element) that remains after monophthongisation towards /æ/. Subsequently, /eɪ/'s nucleus falls to a position similar to that held by the nucleus of /aɪ/ prior to stage one. This is in some areas of the South joined by the lowering of /i/. At the same time or subsquently as /eɪ/'s nucleus is pulled down, /e/ moves into the position of shifted /eɪ/, developing a front-closing off-glide, and /æ/ and /ɪ/ join the pattern of raising and off-glide development exhibited by /e/. The monophthongisation of /aɪ/ causes a drag chain process pulling /eɪ/ and sometimes /i/ down. The vacated slots are then filled by other front vowels. The best candidate for a push mechanism is the movement of /æ/ whose position comes under pressure because of the intial shift of /aɪ/, but the evidence is inconclusive as the movement of /æ/ can also been seen as a shift caused by the vacation of slots above it. The phonological classification, in particular the interaction of contiguous slot filling segments within the vowel space, is the mechanism which explains the rotation of vowels in SVS. Unlike NCS, SVS involves all vowels, monophthongs and diphthongs alike, emphasising the unity of this class of sounds. Phonological structure, in particular how slots help preserve meaning differences, is thus pivotal in understanding the mechanism of SVS.

Both NCS and SVS, as well as the Great Vowel Shift, are system-dependent shifts. The shift of one vowel is the result of the movement of contiguous vowels within a close-knit system, in particular either vowels are pushed out of position or dragged into slots vacated by others or both. The triggering event of each shift is not always clear. The Great Vowel Shift was probably triggered by social factors like prestige. The triggering event of NCS, the raising of /æ/, has been suggested to be a result of the construction of the Erie Canal. This construction brought many North American speakers together who did not pronounce /æ/ in the same way. In such a situation of dialect mixture, it is not uncommon to see simplification so one form becomes the predominant one, which in the Inland North resulted in the general raising of /æ/. What triggered SVS is less clear, but the initial stage in which /aɪ/ becomes a monophthong is not sociolinguistically uniform so prestige cannot be ruled out as a triggering factor. Whatever the triggering factors, the driving force of all three shifts once a vowel has been set in motion is to preserve meaning. For example, prior to SVS the vowel of words like *hide, my* have /aɪ/, but after SVS they are associated with /æ/, so *hide* sounds like *had*. To avoid confusion and preserve meaning, the system responds and the vowel of *had* changes so it approaches the vowel of *made*. To avoid confusion with *mad*, the vowel of *made* subsequently shifts and becomes similar to the vowel of *hide*. In this way meaning differences are preserved, but the result is a sometimes quite drastic reshuffling of vowels in series of words. Similar reshuffling characterised The Great Vowel Shift which is clearly a diachronic change with input and output temporally ordered. Here NCS and SVS have been treated as potentially diachronic too. Since some speakers seem to exhibit full implementation of either shift (in the most advanced inland areas see Ch. 10 below), this option is defensible. But they are for many speakers merely shifts in progress. Vowel shifts have also occurred in London English in which such a shift has reshuffled the diphthongs quite extensively. Vowel shifts can lead to confusing and comical situations, as when a World War II soldier with a fully implemented London English diphthong shift, in which /eɪ/->/aɪ/ so in his pronunciation *lay* sounds like *lie*, responded to the remark 'I came here to die' from his fellow American soldier with the comment, 'I came here yesterday'.

9.4.5 Closing remarks

Two issues should be touched on briefly before this short discussion of change is concluded. The first concerns phonologicalisation. In its classic form, phonologicalisation involves promotion of allophones to phonemes following the loss of the inducing context as in Old English *i*-umlaut. But only such additions of new phonemes normally count as phonologicalisations. Chain shifts do not involve phonologicalisations in the traditional use of this term, because chain shifts merely reshuffle the inventory of vowels without typically increasing the number of contrasting phonemes. But it is not obvious why only combinatorial changes like *i*-umlaut but not system-dependent vowel shifts such as NCS or SVS involve phonologicalisation. NCS and SVS clearly change the vowel phoneme inventories drastically, so large sets of words are assigned new root vowels. As evidenced by the exchange of remarks between soldiers with different phonologies cited above (see end of previous section), such reshufflings of inventories caused by system-dependent shifts affect the meaning to a point of misunderstanding. Phonemes are the smallest meaning-differenciating units of language and as such contribute in an important way to the encoding and decoding of information. Any change affecting this central property of sounds, the property that makes us call them phonemes, should then be an instance of phonologicalisation. Both combinatorial and system-dependent changes are then best categorised as instances of phonologicalisation.

The other issue that requires a brief comment is the kinds of variation and change that have been considered in this chapter. The assimilations of the first sections are all present-day variations triggered by the interaction of contiguous sounds. The diachronic processes such as *i*-umlat or NCS or SVS (in so far as the latter two can be considered diachronic) likewise are the result of factors of contiguity. *i*-umlaut is similar to assimilations, as it is the result of the interaction of contiguous sounds which follow after one another in a string. In the chain shifts, changes occur as a result of sounds being contiguous in close-knit systems of contrasting phonemes. In either case, change happens as a result of interaction between linguistic units. One term used about linguistic phenomena inducing variation and change as in these cases is **internal** factors. But factors such as speech style, register (speech situation), ethnicity or social class and prestige can also influence the pronunciation (and other components of language) and cause change and variation. Such factors are known as **external** factors. North American English /r/, specifically in New York City, is an often cited example of a phoneme whose pronunciation fluctuates because of the prestige that specific social classes assign to a rhotic or non-rhotic pronunciation. Similarly, a wider distribution of clear-*l* than typically before half-close and close front vowels seems to be dependent on ethnicity. Flapping, i.e. no distinct releasing of /t/ and /d/, varies according to external factors like style and register. So external factors clearly contribute to variation and change just like internal factors. Nonetheless, internal factors have received most attention here. This is a consequence of focusing on the sound system of North American English and a result of an endeavour to limit the scope of the book. But this choice should not be taken as a rejection of the importance of external factors, nor as ignorance of how the two factors often jointly cause sounds and language to change.

Variation can also be determined by other factors than neighbouring sounds in a broad sense, or issues like prestige, register and ethnicity. Geography has an impact on language variation too, as is clear from the short discussion of North American regional dialects in Ch. 1. Chapter 10 deals in greater detail with the interaction of region and pronunciation, and lays out the the main dialects of North American English on the basis of specifically, but not exclusively, the pronunciation of vowels and as presented in ANAE. This chapter concludes with a summary of the main features of diachronic change such as this term has been used in this chapter:

- In a diachronic change input and output to the change are temporally ordered
- Two types of diachronic change are recognised: combinatorial (segment-induced) and system-dependent (phoneme slot-induced) changes
- A combinatorial change involves the spreading of one or more phonetic features from one to another segment so the induced segment becomes more like or identical with the inducing segment
- A system-dependent change involves the change of one or a series of segments as a result of the restructurings in the phoneme system of which the segment or the series is a part
- Some system-dependent changes are chain processes, involving either push or drag mechanisms
- In North American English there exist both combinatorial and system-dependent changes. /æ/-splitting in the East is an example of the former and NCS and SVS are examples of the latter.

Further reading

Lass 1984 has a very good account of assimilation processes. On diachronic processes, specifically such as are described here, see Lass 1976, 1984, Lass and Anderson 1975. On historical descriptions in general see Bynon 1977 or Joseph and Janda 2003. For a detailed discussion of the American English phenomena discussed in this chapter see Labov et al. 2006. On English English change shifts, see Wells 1982.

CHAPTER 10

Survey of American English dialects

10.1 Introduction

So far this book's centre of focus has been on NAERD, the reference pronunciation, which has been taken as representative of English pronunciation in present-day North America. This narrow focus has been dictated by the aim of writing an introductory text-book to North American English pronunciation whose reader is expected to have no or little prior knowledge of phonetics and phonology. But focusing on one allegedly representative reference dialect inevitably leads to generalisation and simplification. The selection of what has been called NAERD has left out important detail with regard to the pronunciation of especially vowels, excluding not only certain northern and eastern features but also characteristic vowel pronunciations of the South. This chapter is intended to make up for the lack of dialect diversity which the choice of NAERD has brought about and describe the dialects of present-day North American English. Ch. 1 briefly outlined the main North American English regional dialects and linked these with settlement history, but the dialect variation presented there was discussed without attention to detail. As it was the topic of Ch. 9, variation is then also the topic of this chapter. However, in this chapter variation does not refer to the present-day consonant and vowel variation which is motivated by contiguous sounds such as in assimilations (cf. Ch. 9), nor variation resulting from diachronic change, let alone such as concerns the free and bound allophones of individual phonemes. Instead variation in this chapter stands for the fluctuation in North American English pronunciation which is solely determined by geographical region.

The description of North American dialects of this chapter will be based on the results provided by the so-called TELSUR project and presented in ANAE, the Atlas of North American English, which is predominantly based on the urban pronunciation of vowels (see Ch. 1). The present account thus assumes that dialect stands for a geographical variety defined on the basis of sound system – as has been the assumption throughout this book – specifically, but not exclusively, on vowel system. Lexical evidence and other evidence is not taken into consideration in the present account, but as pointed out in Ch. 1 there often exists a surprising concurrence of lexical and phonological dialect boundaries in North America.

A description of dialect geography on the basis of pronunciation requires that some phonological features are selected as particularly important and diagnostic. It is also necessary to posit a set of non-phonological but general criteria defining when a variety can be called a dialect. The first set of criteria is those listed in (10.1). In ANAE these suffice to define North American dialects in terms of sound system:

(10.1)

- Northern Cities Shift (NCS)
- Southern Vowel Shift (SCS)
- the relative backness of /u/
- the relative backness of /oʊ/
- the low back merger
- /æ/-splitting
- back-closing realisation of /ɔ/
- Canadian raising/shift
- rhoticity

The second set of criteria refers to the presence, the absence or the relative contribution of the defining phonological criteria which identify a regional dialect. Here it will be assumed, following the general opinion of many specialists, that a regional variety can be called a dialect if

(10.2)

- it encompasses an area which is geographically uniform and continuous
- a given defining phonological feature is found frequently in every community within this area and no community outside the area is marked by the same phonological feature
- it is also characterised by a defining pronunciation feature expanding from a centre, a property often incompatible with full satisfaction of occurrence in every community
- a defining pronunciation feature fills a slot in a phonological system in which the feature interacts with other features filling other slots

These four properties, high frequency, exclusiveness, distribution from a centre and systemic membership, will be referred to as the generally defining criteria of a dialect, whereas the list in (10.1) comprises the set of defining phonological features. As expected, the former all concern the phonological properties of vowels except for the last criterion. Thus among consonants, sonorants only play a marginal role in the definition of North American English dialects, and solely with respect to distribution and realisation not phonological contrast, as rhoticity, the only diagnostically relevant property of sonorants, and ensuing *r*-colouring, concerns the presence versus the absence of post-vocalic *r*. Vowels vary considerably diachronically, so much that this variation can identify epochs in the history of English (see Ch. 9), whereas, diachronically, consonants vary least. It is not surprising, then, that vowels, as specified in (10.1), serve as the most important sign posts pointing to different present-day regional dialects in North America. The joint application of the defining criteria, both phonological and general, enables us to draw borderlines between regional dialects. Such borderlines are referred to as **isogloss**es.

10.2 The main dialect areas

As pointed out in Ch. 1, settlement history laid the foundation of present-day dialect geography of North American English, a map of which was gradually drawn in the course of the 20th century culminating with the publication of ANAE in 2007, which established one Canadian and five main phonological dialects in the US. NAERD, the reference dialect which has been described in the preceding chapters, includes and excludes to a varying degree features characteristic of all of these main dialects. NAERD represents a pronunciation which with respect to vowels is not affected by the two major vowel shifts occurring in the North and the South, NCS (The Northern Cities Shift) and SVS (The Southern Vowel Shift) (see Ch. 5 and below), nor does its vowels exhibit typical eastern features. On the other hand, it is marked by the increasing low back vowel merger, merging the *cot – caught* vowels, which is either quite common or spreading in the West and the Midland as well as in some eastern areas. With regard to consonants and prosody, NAERD is not defined as narrowly by excluding particular areas. Instead, most of North America, including Canada, is covered by NAERD when both consonants and prosodic features are taken into account. But clearly such a strategy of excluding certain areas is not appropriate when the aim is to describe dialect diversity. Obviously, this aim dictates the opposite strategy and to leave out, say, the The North and The South would ignore NCS and SVS, two vowel shifts which play a very important part in establishing the present-day main dialect geography of North American English.

NCS defines a northern dialect area whose core area around the great lakes is characterised by full implementation of NCS. SVS, on the other hand, outlines the boundaries of a southern dialect area extending roughly from south-west Texas to East Virginia with two inland core areas characterised by fuller implementations of SVS. By delimiting the North and the South, NCS and SVS also jointly define a non-northern and a non-southern dialect region within which neither shift applies. This region, extending from the eastern seaboard to the west coast, becomes larger as it extends westwards and contains the dialects of the West and the Midland. But this is not the only area in which NCS and SVS fail to apply. The eastern seaboard, more specifically the Mid-Atlantic States including New York City, constitutes an independent dialect area, as does the Northeast. Both these eastern dialects differ from the dialects of the West and the Midland, as well as from one another, so that they will be regarded as belonging to an Eastern dialect region. Neither NCS nor SVS applies in Canada which, moreover, is characterised by a unique process known as Canadian Raising. North American English can then be divided into five main areas as shown on the following map:

(10.3)

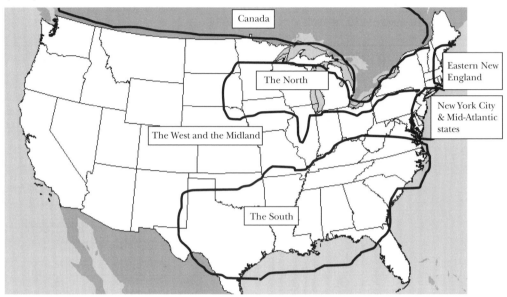

Since the borderlines between the main dialects regions are largely drawn on the basis of NCS and SVS, the dialects of the Midland and the West and other areas outside the North and the South become negatively defined, if no other features than NCS and SVS are invoked. But as is apparent from the defining list in (10.1), such features will be invoked. With the exception of NCS and SVS, these features define dialects of North America outside the North and the South positively. One feature almost plays as important a role as NCS and SVS. This is the low back merger which helps define the West and the Midland, as well as Canada. Within the areas of the West and the Midland, this merger is widespread and increasing, but not yet complete. It is widespread in Canadian English as well as in eastern New England. Because it is found outside the Midland and the West, the low back merger does not define these areas, but it defines the North and the South negatively by not occurring in these regions, just like NCS and SVS define areas outside the North and the South negatively by not occurring outside these areas. Although it is often assumed to be almost diagnostic of the West and the Midland, the low back merger on closer examination does not define and unite the West and the Midland. The inconsistency of this otherwise widespread feature is one indication of the need for a more refined description of North American dialect geography and that the West and the Midland cannot be considered one uniform dialect area, but should be regarded as consisting of several independent dialects. Such more subtle distinctions both within the West and the Midland and such as follows from the major shifts of the North and South follow below.

10.3 The North

10.3.1 The northern area

In the present account, the North will be assumed to encompass any US territory north and east of the West and Midland areas except for Eastern New England. Thus the north extends from Providence westwards just south of the large cities around the great lakes, with a southern detour to include St. Louis, across into Nebraska and from there northwards to the Dakotas state border which marks the level of the northern isogloss of the northern region as this travels eastwards to include the southern half of Minnesota and most of Wisconsin and Michigan. Canada is not part of this area, but constitutes the northern border of another area squeezed in between the North and Canada extending as far westwards as the north-eastern corner of the state of Montana, referred to as the North Central (see below). In the present description, the North Central is considered to be an area of the reference dialect, because of its close affinity with the West and the Midland and because it lacks diagnostic northern features. In other treatments, such as ANAE, the North Central belongs to the North at the same time as it is considered a residual area. Internally, the northern area consists of three sub-areas: the North, including the Inland North around the great lakes, and Western New England. The map below outlines the dialect areas within in the northern area:

(10.4)

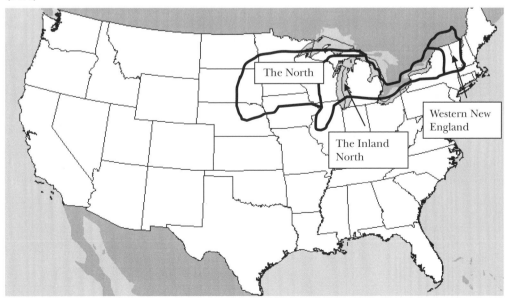

The northern area thus consists of a core area, the Inland North, flanked by two northern areas which are less obviously northern than the Inland, the easternmost one of which includes Western but not Eastern New England.

10.3.2 Diagnosing the North

Of the phonologically defining features listed in (10.1), NCS defines the North. NCS is a chain shift, as discussed in Ch. 9, and is quite unique among English vowel shifts as only monophthongs are shifted. As in other chain shifts, in NCS the displacement of one vowel sets about a massive change of other vowels as some are forced to leave the slots they occupy and others fill the vacated slots. To recapitulate, NCS leads to the following restructuring of the system of monophthongs in the North, a representation repeated from Ch.5:

(10.5)

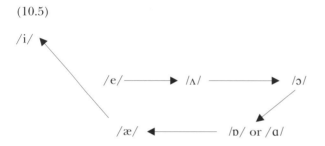

NCS is started by the general raising of /æ/. This raising is followed by the fronting of the merged /ɒ///ɑ/ class and /ɔ/ then responds by moving into the slot vacated by /ɒ///ɑ/. /e/, under pressure from the general raising of /æ/, shifts backward towards /ʌ/ which in turns moves into the position formerly occupied by /ɔ/. Finally, /i/ often moves back and down as a reaction to the shift of /e/.

In the North word pairs like *dawn – don, hawk – hock* are not the same. Unlike in NAERD, the low back merger is then not found in the North. The presence of a low back contrast is not only a pre-condition for NCS; it also provides a way of measuring the relative progression of NCS. The presence of the low back vowel contrast, /ɒ//ɑ/ versus /ɔ/, allows /ɒ//ɑ/ to move forward because its vacated slot can be filled by /ɔ/. The forward movement of /ɒ//ɑ/ is paralleled by the backward movement of /e/ responding to the general raising of /æ/. These parallel, but reverse, movements provide the measuring standard or relative progression of NCS. In its most extreme form, NCS aligns /e/ and /ɒ//ɑ/ along the same front-back dimension. This almost complete /e/-/ɒ//ɑ/ **alignment** defines the core area of the North, the Inland North. In other areas of the North, this alignment is not as advanced. Western New England is one such area, which then along with the northern area west of the great lakes will not be considered a core member of the North, showing only partial /e/-/ɒ//ɑ/ alignment.

Other diagnostic features of the North are the absence of /æ/-splitting and a retracted realisation of /oʊ/. /æ/-splitting is not found outside what above was referred to as the East. The realisation of /oʊ/, on the other hand, is important because this vowel's realisation fluctuates considerably. /oʊ/ is generally moving forward in North America, except in the West and Canada, as pointed out in connection with the discussion of this diphthong in Ch. 5. The relative backness of /oʊ/ in the North provides another measuring standard, parallel to /e/-/ɒ///ɑ/ alignment, which helps diagnose the North. This standard concerns the position of /ʌ/ and /oʊ/ relative to /ɒ///ɑ/. In the North where retracted /oʊ/ is common and /ʌ/ is moving backwards as a result of NCS, as is apparent from (10.4), both vowels are backer than /ɒ///ɑ/ which moves forward. In areas where /oʊ/ is fronted and NCS does not apply, both /ʌ/ and /oʊ/ are fronter. The latter pattern is then characteristic of non-northern dialects with fronted /oʊ/.

As in the case of /e/-/ɒ///ɑ/ alignment, this **non-low – /ɒ///ɑ/ alignment**, as it will be referred to, involving /oʊ/- /ʌ/, on the one hand, and /ɒ///ɑ/, on the other, is then advanced in the Inland North where NCS is in full operation, but less advanced in other Northern areas. The picture which begins to emerge from this complicated interaction of vowels and the slots they occupy in the vowel space may be summarised as follows:

(10.6)

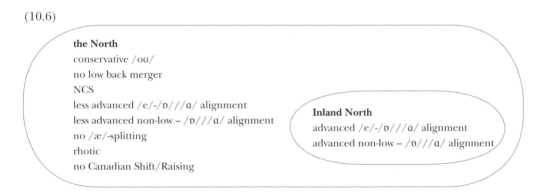

in which the features listed under the North are repeated in subareas if they exhibit a diagnostically important manifestation here. Both advanced /e/-/ɒ//ɑ/ alignment and advanced non-low – /ɒ//ɑ/ alignment exhibit this property. What (10.6) then summaries is that there is a core area within the North. This core area is the Inland North defined by an advanced stage of NCS. Elsewhere in the North, NCS also applies but in a less advanced form and all other defining features characterise the North. In (10.6) the North is also diagnosed by the absence of some defining phonological features. In the treatment of each main dialect area below, the absence of defining features will also be taken as diagnostic of dialects. But dialects are only delimited negatively by referring to features of contiguous dialects and typically only by referring to one defining feature of a contiguous dialect. Thus, for example, the absence of Canadian Raising/Shift delimits the North from Canada, and the absence of /æ/-splitting delimits it from the Mid-Atlantic East.

The features listed in (10.6) are the defining phonological criteria of the North. But do these features then define a dialect as described by the generally defining criteria listed in (10.2)? As for uniformity and continuity, the answer is yes. The North is geographically bound together by NCS, in as much as it is continuous. The uniformity of no low back merger supports this picture of continuity. NCS is also found frequently within all parts of the area and is rare outside. Furthermore, the North has a central area with advanced or full implementation of NCS. From this centre less advanced forms of NCS are spread out to the western and eastern areas within the North. Finally, the North also satisfies the last criterion: diagnostic NCS involves vowel shifts occurring as a result of these vowels' membership of a phonological system of sound slots. The North then seems to live up to the expectations of a regional dialect.

10.3.3 The vowel system of a northern speaker

It is common practice in descriptions of at least English dialects to conclude each dialect description with an overview of its defining sound system. This survey chapter will follow this practice and list the most advanced vowel system of each dialect except for the dialect of the West and the Midland whose system is fairly similar to the reference dialect, NAERD. The overview of each dialect concerns only vowels (for reasons mentioned earlier) and allows for easy comparison with the reference dialect and other dialects of North America.

The quite extensive rotations among the vowels of the North automatically entails that the vowel system of the North in its most advanced form must differ quite significantly from the system of the reference dialect. Given that NCS affects monophthongs only, this difference concerns subsystems A and B of the subclassification system used in Ch. 5, leaving subsystems C and D, the diphthongs, unchanged. In particular, after NCS has applied the A and B systems appear as shown in the following diagram which assumes the most advanced form of NCS:

(10.7)

subsystem A   subsystem B
after NCS   after NCS

   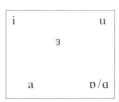

At first sight this system is not significantly different from the system of the reference dialect. Subsystem A and subsystem B of both the reference dialect and the North contain 5 phonemes each, and the slots these phonemes occupy in the vowel space are by and large the same in the two dialects. Nonetheless, the two dialects differ in a significant way. What is significant is that after the application of NCS, all the rotated vowels are associated with a different set of words than they were prior to NCS and that the distinction checked and free no longer follows subsystem A and B strictly. For example, before NCS /æ/ is the vowel of the lexical set to which, among many others, *trap, trash, match* belong, but after NCS this lexical set is associated with /e/ or even the higher /ɪ/ (often realised as the second vowel of *idea*). Similarly, before NCS /ʌ/, for example, is the vowel of the lexical set to which, among many others, *strut, lush, much* belong, but after NCS this lexical set comes to be associated with /ɔ/. Given that NCS is a chain shift, involving a rotation of all non-close monophthongs, this effect on the lexical sets is to be expected just as no directly observable restructuring of the phonological system of monophthongs is obvious when all vowels participate in the rotation. The difference between an advanced northern speaker and a speaker of, say, the reference dialect is then really only apparent from the lexical set with which a given vowel is associated and, as mentioned, the checked/free distribution. An appropriate defining overview of the subsystem A and B vowels of the North then requires that the input-to-NCS qualities are listed with examples of lexical sets. (10.8) summarises this information which then represents the vowel system of a speaker from the Inland North.

Clearly, the lexical sets associated with a northern speaker after NCS highlight the difference between a speaker from the Inland North and other speakers of English both inside and outside of North America.

(10.8)

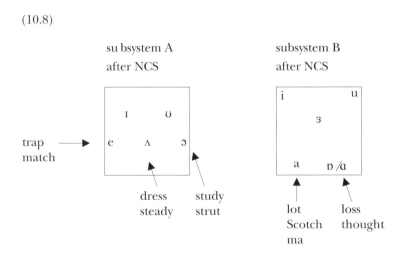

10.4 The Midland and the West

10.4.1 The area of the Midland and the West

As will have become apparent, the Midland and the West is not one uniform dialect area, but consists of several sub-areas of which the West is one and the Midland is another. Although they make up the most of the area of the Midland and the West, there is also a third dialect area within this very large area. The easternmost Midland extends not all the way to the Mid-Atlantic states, but in-between lies an area which, like the Midland and the West, is assumed to constitute an independent dialect area. This is referred to as Western Pennsylvania, so the super area of the Midland and West is here assumed to comprise the following three dialects: The West, the Midland and Western Pennsylvania.

Geographically, the West, spanning an area from the Canadian to the Mexican border, extends eastwards from the pacific coast to where the North begins, approximately midway between the east and the west coasts of the United States. In the South it does not include the state of Texas, whilst in the North it is in the present treatment regarded as including the area squeezed in between the North and the Canadian border, the area commonly referred to as the North Central. The Midland starts where the West stops – midway between the east and the west coast – following the southern border of the North to the Ohio-Pennsylvania state border, except that the St. Louis corridor belongs to the North. In the East, the Midland covers most of the state of Ohio, and its southern border follows approximately the Ohio-Kentucky and Indiana-Kentucky state borders. The southern Midland border cuts off the southern part of the state of Missouri, but includes the northern half of Oklahoma except for the panhandle. Most of the state of Kansas belongs to the Midland as does the southeastern part of Nebraska where the Midland border is united with the border of the North. Western Pennsylvania, the last and smallest dialect area within the area of the West and the Midland, covers as the name suggests Western Pennsylvania. It extends into the northern part of West Virginia and the eastern part of Ohio and includes in the North the city of Erie. The northern and eastern borders of this area are those defined by the North and the Mid-Atlantic states. The map below displays the dialect areas of the Midland and the West:

(10.9)

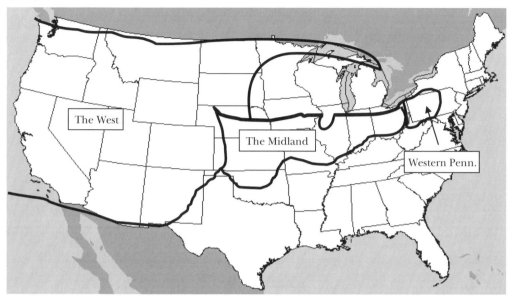

Unlike the North, the West and Midland area does not contain a core dialect flanked by less typical, less advanced West and Midland dialects. Instead the area contains three dialects which obviously are bound together by jointly having many features in common, and with the reference dialect NAERD, at the same time as each dialect area has its own defining features. How they are similar and how they differ will become clear presently.

10.4.2 Diagnosing the West and the Midland

It has been pointed out several times that the West and the Midland is defined negatively by not being affected by NCS and SVS. The absence of these shifts is thus a defining feature of all dialects within this large area. But the absence of NCS and SVS means that the low back merger is a possibility. Fusion of the /ɔ/-/ɒ//ɑ/ contrast is exactly what we find too. Positively, the dialects of the West and the Midland are then characterised by the low back merger, but, strictly speaking, the low back merger is not found consistently within all three West and Midland dialects. Its distribution is then an appropriate starting-point for establishing the defining features for each of the West and Midland dialects.

The dialect of the West and only the West is marked by the low back merger which is found sufficiently consistently to define it. Another feature of the West is the conservative, retracted realisation of /oʊ/ like that of the North, whilst /u/ in the West has joined the general fronting found in many North American dialects. The residual North Central area, extending from Montana westwards along the US-Canadian border, is also – somewhat controversially – categorised as western in the present treatment. For the Central North to be considered western requires that the fronted /u/-criterion be relaxed, a vowel which, unlike in the remaining part of the West, remains fairly back within this area. On the other hand, the North Central has the low back merger and no NCS and SVS, at the same time as it lacks distinctive Canadian features like the remaining part of the West (for Canada see further below).

The Midland, that is, the middle part of the West and Midland area, is characterised by not having fully merged the pronunciations of the /ɔ/-/ɒ//ɑ/ contrast. Instead the low back merger is in transition in the Midland, whilst the West to the west and Western Pennsylvania to the east of the Midland both exhibit advanced stages of the merger. This fluctuation flanked by completion is likely to lead to full merging of these low back vowels in a not too distant future in the Midland. What sets the Midland off from the West is /oʊ/ which in the Midland is distinctly fronted, while the pronunciation of this vowel is more retracted and conservative in the West. Fronting of /u/ is also characteristic of the Midland. Other signs of heterogeneity than transient low back merger in the Midland are the presence of the St. Louis corridor which is a northern protrusion with northern features into the Midland.

Lastly, Western Pennsylvania, the third West and Midland dialect, is characterised by solid completion of the low back merger. Fronted /oʊ/ and /u/ also help define this dialect and its eastern border is drawn where /æ/-splitting begins to occur in the Mid-Atlantic states. As in the Midland, there are also areas within Western Pennsylvania with unique phonological features. One such area is the city of Pittsburgh in which monophthongisation of /aʊ/ to /a/ is common. But the Pittsburgh pronunciation of *downtown* as [ˌdanˈtan] is rare in the Midland outside this city. The defining criteria of the three West and Midland dialects are summarised in (10.10)

(10.10)

The West	The Midland	Western Pennsylvania
low back merger	incomplete low back	low back merger
retracted /oʊ/	merger	fronted /oʊ/
no NCS and SVS	fronted /oʊ/	no /æ/-splitting
no Canadian	no NCS and SVS	no NCS and SVS
Raising/Shift	rhotic	rhotic
rhotic		

Not all the defining criteria from the list in (10.1) are listed under each dialect. Thus /æ/-splitting is listed as distinctive for Western Pennsylvania and Canadian Raising/shift for the West. This is because Western Pennsylvania borders on a dialect for which /æ/-splitting is criterial, viz. the Mid-Atlantic states, and the West borders on a dialect, viz. that of Canada, defined by Canadian Raising/

shift. It is clear from (10.10) as pointed out at the beginning of this section that all three dialects are defined by the absence of NCS and SVS and by rhoticity. Individually, they are differentiated by different applications of the low back merger and /oʊ/-fronting.

As in the case of the northern dialects, it is also necessary to ask whether these three dialects satisfy the generally defining criteria listed in (10.2). Not all three dialects satisfy the criterion that a dialect should encompass a continuous and uniform geographical area equally well. The West meets this demand fully. The Midland less obviously so, being almost halved by the St. Louis corridor. Western Pennsylvania cannot fully live up to this requirement either. The special Pittsburgh monophthongisation is a discontinuing factor. On the other hand, all three satisfy the requirement that the defining criteria are found frequently within each area – for the Midland this means that full completion of the defining low back merger is irregular. The last two criteria are less obviously fulfilled. In the West and Midland, it is not possible to speak of a feature expanding from a centre as in the North and the South (see § 10.4.3), nor that one or more particular defining features interact systemicly with other features of the sound system. In this regard, a less optimal satisfaction of the generally defining features for the West and Midland has to be accepted.

It is no accident that the West and Midland dialects less readily satisfy the last two generally defining criteria. Unlike the North and the South, the West and the Midland lack a single unifying property which distinguishes them as one obvious dialect area. NCS and in the South, as will become clear presently, SVS serve these purposes in these regions. It is true, the low back merger does offer itself as a candidate uniting the area of the West and Midland, but the low back merger is also characteristic of Canada and Eastern New England, whereas NCS and SVS are restricted to their defining areas. The absence of a unifying sound shift also makes it easier for neighbouring dialect features to invade and for isolated phonological systems to develop. The St. Louis corridor and the Pittsburgh peculiarity illustrate this side of an absent unity. Conversely, it is also not so difficult to incorporate neighbouring areas into the West and the Midland when it is not united by one property. This explains why the temptation to incorporate the North Central in the West and Midland area could not be resisted in the present description. As an area without a single unifying property and with more flexible and less rigid borders than other dialect regions, the West and the Midland become the default dialect area, possibly even the default dialect *par excellence*. When at the same time it has a fairly main-stream and familiar vowel system, the West and the Midland dialect area also could be an obvious choice as reference dialect. The fact that the vowel system of NAERD is more like the vowel systems found in this very large area than in any other dialect area confirms this view, as does the view expressed in ANAE that if any North American dialects were to be regarded as constituting one reference dialect area then this area should include the West, the Midland and Canada. The relative affinity of the West and the Midland with NAERD entails that this section on the West and the Midland will not be concluded with a summary of the vowel systems of speakers of these two areas. These systems have already, by and large, been listed in specifically Ch.5.

10.5 The South

10.5.1 The southern area

Geographically, the South encompasses all US territory south and south-east of the West and the Midland dialect areas except for almost all of the state of Florida. On the east coast, the northern border of the South starts approximately where the Maryland – Virginia state borders meet. From there the northern isogloss runs westward south of Washington DC until it meets the southern Midland border which it joins until the eastern border of the West is encountered. The South includes almost all of the state of Texas from where the Gulf coast marks the southern border of the South. Florida is cut off as non-southern, as is on the east coast a small area around the city of Charleston. Otherwise the east-coast line represents the eastern border of the South until it reaches the Maryland state border in Chesapeake Bay. Inside the South, two enclaves differ so much from the South in general that they are considered independent subdialects: one is the Texas-based Texas South, the other is the Inland South, encompassing an area put together by parts of the states of Alabama, Georgia, the Carolinas and Tennessee. The southern dialect area and sub-areas are shown in the following map:

(10.11)

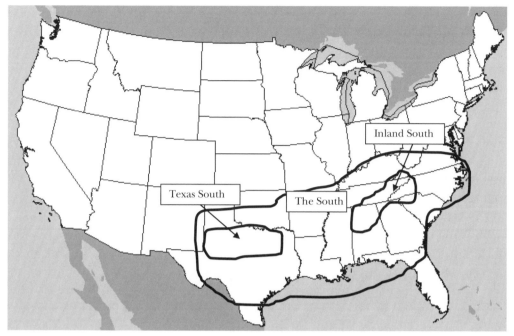

SVS is pivotal in defining the South. How it contributes to its delimitation and the definition of the two internal sub-areas will be considered presently.

10.5.2 Diagnosing the South

Of the phonologically defining features listed in (10.1), SVS defines the South. SVS is a chain shift, but unlike NCS, SVS affects monophthongs and diphthongs alike. As in NCS, the displacement of one vowel from the slot it occupies triggers a wholesale restructuring of the vowel space system of the South. To recapitulate, SVS involves the following shifts (repeated from (5.20)):

(10.12)

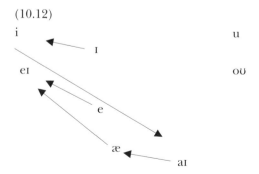

SVS is triggered by the monophthongisation of /aɪ/, whose resulting nucleus often at the same time is fronted approaching the position of /æ/. Following this **off-glide deletion** (deletion of the second less prominent off-glide /ɪ/),

/eɪ/ falls along a non-peripheral track so its first element occupies the phonological area taken up by the nucleus of /aɪ/ after off-glide deletion. This **1st non-peripheral lowering** is in some areas joined by **2nd non-peripheral lowering** when /i/, frequently realised as a diphthong, approaches /e/. Either at the same time or after these lowerings, /æ/, /e/ and /ɪ/ in response to off-glide deletion and non-peripheral lowering are fronted and raised, frequently developing inglides simultaneously so /e/ comes to occupy the slot formerly taken up by /eɪ/, /ɪ/ the slot taken up by /i/ and /æ/ the slot held by /e/. In the case of /æ/, it is also possible that breaking steps in, splitting /æ/ into [æ] + [ə] intercepted by [j], see Ch. 9 above. Finally, although not obviously related with these shifts among front and central vowels, /u/ and /oʊ/ are shifted forward to more fronted positions.

The successive stages of SVS, involving the lowering of some and the fronting and raising of other vowels, provide a way of measuring the relative progression of SVS in the South and relate this progression to specific areas. The first stage of SVS, off-glide deletion, in particular such as occurs before weak obstruents and finally, serves as the feature delimiting and diagnosing Southern speakers in general. The outer boundaries of the South as indicated in (10.11) are drawn on the basis of off-glide deletion in this environment as in, for example, *side, size, tie, high*. 1st non-peripheral lowering outlines a very similar area as off-glide deletion. This lowering of SVS reverses the relative height of the nuclei of /eɪ/ and /e/. The area where this reversal is found does not extend all the way out to the Atlantic seaboard, nor is it typical of southern Texas, but otherwise concurrent with the off-glide deletion isogloss. 2nd peripheral lowering, by contrast, has a much more limited distribution. This lowering which reverses the relative height of the nuclei of /i/ and /ɪ/ is only found in a much smaller area with the Inland South as the centre. Off-glide deletion before weak obstruents and finally thus delimits what could be called the Outer South, off-glide deletion and 1st non-peripheral lowering mark the boundaries of what could be called the Inner South (a slightly smaller area excluding the Atlantic seaboard and the Gulf coast) and off-glide deletion, 1st non-peripheral lowering and 2nd non-peripheral lowering identify an area of the Inland South centred on Alabama and western Tennessee.

Off-glide deletion also takes place before strong obstruents as in, for example, *kite, like, life, price*. This 'strong' off-glide deletion occurs by and large within all of the Inner South, but it is particularly frequent in the northern part of Texas and in that part of the Inland South which is also the centre of the most advanced stages of SVS, i.e. Alabama and Tennessee. This restricted form of off-glide deletion thus refines as well as solidifies the picture of southern dialect geography established by other aspects of SVS.

The dialect geography established by SVS is also solidified by the fact that it is an area resistant to the low back merger. The presence of (unmerged) /ɔ/ also affects the vowel system in a diagnostically significant way, triggering a shift among diphthongs in the South not found elsewhere in North America. Frequently, /ɔ/ is realised in the South as a diphthong (see Ch. 5 above), specifically a diphthong with a back-closing off-glide, [ʊ] or [u]. In the combination /ɔ/ plus back-closing off-glide, /ɔ/ often unrounds to /a/, so /ɔ/ comes to be pronounced as the diphthong [au]. This back-closing pronunciation of /ɔ/ brings /ɔ/ into conflict with the diphthong /aʊ/ found in *now, house* etc. Consequently, /aʊ/ is pushed forward so it is pronounced [æʊ]/[æo] or sometimes [eo] (in the South the nucleus of /aʊ/ is front of centre in any case (see Ch. 5 above)). Thus the presence of /ɔ/, frequently realised as a back-closing diphthong, triggers the diphthong shift: /ɔ/ → /aʊ/ → /æo/ or /eo/. This clockwise **back-closing diphthong shift** is, like SVS, diagnostically important because it solidifies the isoglosess drawn on the basis of SVS. The most advanced stage of the back-closing diphthong shift is found in the inner South which is also the centre of the most advanced form of SVS. This area is shown on the map in (10.11) and referred to as the Inland South.

The dialect picture which begins to crystallise is then that the boundary of the outer South follows the Atlantic and Gulf coasts, excluding Florida, and after it has reached the New Mexico-Texas state border joins the southern Midland border to Chesapeake Bay. Inside this area is an Inner South area which does not extend to the Atlantic and Gulf coasts and encapsulated inside these two areas are the Texas South and the Inland South. The dialect features that define these southern dialect areas are summarised in the following diagram:

(10.13)

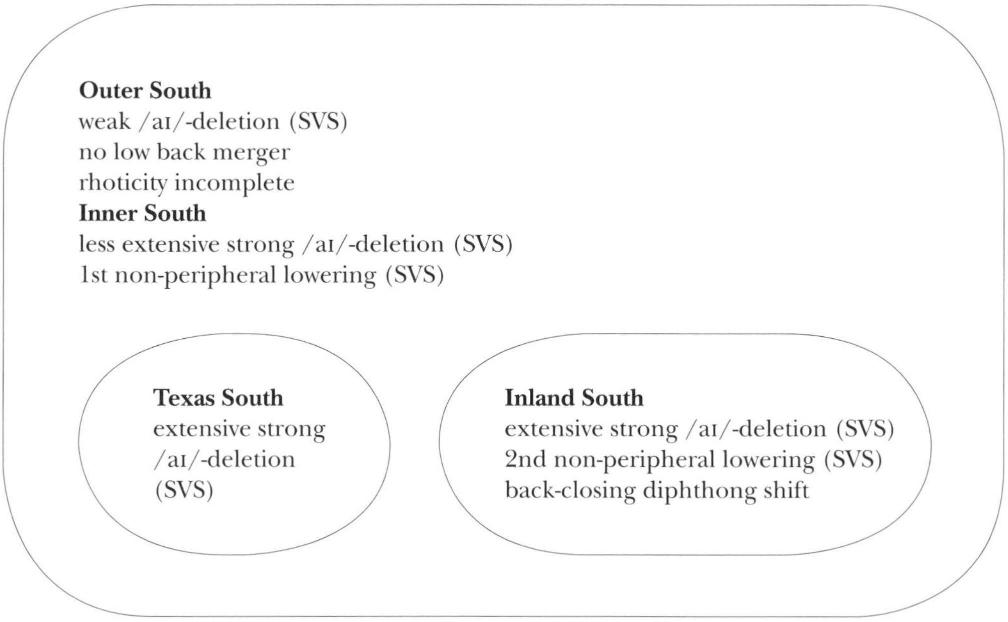

Outer South
weak /aɪ/-deletion (SVS)
no low back merger
rhoticity incomplete
Inner South
less extensive strong /aɪ/-deletion (SVS)
1st non-peripheral lowering (SVS)

Texas South
extensive strong
/aɪ/-deletion
(SVS)

Inland South
extensive strong /aɪ/-deletion (SVS)
2nd non-peripheral lowering (SVS)
back-closing diphthong shift

in which the features listed under Outer South are repeated under the sub-areas if they show up in a diagnostically important way within the sub-areas. Those diagnostic features which are part of SVS are marked by (SVS), i.e. SVS in brackets.

Among the phonologically defining features, the low back merger (or the absence of this to be more accurate), rhoticity (in part) and SVS (predominantly) are then diagnostic of the South. The back-closing realisation of /ɔ/, a feature not drawn on so far, also helps identify southern phonology. The pronunciation of /ɔ/ as [ɔu] triggers the back-closing diphthong shift. This feature should then also be listed as diagnostic of the South. One question only remains now: do these features then define a dialect as described by the generally defining criteria listed in (10.2)?

The important SVS delimits the South as geographically continuous, /aɪ/-deletion being found all over the South. The uniformity of no low back merger supports this picture of continuity. SVS is also frequent within the boundaries of the South and rare outside as demanded by the second requirement. Furthermore, the South can be said to have one or possibly two core areas from which SVS spreads out. In these core areas SVS applies more fully than in the areas not recognised as central, and in one core area a diphthong shift occurs which is a more advanced shift resulting from the absence of the low back merger. Finally, the defining SVS and, for one core area, the diphthong shift satisfy the last requirement. Both vowel rotations occur as a result of the involved vowels' membership of a phonological system of sound slots. Like the North, the South then lives well up to the generally defining criteria of a regional dialect

10.5.3 The vowel system of a southern speaker

The extensive rotations among the vowels of the South shift both monophthongs and diphthongs. The effect of SVS and the back-closing diphthong shift is thus more extensive than the effect of NCS in the North. Not only subsystems A and B undergo change, but subsystems C and D are also altered, making the southern vowel system significantly different from those of other North American dialects, including that of the reference dialect. This section provides an overview of all four vowel subsystems of the South, assuming an advanced stage like that found in the Inland South.

Given the summary in (10.13), the A, B and C, D subsystems (for these subsystems see Ch. 5 above) of an advanced southern speaker appear as shown in (10.14)(BCDS is an abbreviation of the back-closing diphthong shift):

(10.14)

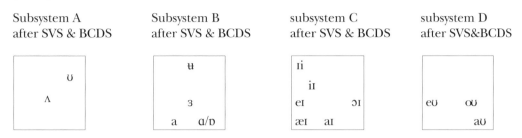

| Subsystem A
after SVS & BCDS | Subsystem B
after SVS & BCDS | subsystem C
after SVS & BCDS | subsystem D
after SVS&BCDS |

Clearly, this advanced southern system is significantly different when compared to the vowel system of NAERD. Subsystem A is considerably reduced in the South containing only two members, as /ɪ/, /e/ and /æ/ have diphthongised and become members of subsystem C. The number of subsystem B members has also been cut down, /i/ having changed to /iɪ/, /ɪ/ to /ɪi/ and /ɔ/ diphthongised to /aʊ/, the latter shift triggering the back-closing diphthong shift. The potent subsystems of the South are then C and D, in particular C which has three members added to it by the diphthongisation of monophthongs. Although a significant rotation occurs, the number of vowel phonemes in the South is still fifteen after SVS and the back closing diphthong shift as it is in NAERD as well as in the South prior to SVS. No change in the number of vowels is to be expected when SVS and the back closing diphthong shift are chain shifts, restructuring or reshuffling the inventory of vowels. Like NCS in the North, the outcome of comprehensive SVS and the back-closing diphthong shift is then a reassociation of vowels with new lexical sets. But unlike NCS, SVS and the back-closing diphthong shift also alter the phonetic realisation and distributional properties of the vowels significantly, so that a southern speaker using an advanced southern vowel system will be perceived as having not only other vowels in specific lexical sets, but also as pronouncing many of these vowels in a way not heard prior to SVS in any lexical set also outside the South.

The object of this section is to present an overview of the vowel system of the South. As in the description of the North, such an overview is best obtained by also listing the lexical sets associated with the vowels if these are different from those prior to SVS and the back-closing diphthong shift. Given the system outlined in (10.14) and the general description of the two important shifts of the South presented above, the overview of the vowels of the South looks as follows:

(10.15)

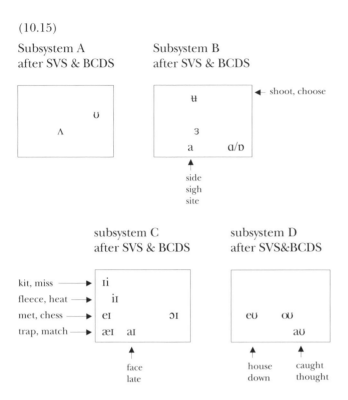

Needless to say, the advanced southern vowel system differs significantly from both the system of the North and the system of the reference dialect. With just under ten lexical sets reassociated with other vowels than in these two dialects, it is not surprising that the pronunciation of southern speakers deviates, often in an obvious way from that of other North American speakers. Even without the mention of /æ/-breaking (see Ch. 9), which more than any other feature creates the characteristic southern drawl, there exists sufficient vowel change material to identify the sound of an advanced southern speaker.

10.6 The East

10.6.1 The eastern area

The East comprises in the present broad account two detached areas in the north-eastern corner of the United States: the Mid-Atlantic States and Eastern New England. The former is assumed to include New York City, whilst Eastern New England is not continuous with New York City and the Mid-Atlantic States, but detached from theses areas by an intervening northern corridor. Nor do the Mid-Atlantic States extend as far south as to the northern border of the South. The adjoining area south of the Mid-Atlantic States lacks core dialect features of other dialects. Washington DC belongs to this transitional but marginally southern area. The East is then not one continuous area in the same way as the North or the South is one continuous area, and it is therefore not possible to refer to one eastern dialect in the same sense as it was possible to speak of a northern or a southern dialect.

Geographically, Eastern New England covers an area extending from the easternmost border of the North, approximately the Vermont-New Hampshire state border, from where it extends eastwards to the Atlantic coast. In the North, it stretches as far north as to include Bangor in Maine, whereas in the South it includes Rhode Island and the eastern halves of the states of Massachusetts and Connecticut.

New York City and the Mid-Atlantic states, on the other hand, are detached geographically from Eastern New England as pointed out above by a northern corridor. The area of New York City obviously includes the city as such and very little else outside the city's limits except for neighbouring areas of Long Island and New Jersey. Although not completely accurate, the Mid-Atlantic area will be assumed to border on New York City. From here it extends southwards including an area from the east coast to approximately the eastern border of Western Pennsylvania. On the southern boundary, the city of Baltimore is included in the Mid-Atlantic area, but as pointed out above Washington DC is neither part of this dialect area nor the South proper. The isoglosess of the eastern dialect areas are shown on the following map:

(10.16)

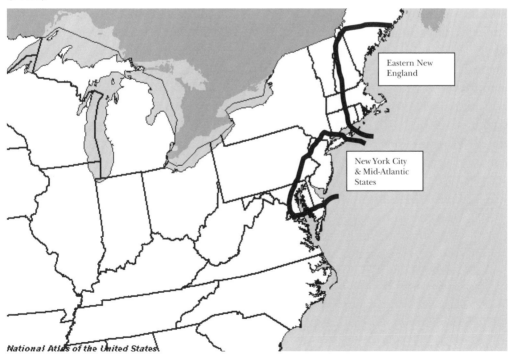

Since it consists of two discontinued areas, the East will here be assumed to comprise two separate dialects: that of Eastern New England and that of New York City and the Mid-Atlantic states. The latter has two sub-dialects, obviously New York City, on the one hand, and the Mid-Atlantic states on the other. As is a possibility in a noncontinuous dialect area, no single phonological feature is pivotal in delimiting the East like NCS and SVS are pivotal in the North and the South. Instead a multitude of features contributes to the definition of the eastern dialects. The behaviour of /ɔ/, including the low back merger, rhoticity and the splitting of /æ/ all play prominent parts in this definition.

10.6.2 Diagnosing the East

The reason that Eastern New England will be considered one dialect of the East and New York City and the Mid-Atlantic States another is that Eastern New England differs more from the sound system of New York City and the Mid-Atlantic States than the latter two differ from one another. To call all three dialects eastern is primarily motivated by geography. Phonologically they are united, if the word united is at all appropriate, by Eastern New England and New York City sharing one or two features and New York City and the Mid-Atlantic states sharing other features. The defining and diagnostic features of the dialect of Eastern New England will be considered first.

Eastern New England is the only consistently non-rhotic dialect area in North America. Thus, as described in Ch. 4 above, post-vocalic *r* is not pronounced before a consonant and before a tone group boundary in this part of North America. A pronunciation of a string like *park the car!* has then no *r* in it: [ˈpɑk ðə ˈkɑ|]. As in other non-rhotic varieties of English, *r*-sandhi such as linking-*r* (see Ch. 4 for discussion) is also frequent in Eastern New England. Thus before a following vowel with no intervening prosodic boundary but across a word boundary, *r* may, but is not always, pronounced as in *park the car in the yard* [ˈpɑk ðə ˈkɑ rɪn ðə ˈjɑd|] (linking-*r*), just like a historically unattested *r* may be inserted in, for example, *law and order* [ˈlɔr ən ˈɔdə] (intrusive-*r*). Probably, Eastern New England speakers adopted *r*-lessness, and *r*-sandhi with it, from English English RP because of the close post-settlement ties that existed between Eastern New England and the 'old motherland'.

As a non-rhotic dialect, Eastern New England, like English English RP, also has three diphthongs not found in rhotic dialects of North America. The pronunciation of *fear, care, sure* illustrates these diphthongs as shown in (10.17) (repeated from (4.8); rhotic NAERD pronunciations are listed for comparison):

(10.17)

	Eastern New England	NAERD
fear	[fɪə]	[fɪr]
care	[keə]	[ker]
sure	[ʃʊə]	[ʃʊr]

The presence of such *r*-less pronunciations adds a new sub-class of vowels termed centring diphthongs whose second off-glide is /ə/, a residue of the lost /r/.

r-lessness and centring diphthongs are due to English English influence, some would even say English English relics. But despite its clearly distinct English English-oriented sound system, the dialect of Eastern New England also participates in some of the general sound restructurings characterising North American English in these years. This participation involves neither NCS nor SVS. Instead Eastern New England is affected by the low back merger, but the neutralisation of the /ɔ/-/ɒ//ɑ/ contrast is manifested differently here than elsewhere in North America. Where this merger typically results in *caught*, *lot* and *start*-words all being pronounced with the unrounded [ɑ]-vowel (see Ch. 5), in Eastern New England the outcome of this merger is the rounded vowel /ɔ/, at the same time as [ɑ] also occurs as the realisation of /ɑ/ in such words as *start*, *father*, *palm*. The class of /ɑ/-words is also larger in Eastern New England than elsewhere in North America. Like in English English RP, many words fail to be pronounced with the [æ], sometimes referred to as the flat-*a* and so typical of American English, so that *half, aunt, bath*, for example, and many more words have /ɑ/ in the dialect of Eastern New England. The flat-*a* pronunciation was the norm in 'settlement English', but subsequently changed in English English to [ɑ] which was then adopted in Eastern New England where the ties with England were closest. Two more phonological features require mention. The first concerns the important /æ/-splitting characteristic of some but not all parts of the East. In Eastern New England /æ/ does not split, the absence of which distinguishes it from the Mid-Atlantic States and New York City. The second feature concerns the realisation of /u/ and /oʊ/ which in large parts of North America become fronted. Again not so in Eastern New England, which has preserved the conservative retracted qualities of these vowels. The defining phonological features of Eastern New England are then the following:

(10.18)

> **Eastern New England**
> non-rhotic (and *r*-sandhi)
> centring diphthongs
> low back merger
> no /æ/-splitting
> no NCS
> conservative non-fronted /u/ and /oʊ/
> extended /ɑ/-class

NCS is listed as absent in Eastern New England, whereas SVS is not mentioned at all. This follows the practice used so far that diagnostic features of contiguous dialect areas are used as important in delimiting a dialect.

New York City and the Mid-Atlantic states are separated by a northern corridor from Eastern New England. In terms of phonological features there is also some distance between the two areas, at the same time as the latter two differ from one another. New York City, like Eastern New England, is basically non-rhotic, but an *r*-ful pronunciation is gradually spreading specifically among middle and upper class speakers. In the Mid-Atlantic states, on the other hand, rhoticity is the norm. With Eastern New England, New York City also shares a conservative pronunciation of /oʊ/, whereas /u/ is much fronter than in Eastern New England. In the Mid-Atlantic States both vowels show considerable fronting. Unlike in Eastern New England, the low back merger is absent in both New York City and the Mid-Atlantic states. Instead, as the result of a contrast among the low back vowels, the path is open for the further development of /ɔ/, just like in the South where this vowel in the absence of the low back merger participates in the back-closing diphthong shift, as discussed earlier in this chapter. But in New York City and the Mid-Atlantic States, /ɔ/ is raised and diphthongised to a vowel not unlike that found in an Eastern New England pronunciation of *sure, tour*. This centring [ʊə] underlies dialect spellings of *New York* as *Noo Yawk* and is heard in words like *talk, coffee*, [tʊək], [ˈkʊəfi]. Finally, one more feature unites New York City and the Mid-Atlantic states. This is the often mentioned and diagnostically important /æ/-splitting, not occurring anywhere else in North America. Both eastern areas split /æ/ into two phonemes: /æ/ and /æ:/ where the latter is long and frequently raised so it is pronounced not unlike [ɪə]. This lengthening and raising occur typically before the nasals /m, n/ and before the strong fricatives, /f, s, θ/ and sometimes before weak fricatives. In some words it is also found before weak stops, but /æ:/ does not crop up before strong stops and /ŋ/ and /l/. Given the properties outlined so far, the East outside Eastern New England may then be summarised as having the following defining phonological features:

(10.19)

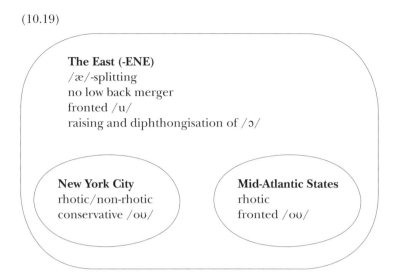

where the specific features differentiating New York City from the Mid-Atlantic states are those listed underneath each of these, whilst those listed in the larger box are shared by both eastern subdialects. Unlike the North and the South, the East, outside Eastern New England, consists of two independent dialects which do not constitute pockets within a larger area. As indicated by the diagram in (10.19), New York City and the Mid-Atlantic states exhaust the non-northern part of the East.

Given the summaries in (10.18) and (10.19), one question must now be addressed: how well can the dialects of the East be said to satisfy the generally defining criteria of dialects? Starting with Eastern New England, clearly the dialect of this area does not comply with all of the general criteria. Although it forms one continuous geographical region, all of its defining features, except perhaps for conservative retracted /u/, occur outside Eastern New England. Consistency is then not complete in the dialect of Eastern New England. But some of its most characteristic features like non-rhoticity and accompanying centring diphthongs are only found outside its boundaries in New York City and in the coastal South and often only as a social/ethnic variable. Likewise the enlarged /ɑ/-class is restricted to Eastern New England, just like a retracted /oʊ/ and a similarly fairly retracted /u/ is not as salient anywhere else, including the North. But the low back merger, characteristic of Eastern New England, is far from only found within this dialect area, nor does Eastern New England have a defining feature expanding from a centre like NCS and SVS. For the same reason, it is difficult to demonstrate that a defining feature fills a slot in a phonological system and that ensuing system restructurings characterise the dialect of Eastern New England (like NCS and SVS in the North and the South respectively). The absence of a conspicuous vowel shift clearly blurs the contour of a distinct dialect. However, the almost unique presence in North America of a non-rhotic pronunciation as well as a conservative rendering of both /u/ and /oʊ/ consolidate the boundaries of an Eastern New England dialect.

Now, how about the dialect of the Mid-Atlantic States, the other dialect of the East? Again this dialect is geographically continuous (or almost continuous as there is a very narrow corridor separating New York City and the Mid-Atlantic area, but this corridor is ignored here). As for consistency, two features, /æ/-splitting and diphthongal realisation of /ɔ/, are only found here and not outside (the diphthongal realisation of /ɔ/ in the South is different), whereas the low back merger is absent in the North and the South too, and fronted /u/ is also found elsewhere. Whilst only two of the defining features satisfy the consistency criterion of not occurring outside the boundaries, there is also no major shift emanating from a centre with obvious restructurings that involve phoneme slots. As in the case of the dialect of Eastern New England, not all generally defining criteria sustain the dialect boundaries of the Mid-Atlantic States. Again it is necessary to accept that two features, /æ/-splitting and diphthongal realisation of /ɔ/, play a vital part in consolidating the dialect's boundaries. The absence of systemic features is then compensated for by the quite unique position of /æ/-splitting and /ɔ/ realisation in this part of North America.

10.6.3 The vowel systems of eastern speakers

Despite the absence of a radical vowel shift, like NCS or SVS, in the East, the vowel system of an eastern speaker is not completely the same as that of a speaker of NAERD. The difference can be related to the three important areas outlined above: the realisation of /æ/, the realisation of /ɔ/ and non-rhoticity.

In non-rhotic speakers, the absence of post-vocalic *r* creates a new system of centring diphthongs, the second element of which is /ə/. Thus in Eastern New England the vowel system has an extra class of centring diphthongs whose second element is a residue of the lost *r*. This is system E in the system overview shown in (10.20) which leaves out subsystems A, C and D which in Eastern New England do not differ from those of NAERD:

(10.20)

subsystem B   subsystem E

Although it is not really different from that of NAERD, subsystem B is included here because with respect to the lexical sets associated with /ɔ/ and /ɑ/ the two systems do differ. The following diagram summaries the typical distribution of these two vowels in Eastern New England as well as examples of words with /ɪə/, /eə/ and /ʊə/:

(10.21)

subsystem B   subsystem E

As pointed out above, it is characteristic of Eastern New England that *caught/ cot*-words are pronounced with a rounded back vowel and thus not identified with unrounded /ɑ/, unlike in other dialect areas with the low back merger where this possibility exists. Similarly, /ɑ/'s distribution is not as in NAERD, occurring not only not in *caught/cot*-words, but also in quite a large set of words which outside Eastern New England have /æ/. The presence of /ɔ/ follows from the low back merger not involving further unrounding of /ɔ/, and the extended occurrence of /ɑ/ is the result of English English influence.

   Turning to the Mid-Atlantic States, speakers of this dialect will also have subsystem E, in so far as they are non-rhotic (like some New Yorkers). But non-rhoticity aside, the main characteristics of this eastern dialect concern the realisation of /ɔ/ and the splitting of /æ/. As an area unaffected by the low back merger, /ɔ/ is free to follow its own course of development as in the South. This explains /ɔ/'s development into the diphthong [ʊə]. Thus in the pronunciation of non-rhotic New Yorkers, words like *sure, tour,* and *walk, lost, coffee* have very similar vowels. In non-rhotic speakers, [ʊə] is also found, but only associated with words like *walk, lost, coffee.* But arguably, [ʊə] is not the only centring diphthong of this eastern dialect. The splitting of /æ/ into two vowels can also be interpreted as involving the formation of a centring diphthong. When /æ/ splits one vowel is short, checked and in low front position. This is represented as /æ/. But the other vowel typically involves raising and lengthening. The realisation of this other vowel is diphthongal so *ham, staff, path* are pronounced like the vowels of *idea* and *yeah*, i.e. [ɪə]. Given these specific realisations of what in NAERD is represented as /æ/ and /ɔ/, the vowel system of a (non-rhotic) Mid-Atlantic speaker could look as follows which lists only subsystems B and E, subsystems A, C and D being the same as in NAERD:

(10.22)

subsystem B   subsystem E

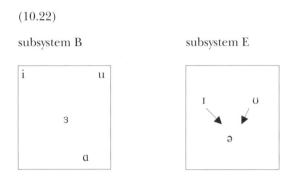

Subsystem B differs then by lacking /ɔ/. Instead a Mid-Atlantic speaker invokes subsystem E in which /ʊə/ does the job of /ɔ/. Notice in this connection that /ɑ/ is the vowel of many words which in dialects with the low back merger may be identified with /ɔ/, such as *cot, don, hot, hock*. The following diagram summaries the lexical sets associated with the vowels of subsystem E and with /ɑ/ of subsystem B:

(10.23)

subsystem B   subsystem E

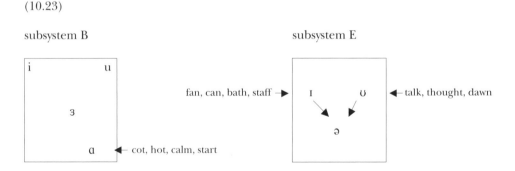

The lexical set associated with /ɪə/ varies somewhat, the general rule being that it is found before /m, n/ and the fricatives /f, θ, s/, but as pointed out above not any word meeting the required input structure exhibits splitting to /ɪə/.

Simultaneous occurrence of all centring diphthongs is then only found in eastern non-rhotic varieties. The presence of /ɪə/ and /ʊə/, but not centring /eə/, also characterises this area, but /ɪə/ is also found outside the East but typically only before /m, n/ and in the North where [ɪə] can be the realisation of /æ/, the first stage of NCS. The most distinctive vowel feature of the East is then the use of diphthongs which are rare elsewhere in North America and /æ/-splitting.

10.7 Canada

10.7.1 The Canadian area

In this broad outline, Canada will be assumed to encompass approximately an area extending from Montreal in the East to the Pacific coast in the West whose southern border follows the Canadian/US border and whose northern border does not extend much further north than a line drawn between Montreal in the East and Edmonton in the West. The area does not include the Atlantic provinces in the East, that is, all of Nova Scotia and most of New Brunswick. Although it shares some features with the rest of Canada, this Atlantic area is considered to be separate from the rest of Canada, lacking the two most characteristic features of Canadian English, the Canadian Shift and Canadian Raising. Geographically, it is also separated from non-Atlantic Canada by a corridor whose width is approximately the distance between the cities of Montreal and Saint John. The map in (10.24) outlines the provinces considered to be included in the Canadian dialect area (the Atlantic provinces are marked with broken lines to indicate their exceptional status):

(10.24)

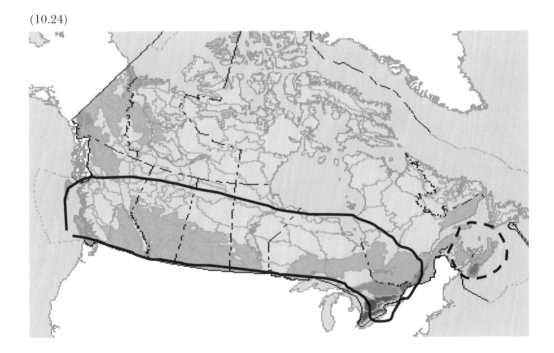

Atlantic Canada shares with Canada proper the low back merger and fronted /u/. But more shared features are necessary for Atlantic Canada to be considered part of the Canadian English area. Western Pennsylvania, for example, also merges the low back vowels at the same time as /u/ is fronted. But Western

Pennsylvania is not interpreted as part of Canada. Western Pennsylvania, like Atlantic Canada, lacks Canadian Raising and the Canadian Shift. The Atlantic provinces of Canada are then best viewed as a residual area.

10.7.2 Diagnosing Canadian English

As indicated already, of the phonologically defining features listed in (10.1), the low back merger, **Canadian Raising**, the **Canadian Shift** and fronted /u/ characterise Canadian speech. Canadian raising is the feature most often associated with Canadian speakers. This shift raises and centralises the nuclei of /aɪ/ and /aʊ/ before strong consonants, so that these diphthongs are pronounced [əɪ] in words like *mice*, *height* and [əʊ] in words like *house* and *shout*. However characteristic it may be, Canadian Raising does not affect the phoneme inventory of Canadian speech. Instead it assigns for Canada typical bound allophones to /aɪ/ and /aʊ/. Nor is Canadian raising found everywhere in Canada or completely absent outside its boundaries. The Canadian Shift, by contrast, not only alters the phoneme inventory but also is a better diagnostic candidate feature occurring with high consistency inside Canada. The Canadian Shift is closely linked with the presence of the low back merger in Canada. The coalescence of the /ɒ///ɑ/-/ɔ/-contrast leaves space for /æ/ to shift backwards, upon which /e/ is lowered and backed, taking up the position formerly occupied by backed /æ/. Schematically, this Canadian Shift looks as shown in the following diagram:

(10.25)

e

↘

æ   →   ɒ/ɑ   →   ɔ

In addition to the low back merger and the Canadian Shift, Canada has fronted /u/, in fact the most fronted quality among the North American dialects that also exhibit conservative non-fronted /oʊ/. Like the West and the North, Canada is then also characterised by retracted /oʊ/. The defining phonological features of Canadian speech are then the following:

(10.26)

Canada
the low back merger
the Canadian Shift
Canadian Raising
fronted /u/
conservative /oʊ/
rhoticity

How well does Canadian English then satisfy the generally defining features of a dialect? Disregarding for the moment the realisation of /u/ and /oʊ/, both Canadian raising and the low back merger fail to satisfy the first two criteria well. Although typically assumed to be diagnostic of Canadian speech, Canadian Raising is not found everywhere within the boundaries of the Canadian area, at the same time as it also occurs in speakers of the North. Similarly, the low back merger is far from restricted to Canada. The Canadian Shift, on the other hand, has high consistency within the Canadian dialect boundaries. Unfortunately, speakers of the West, who also merge the low back vowels, can be heard to have the shift too. The first two criteria are then fulfilled better by the Canadian Shift than by Canadian Raising, whilst the low back merger is of secondary value. Fullest satisfaction of the continuity and consistency criteria is best achieved if the interaction of /u/ and /oʊ/ is utilised. No other North American dialect has a so fronted /u/ at the same time as /oʊ/ remains conservative in quality. Thus an interplay of the Canadian Shift and /u/-/oʊ/ interaction establish Canada as a continuous dialect area and serve to solidify the boundaries of Canada best.

As for the two other general criteria, the Canadian Shift is a potential defining candidate, but Canada does not seem to have a core area from where it can be said to expand. Instead, as just pointed out, the Canadian Shift is very consistent throughout Canada. But although it does not expand from a centre, the Canadian Shift is similar to NCS and SVS, which typically expand from a centre. Like these two massive chain shifts, the Canadian Shift involves a rotation, although much less extensive than both NCS and SVS, which is determined by vowels filling slots in a phonological system. The last two general criteria are then in part satisfied by the phonological properties of Canadian English.

10.7.3 The vowel system of a Canadian speaker

As a rhotic dialect with the low back merger, the vowel system of a Canadian speaker really only differs from that of the reference dialect with respect to the vowels affected by the Canadian Shift. As pointed out above, this shift affects subsystem A, in particular it retracts /æ/ and lowers and backs /e/. Thus after the implementation of the Canadian Shift, subsystem A looks as shown below:

(10.27)

Subsystem A

In the extreme case, /e/ is then absent from subsystem A, but the number of vowel phonemes has not changed. The loss of /e/ is a result of the new open class /a/ which pulls /e/ into the position formerly occupied by /æ/. But the appearance of /a/ affects the association of /æ/ and /a/ with lexical sets. The lexical set formerly associated with /e/ is after the shift associated with /æ/, whose pre-shift set in turn is associated with /a/ after the shift.

   With respect to two sets of words and the checked vowels associated with them, Canadian English then differs from the rest of North America. Those Canadian speakers who also have Canadian raising will exhibit further deviance. Canadian raising does not pertain to the phonological system as such, but concerns the pronunciation of /aɪ/ and /aʊ/ before strong consonants. However, those who raise the nuclei of these diphthongs allophonically in this environment will be identified as typically Canadian.

10.8 Summing up North American dialects

This last section of chapter 10 will focus on two issues. First, as is appropriate after the description of five dialect areas, it will summarise the main phonological features of North American English and provide a schematic overview of the dialect geography of North America. Second, since the description above has not covered all of North America, this section will also deal with residual areas not included within the five main North American English dialect areas discussed above. The second issue will be dealt with first, but the treatment will be brief, as residual areas deviate little from contiguous uniform dialect areas except that the residual areas typically show fewer defining features.

10.8.1 Three residual areas

Three residual areas will be dealt with here, all of which encompass quite large territories. It should be emphasised that these are not the only areas that fall under the heading residual. There are pockets constituted by individual cities such as, for example, Boston and St. Louis, as well as enclosures in California and enclosures on the east coast such as Charleston which do not fit into the patterns of the main dialect areas. Such relatively small residual pockets will not be discussed in this very general overview. The discussion will instead restrict itself to three fairly large areas that have not been included so far. These are: Florida, the North Central and the Atlantic Provinces. Alaska, which covers a very large territory, will then also be left out of consideration.

   Two of these have been dealt with already if not exhaustively then to such an extent that very little can be added to make the phonological description of them complete. First the Atlantic Provinces. As stated in §10.7.1, the Atlantic Provinces, which encompass all of Nova Scotia and most of New Brunswick, are an area which like the rest of Canada has the low back merger and fronted /u/.

But it does not share with the rest of Canada the diagnostic Canadian Shift nor the typical Canadian Raising. However, the low back merger and fronted /u/ are not sufficient phonological properties to define the Atlantic provinces as an independent dialect area. The second area is the North Central. The North Central area constitutes an area squeezed in between the North and Canada. It extends as far westwards as the north-eastern corner of the State of Montana, and as far eastwards as Lake Huron. Lacking NCS, the North central is not included in the North. The present description has included it in the large West and Midland dialect area, and thus with regard to vowel system, close to the reference dialect. As part of the West and the Midland dialect areas, the North Central is characterised by the low back merger, no Canadian Shift or Raising at the same time as it, like the West, also has conservative /oʊ/. But the absence of NCS makes the North Central non-northern at its core. This is the reason that it has been placed in the large West and Midland dialect areas in the present description and the reason that in other accounts it is treated as a residual area rather than as an individual dialect.

The third residual area is Florida. It comprises all of Florida, the northern border of this area running north of Tallahassee but south of Jacksonville. Although sufficiently large to constitute an independent dialect area, Florida lacks clearly defining features. It is best defined as a southern dialect with fronted /oʊ/ which does not have the low back merger, at the same time as SVS is absent. SVS is absent in any form in Florida. The absence of even weak /aɪ/-deletion makes Florida as much a midland dialect as a southern dialect, a fact which underpins the propriety of classifying it as residual. With this brief description, it is now possible to summarise the main characteristics of the not all too clearly definable residual areas:

(10.28)
Three Residual areas

Atlantic Provinces
low back merger
fronted /u/
no Canadian Shift/
raising

North Central
low back merger
no NCS
conservative /oʊ/
no Canadian Shift/
raising

Florida
no low back merger
no SVS
fronted /oʊ/

10.8.2 Summary of the main North American English dialects

The preceding survey has described North American English as having five main dialects: the North, the West and Midland, the South, the East and Canada. With the exception of Canada, these main dialects can be divided into subdialects. This subdivision can be one of two kinds. Either the subdialects are parallel or the subdialects involve embedding. Parallel subdivision is what we find in the West and the Midland which is split up into three separate and geographically non-overlapping dialects which are united by some features and distinguished from one another by others. Subdivision involving embedding is characteristic of, for example, the South. In the South two sub-dialects are contained within the main dialect area, overlapping with the main dialect area without completely exhausting it. Such embedded subdialects constitute geographical pockets and exhibit typically more advanced forms of one or more of the phonological features defining the main area. Either parallel or embedded dialect structure is the norm for a main dialect area, the North and South exemplifying the latter and the East and the West and the Midland the former. The following diagram summarises the main pattern of North American dialects where embedding is represented in terms of embedded and overlapping figures, parallelism in terms of separate non-overlapping representations:

(10.29)

Canada	low back merger Canadian Shift/Raising fronted /u/ conservative /oʊ/ rhotic	

The North	conservative /oʊ/ no low back merger NCS rhotic no Canadian Shift/Raising no /æ/-splitting	**The Inland North** advanced /e/-/ɒ///ɑ/ alignment advanced non-low /ɒ///ɑ/ alignment

The East	**Eastern New England** non-rhotic (and *r*-sandhi) centring diphthongs low back merger no /æ/-splitting no NCS conservative /u/ and /oʊ/ extended /ɑ/-class	
	East (non-northern) /æ/-splitting low back merger fronted /u/ raising and diphthongisation of /ɔ/	**New York City** rhotic/non-rhotic conservative /oʊ/ **Mid-Atlantic States** rhotic fronted /oʊ/

The West and Midland	**The West** low back merger conservative /oʊ/ no NCS and SVS no Canadian Shift/Raising rhotic
	The Midland incomplete low back merger fronted /oʊ/ no NCS and SVS rhotic
	Western Pensylvania low back merger fronted /oʊ/ no NCS and SVS no /æ/-splitting rhotic

The South	SVS weak /aɪ/-deletion no low back merger rhotic	**Texas South** extensive strong /aɪ/-deletion
		Inland South: extensive strong /aɪ/-deletion back-closing diphthong shift

Further reading

American English dialect geography based primarily on the phonology of vowels is discussed in detail in ANAE (Labov et al. 2006). Wells 1982 also contains a comprehensive but now somewhat outdated description. The reader is also referred to the numerous dialect projects mentioned in Ch. 1 which lead up to ANAE and which are listed under further reading in Ch. 1.

Bibliography

Aitchinson, J. 1991. *Language Change: Progress or Decay?* Cambridge: Cambridge University Press.

Algeo, J. 2001. *The Cambridge History of the English Language. Vol. VI. English in North America.* Cambridge: Cambridge University Press

Bauer, L., J.M. Dienhart, H.H. Hartvigson & L. Kvistgaard Jacobsen. 1980. *American English Pronunciation.* Copenhagen: Gyldendal.

Bolinger, D. 1972. *Intonation.* Harmondsworth: Penguin

– 1986. *Intonation and its Parts. Melody in Spoken English.* London: Edward Arnold

– 1989. *Intonation and its Uses. Melody in Grammar and Discourse.* London: Edward Arnold.

Bynon, T. 1977. *Historical Linguistics.* Cambridge: Cambridge University Press

Carver, C. M. 1987. *American Regional Dialects: a Word Geography.* Ann Arbor: University of Michigan Press.

Chomsky, N & M. Halle. 1968. *The Sound Pattern of English.* New York: Harper and Row

Fischer, J. H. 1996. *The emergence of standard English.* Lexington: University Press of Kentucky.

Giegerich, H. 1992. *English Phonology: an Introduction.* Cambridge: Cambridge University Press.

Gimson, 1962. *An Introduction to the Pronunciation of English.* London: Edward Arnold.

Green, L. 2002. *African American English.* Cambridge: Cambridge University Press.

Gussenhoven, C. 2004. *The Phonology of Tone and Intonation.* Cambridge: Cambridge University Press.

Halle, M. and S. Keyser. 1971. *English Stress.* New York: Harper and Row.

Halliday, M. 1970. *A Course in Spoken English: Intonation.* Oxford: Oxford University Press.

Joseph, B. and R.D. Janda. 2003. *The Handbook of Historical Linguistics.* Oxford: Blackwell.

Kenstowicz, M. 1994. *Phonology in Generative Grammar.* Oxford: Blackwell.

Kenyon, J. S. and T. A. Knott. 1944. *A Pronouncing Dictionary of American English.* Springfield, MA: Merriam.

Krapp, G. P. 1925. *The English Language in America.* 2 vols. New York: Century.

Kurath, H. 1939-43. *Linguistic Atlas of New England.* 3 vols. in 6. Providence, RI: Brown University and American Council of Learned Societies.

– 1949. *A word Geography of the Eastern United States.* Ann Arbor: University of Michigan Press.

– 1965. 'Some Aspects of Atlantic Seaboard English Considered in their Connections with British English'. *In Communications et rapport de Premier Congris International de Dialectologie Generale, Troesieme Pertie*, 236-40.

Kurath, H. and R. I. McDavid. 1961. *The pronunciation of English in the Atlantic States.* Ann Arbor: University of Michigan Press.

Leech, G. N. 1969. *A Linguistic Guide to English Poetry.* London: Longman.

Labov, W., S. Ash & C. Boberg. 2006. *The Atlas of North American English. Phonetics, Phonology and Sound Change.* Berlin: Mouton.

Ladd, D. R. 1996. *Intonational Phonology.* Cambridge: Cambridge University Press.

Ladefoged, P. 2001. *A Course in Phonetics* (4th edition). Boston: Heinle & Heinle.

Laver, J. 1994. *Principles of phonetics.* Cambridge: Cambridge University Press

Lass, R. (1976). *English Phonology and Phonological Theory: Synchronic and Diachronic Studies.* Cambridge: Cambridge University Press.

Lass, R. 1984. *Phonology.* Cambridge: Cambridge University Press.

Lass, R. and J.M. Anderson. 1975. *Old English Phonology*. Cambridge: Cambridge University Press

Lyons, J. 1968. *Theoretical Linguistics*. Cambridge: Cambridge University Press.

Sommerstein, A. H. 1977. *Modern Phonology*. London: Edward Arnold

Tottie, G. 2002. *An Introduction to American English*. Oxford: Blackwell.

Wales, K. 2001. *A Dictionary of Stylistics*. London: Longman.

Wells, J. C. 1982. *Accents of English*, vol. 1, 2, 3. Cambridge: Cambridge University Press

– 2000. *Longman Pronunciation Dictionary*. London: Longman.

Wolfram, W. and N. Schilling-Estes. 1998. *American English*. Oxford: Blackwell.

Wolfram, W and E. R. Thomas. 2002. *The Development of African American English*. Oxford: Blackwell.

Index

When first introduced or defined, many technical terms are printed in the book in bold face. In this index, the page numbers of these boldened items are also printed in bold.